GONE AWRY

GONE AWRY

The Collision of Property Rights,
Environmentalism
And the American Dream
In the Smart Growth Quest
To Stop Urban Sprawl
In San Diego, California

Parke Troutman

THREE ACRES PRESS
SAN DIEGO, CALIFORNIA

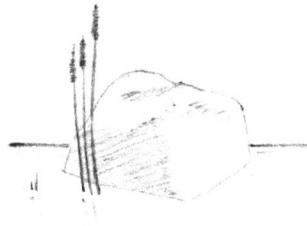

Parke Troutman is a San Diego-based policy advocate and analyst, working primarily on land use and food policy, including reforming the City of San Diego's community garden and urban agriculture ordinances as well as state and federal anti-hunger legislation. He received his PhD in sociology in 2004 from the University of California, San Diego.

Three Acres Press, San Diego, California

For my family, which has been waiting patiently for years for my boxes of City and County planning records to be out of the house.

CONTENTS

Part III
MEANWHILE, BACK AT THE SUBDIVIDED RANCH
The County's Never-ending Effort
to Rein in Backcountry Sprawl

FOREWORD

Planners have found religion, once again. First there was comprehensive planning coupled with urban renewal and then, starting in the 1970s, growth management. This last one was a little tricky. It went against the historical function of planning for accommodating growth while attempting to ameliorate its problems. But in the 1990s the forces of growth reasserted their historic weight and Smart Growth was born. Smart Growth calls for the accommodation of growth because, it is maintained, growth is inevitable but the problems associated with it are not. Smart Growth proponents argue that by creating more compact development patterns, promoting urban reinvestment, and designing communities that are mixed use, higher density, transit oriented and pedestrian-friendly, we can eat the growth cake and have it too.

This vision of a strategy of development that promises growth accommodation while at the same time rejuvenating our decaying communities and saving our endangered ecosystems is a powerful one—but extremely difficult to realize. Regrettably, this aspect of Growth Management is not given much attention. Successes, the rare ones, or the more frequent alleged successes (promoted by self-aggrandizing planners) continue to give legitimacy to Smart Growth. That is natural for the profession to do—but dangerous. Do you remember urban renewal? Planners, allied with the forces of growth and development, uncritically accepted the idea that cities were to be saved by destroying them first, with the results we all know. Smart Growth is certainly less destructive than urban renewal, and in fact one of its major tenets is the revitalization of the inner city, but, with gentrification being the likely result, aren't the effects going to be similar to those of urban renewal?

The point is that we need to be careful: that while appreciating the potential of Smart Growth we need also to understand its potential drawbacks and recognize the obstacles that make its implementation arduous and weak. Planners and practitioners need to analyze what works, or fails, and under what circumstances. To provide such understanding I would want, ideally, somebody outside the planning profession—but that understands it inside out—who can provide a dispassionate account of Smart Growth. That same person would need to possess considerable research skills to be able to navigate through a variety of case studies and show clearly how Smart Growth is faring under different conditions. Not only that. I would also want to be helped to understand what happened and why, and be given an array of possible alternatives. And finally, this miracle man or woman should come with a writing style that is void of jargon, but still profound, breezy, clear and fun to read.

Parke Troutman is that person. He is an urban sociologist who spent years on his dissertation researching and writing about Smart Growth in the San Diego Region, with a particular emphasis on the San Diego Association of Governments (can Smart Growth succeed without regional planning?) and the County and City of San Diego that, at the turn of the century, were engaged at the same time in updating their general plans.

He has shortened and updated the dissertation and the result is a gem of a book that meets all the requirements that I have outlined above. It should be required reading for anybody even tangentially related to planning in San Diego, especially now that SANDAG expects the region to have to accommodate well over a million more people by 2050—presumably on the basis of Smart Growth principles as embodied in plans like those of the City and County of San Diego. But the book's lessons are relevant for other areas experiencing growth as well and of interest to a national audience of planning practitioners, academics and students. You might not agree completely—as I don't—with Troutman's assessment of Smart Growth and all of his prescriptions for the future of planning, but they will surely make you think.

Nico Calavita
Emeritus Professor of City Planning
San Diego State University

ACKNOWLEDGEMENTS

Writing a book is like owning land: it's treated as belonging to one person. Yet this claim to the singular right of ownership is belied by a massive network of people who make such assertions possible. Indeed, it's disconcerting to realize that so much goodwill from so many people is required to write a book, not only to complete the project but to keep you sane in the process. So let me first state that I am grateful to all the friends, family and mentors who helped, from my cohort in grad school, like Maria and Shannon, to my dissertation committee (Richard Madsen, Richard Biernacki, Amy Bridges, Michael Schudson, and Michael Davidson and especially Nico Calavita), to my writers group (Laura, Chris and Lisa), to my family, who endured this far longer than they should have had to. I am also grateful to those who provided feedback on the penultimate draft: Amanda Lasik, Lora Logan, Louann Troutman, Chris Robinson and Susan Yogi.

With considerable misgivings, I have decided not to thank by name the people who helped me the most. I talked to many different people involved in San Diego land use. I am most grateful for their time and patience in answering my questions. I am doubly thankful for those who read the case studies and provided feedback, sometimes incredibly detailed. As the plans grew controversial, however, sensitivities about talking about them dramatically increased.

It was noted in response to early drafts that few people come off looking good in the efforts to update the general plans. Except for one fellow who threatened to destroy me if I repeated anything he said (and who, with hindsight, appears to have been a sociopath), I found it easy to empathize with the people involved. My feeling is that writing general plans is like constructing a house: no matter how beautiful the structure is at the end, the builders are covered in dirt. Gustave Flaubert (in Robert Baldick's translation of *Sentimental Education*) made a similar observation years ago: "Heroes don't smell very nice!" Although I'm not sure that many people involved were actually heroic, they were quietly humane, and, if they sometimes came across as less than charming in public, it was because they felt so threatened by what was happening. To be sure, participants often conceived of each other in negative, sometimes slightly fantastical, terms, but even the slightest slips of the mask gave lie to this. Once, for example, I saw the head of a local chapter of an oft-criticized organization give his three minutes of public testimony at a hearing. Then, when he was done, he went to the back of the meeting room and announced to his friends that he was ready to go outside and throw up.

PART I

CONFRONTING THE PROBLEMS OF URBAN GROWTH

If men were angels, no government would be necessary. If angels were to govern men, neither external nor internal controls on government would be necessary.

—James Madison, *Federalist Papers*, no. 51

INTRODUCTION

I n the early 1990s, planners at SANDAG discovered a problem. Never mind, for the moment, that most of the 2.5 million people living in San Diego County had no idea what SANDAG was or that SANDAG stood for the San Diego Association of Governments. Never mind, either, that the problem the SANDAG planners had discovered was essentially a conceptual glitch in population modeling software. It was a little thing, something they couldn't get people to take seriously for years. But, on an unmarked day shortly after the end of the Cold War, San Diego's demographic canary-in-a-coal-mine died.

SANDAG's staff of planners periodically estimated population growth for the next twenty years for the 4,200 square mile region. In theory, the local cities and the County used the demographic projections to prepare for the anticipated population growth.[1] In practice, the elected officials from the cities and County who made up the SANDAG Board of Directors said the usual pieties about the need for regional cooperation, and, then, if—and only if—they were feeling particularly ambitious, they would go home and pretend to do something about it. What the demographers found in the 1990s was a snag in this charade.

The problem stemmed from how the demographers predicted the San Diego region's population growth. They used a two-step process

---

1. City and County are here capitalized when they refer to the government and left lowercase when referring to a geographic or cultural entity.

to develop their twenty-year estimates. The first step estimated basic economic and population trends. The second step calculated, down to the census tract, where population growth was likely to go, based largely on where future employment growth would occur, on how workers would commute to the new jobs and—this is important—on where the cities and the County had planned for additional housing.[2] This approach traditionally worked fairly well for SANDAG staff, though they knew they better predicted the total population growth than its exact location.[3]

When the planners incorporated the 1990 census data into their models, the modeling process went awry. The first step came up with a population number for the year 2015. That worked fine. The second step of the modeling process, however, couldn't find enough housing in current city plans to accommodate all the people who would either move into the region or be born there. San Diego, which was boxed in by the Pacific Ocean, the Mexican border, Camp Pendleton and its own mountains, was running out of developable land. Yet the demand for that finite land was going to keep growing.

This was quite a problem. Even in the best of times, San Diego had never been good at providing housing. Its journey from quaint border town to military powerhouse to classic Southern California metropolis had been bumpy. In the bursts of growth, demand for housing consistently exceeded supply, leading to skyrocketing living costs and serious problems, such as increased homelessness and children unable to afford to live in the neighborhoods in which they grew up. Expensive housing caused a great silent misery for many, even with wide expanses of coastal shrub still left to bulldoze. If, as SANDAG was predicting for 2015, all the available land from the mountains to the shining sea was going to be used up, then the ratio of supply and demand could only become more unhinged.

San Diego wasn't the only place facing this challenge. True,

2. A detailed description of the modeling process can be found in San Diego Association of Governments, *2020 Cities/County Forecast*, 4 vols. (San Diego, 1998), especially volume one.
3. For a brief historical overview of its growth projections since 1971, see San Diego Association of Governments, *2020 Cities/County Forecast*, 4 vols. (San Diego, 1998): 3.

the region was one of relatively few in the United States reaching its physical limits.[4] But San Diego was typical of California, and California ranked only seventeenth among states in its growth rate.[5] Population growth was a widespread challenge: Salt Lake City and Las Vegas also anticipated a million more inhabitants by 2020; the Atlanta region, 1.5 million; Greater Chicago, 1.78 million; Boston, 600,000 between 2005 and 2025; Los Angeles saw six million more people or "two Chicagos" in its future; Portland expected 1.1 million people by 2040. These major increases in population were merely part of the country's projected growth of 61 million people from 2000 to 2025. This growth was not limited to the United States. For the period 1990 to 2011, Melbourne, Australia anticipated growth of half a million people. A 1999 report indicated that the United Kingdom expected 3.8 million more households from 1996 to 2021. Hong Kong was expected to gain two million people from 2001 to 2031. Indeed, the United Nations anticipated that as the global population rises to 8.11 billion by 2030, "virtually all the population growth… will be concentrated in the urban areas of the world."[6]

In the not-so-distant past, such growth would be cause for celebration. It was a mark of national power and economic success. Bigger was better. But just as portliness used to signify wealth but is now, in an era of cheap calories, seen as a worrisome health hazard, by the late 1990s, growth had lost its shine.

4. The other geographically constrained regions are Los Angeles, Miami, New Orleans, Pittsburgh, San Francisco and Seattle, according to Robert W. Burchell, Anthony Downs, Barbara McCann and Sahan Mukherji, *Sprawl Costs: Economic Impacts of Unchecked Development* (Washington, DC: Island Press, 2005): 150.

5. Woods & Poole Economics, Inc., *The Complete Economic and Demographic Data Source*, vol. 1. (Washington, DC, 1998): 67–68.

6. United Nations Population Division, *World Urbanization Prospects: The 1999 Revision* (1999): 1. For Melbourne, see Pete Newton, "Urban Form and Environmental Performance," in *Achieving Sustainable Urban Form*, ed. Katie Williams, Elizabeth Burton, and Mike Jencks, (London and New York: E & FN Spon, 2000): 48. For the United Kingdom, see Urban Task Force, *Towards an Urban Renaissance* (London: E & FN Spon, 1999): 35. For Hong Kong, see Government of Hong Kong, *Hong Kong Population Projections 2004–2033* (June 30, 2004): http://www.info.gov.hk/gia/general/200406/30/0630094.htm.

This book focuses on one sliver of the question of growth, one that was profoundly controversial in Australia, North America and Europe: how cities should be built to accommodate additional people. Debates about urban growth revolved around one word: *sprawl*. Critics used the term to describe the dispersed low-density, car-dependent housing that had become home to over half of all Americans. *Sprawl* was a rhetorically effective term, carrying much more punch than the neutral *suburbanization* or the yawner *decentralization*. It conjured up images of a slothful, unsightly spreading out, as in "the passed-out drunk sprawled out across the sofa."

Criticisms of sprawl often took the form of a story that was remarkably similar regardless of the country about which it was told. The American version: World War II was about to end and a dam was about to break. Starting in the nineteenth century, improvements in transportation technology made it easier to move out into the countryside and still work in the city.[7] The automobile, becoming popular in the 1910s and 1920s, had the potential to revolutionize where people lived and worked, but the Great Depression, which devastated the housing industry, put that on hold. At the end of World War II, however, almost twenty years of pent-up demand for new housing exploded across the countryside, transforming the American physical and cultural landscape.

The federal government made moving out to the suburbs easy with programs that increased the convenience of cars and lowered the cost of buying a home. This put inner cities on a downward spiral. As whites and their tax dollars were pulled outward to the new suburban settlements, their old neighborhoods suffered from disinvestment, a situation intensified when jobs followed workers out to the suburbs. Inner-city infrastructure declined. Inner-city children grew up in homes disproportionately hurt by poverty

7. The classic description of this is Kenneth T. Jackson, *Crabgrass Frontier: The Suburbanization of the United States* (New York: Oxford University Press, 1985). On the technology behind the freeway system, see Earl Swift, *The Big Road: The Untold Story of the Engineers, Visionaries and Trailblazers who Created the American Superhighways* (New York: Houghton Mifflin Harcourt, 2011).

and crime, attended overcrowded schools and saw few economic opportunities in their own neighborhoods. At the same time, they became sealed off from the growing suburbs, not only by aggressively policed segregation, but also by the difficulties of physically getting to the new jobs on the outskirts of the cities. As far-flung suburbs bloomed, urban mass transit stagnated: whenever someone came to rely exclusively on a car, it meant each remaining bus ticket had to cover more of the infrastructure and maintenance costs. Raising ticket prices only made riding less appealing. Soon, mass transit was the transportation of last resort, a system for people who were too poor to own a car or were physically unable to drive.[8]

According to the critics' story of sprawl, all was not well in the new communities either. To maintain homes in an idyllic state, government regulations started keeping different land uses (residential, industrial, commercial, etc.) separate. This kept the pollution and noise of factories away from the white picket fences, but it had a poorly thought out consequence: people needed cars to get to work, to visit friends, to go grocery shopping—indeed, to do almost anything. That led to (a) exasperating traffic congestion, which produced air pollution of its own, and to (b) dangerously sedentary lifestyles, right at the moment when unhealthy fast food was becoming popular.

The same conditions that made suburban houses cheap made suburbia an expensive proposition for local government. Central cities couldn't support the infrastructure that was being abandoned. If they raised taxes, they drove more people away, accelerating their decline. The new suburbs, for their part, needed entirely new infrastructure (utilities, schools, fire stations and the like), but nobody wanted to pay for them. Developers didn't: they preferred to build

---

8. This story, as all stories do, leaves things out. Something that deserves far more attention is the transformation of rural America at the time. Shifts in farm policy and spectacular technological advances were making many smaller farms uncompetitive, suggesting the possibility that suburbia was flowing into a rural land market vacuum. See Paul K. Conkin, *A Revolution Down on the Farm: The Transformation of American Agriculture Since 1929* (Lexington, KY: The University Press of Kentucky, 2008).

cookie cutter houses and then move on. Residents didn't want to pay either: they turned their wrath on anyone newer than themselves, blaming them for crowding the clean and spacious amenities that were the reason for moving out of the city in the first place. Residents pressed their local governments to use urban planning regulations to limit growth and to require that developers pay for the infrastructure. In response, developers cultivated the political power to resist regulations and fees by becoming the biggest contributors to local political campaigns. New developments were still often built ahead of the infrastructure.

But, as the critics of sprawl note, the segregation, the monotony of the new suburbs, the infrastructure problems—they were only the human costs of sprawl. When cities rippled outward, they destroyed farmland and natural habitat: as Edward Johnson has noted, for the first half of the twentieth century, Los Angeles County, now seen as the epitome of sprawl, was the most productive agricultural county in the United States.[9] The destruction extended beyond simply cutting down trees or replacing cornfields with tract homes. Roads became gateways for invasive species; lawns were often laden with dangerous chemicals; parking lots turned rain into oily high-velocity rushes of water that eroded creeks and streams; and suburban cats and dogs wreaked havoc with the smaller native fauna. In short, moving out to be closer to Nature was destroying it.

These criticisms remained all but constant from the early 1970s to the Great Recession. So, too, was the proffered solution: return to the denser, more pedestrian-friendly development patterns that existed before cars were widely available. This old-school solution *was* elegantly simple. The first step was key: redirect future growth from the urban fringe and back towards older, neglected areas of cities. This could be done in a variety of ways, such as reducing the amount of development allowed on the urban fringe, providing incentives to developers to build in older neighborhoods and shifting

9. Edward J. Johnson, "The Effect of Historic Parcels on Agriculture: Harvesting Homes," *San Joaquin Agricultural Law Review* 12 (2002): 56.

transportation funding from suburbs to older cities.[10]

Start reversing sprawl, and everything would fall back into place like a zipper being zipped up. Neglected older neighborhoods would receive more public and private investment, which would make them more appealing. The additional people would make mass transit more viable and the availability of stores, restaurants, parks and friends within walking distance would reduce the need to drive or even own a car. This would start mass transit upward on a virtuous cycle: as more and more people used it, it would have the funds to expand while lowering ticket prices, which would increase its appeal and ridership even further. The advantages of scale economies would work with other infrastructure too—it takes less asphalt, pipe and wiring to connect a group of condo units than it does houses separated by wide lawns—and that would lower costs for local government. And less construction on the suburban fringe would mean less habitat destruction, less watershed damage and fewer cars commuting in from the boondocks. The combined effect of all these changes would be vibrant cities, healthy ecosystems and freedom from foreign oil. The icing on the cake would be that you still got to eat the cake: the opportunity to walk more places would help keep people fit. We would in effect have the glory of early twentieth-century cities without the smoky factories (which were all moving to China anyway).

This roll-back-the-clock fantasy was first called *growth management* in the 1970s and 1980s. During the 1990s, this vision of the good city, this alternative to sprawl, was repackaged and relabeled *Smart Growth*.[11] There were modest differences, some the result of planning

10. For a catalogue of Smart Growth techniques, see Elizabeth Gearin, "Smart Growth or Smart Growth Machine? The Smart Growth Movement and Its Implications," in *Up Against the Sprawl: Public Policy and the Making of Southern California*, ed. Jennifer Wolch, Manuel Pastor, Jr. and Peter Dreier, 279–307 (Minneapolis: University of Minnesota Press, 2004).
11. For an early analysis comparing Smart Growth to its predecessors, see Robert W. Burchell, D. Listokin, and C. Galley, "Smart Growth: More than a Ghost of Urban Policy Past, Less Than a Bold New Horizon," *Housing Policy Debate* 11 (2001): 821–879. Although critics of sprawl play up the interconnections between the different problems they wish to address, some at least do recognize that Smart Growth will not solve them all. Robert

innovations and some the result of the country moving politically to the right. First, growth management's emphasis on expensive light rail government projects, which frequently generated only limited ridership, slowly began to give way to more creative approaches to mass transit.[12] Second, frustrations at the lack of coordination among cities made regional cooperation a central tenet of Smart Growth. Third was a shift in attitude. A number of advocates of earlier growth management plans were candid in their opposition to new growth. This was banished. Whatever reservations advocates of Smart Growth privately had about more development, in public the question was not whether growth was good but solely where to put it: more growth made possible the advantages of higher densities, such as better mass transit. This made urban planning more palatable to business people, who were sometimes uneasy about the hostility directed towards them by earlier critics of growth, but it put Smart Growth advocates in the awkward position of arguing that the cause of the problem was also the solution.[13]

The widened appeal of rebranding growth management was immediately obvious. Typically, urban planners' only allies in the push for more compact cities were environmentalists, good government groups like the League of Women Voters, downtown business interests and the occasional enterprising politician. During the dot-com boom of the late 1990s, however, not only did some business leaders support Smart Growth, but so did public health officials,

---

W. Burchell, Anthony Downs, Barbara McCann and Sahan Mukherji, *Sprawl Costs: Economic Impacts of Unchecked Development* (Washington, DC: Island Press, 2005): 120, 163; Peter Calthorpe and William Fulton, *The Regional City: Planning for the End of Sprawl* (Washington, DC: Island Press, 2001): 11.

12. For a description of light rail obsession in Los Angeles, see Genevieve Guiliano and Elizabeth Gearin, "Where is the 'Region' in Regional Transportation Planning?" in *Up Against the Sprawl: Public Policy and the Making of Southern California*, ed. Jennifer Wolch, Manuel Pastor, Jr., and Peter Dreier, 151–170 (Minneapolis: University of Minnesota Press, 2004).

13. For the early use of the phrase *Smart Growth* in Maryland, see John W. Frece, *Sprawl and Politics: The Inside Story of Smart Growth in Maryland* (Albany: SUNY Press, 2009).

politicians of both parties (especially governors), labor unions, histori-cal preservationists, the Environmental Protection Agency, architects and even the Bank of America. Although property rights advocates and libertarians were critical, the rapid economic growth of the time made Smart Growth, for a brief moment, the political common sense. Everyone knew that we had to do it. It was just a question of how. That question was asked high and low: although too complex to receive much attention on television, Smart Growth became a buzzword to be brandished about in city councils, local newspapers, state legislatures and magazines like *National Geographic*, *Newsweek* and *Time*. Not since the massive surge of environmentalism in the late 1960s had urban planning garnered such national interest and institutional support.

Smart Growth, then, was to be the cavalry coming to the rescue of American cities. It could deal with land supply problems, housing affordability, traffic congestion, crime, health issues, downtown dete-rioration and city budget problems. It could protect natural habitats and keep farms and waistlines where they belonged. Smart Growth was classy. It was sophisticated. It was sexy. It was, uhm, smart. But we never truly found out whether Smart Growth could work. The seemingly unstoppable waves of suburban sprawl were abruptly halted by the Great Recession.

After seven years of real estate doldrums, however, people are now beginning to ask whether we are experiencing another housing bubble because home prices are going up so rapidly. If history is any guide, if growth continues, people will begin clamoring for ways to deal with the problems of suburban development and will likely turn to Smart Growth first. History also suggests that a resurrected Smart Growth will disappoint its backers in countless ways.

To understand why requires looking at one place in great depth. To breeze over what was happening in many cities and pronounce it good, as did books and articles cheerleading Smart Growth during its heyday, won't work because of the tremendous gap between what planners and elected officials claimed would happen as a result of Smart Growth efforts and what was happening on the ground.

Any American city could more or less work for such a study. San Diego, California, however, is perfect. It is large enough to have the experiences of large cities—it was actually the sixth largest city in the country when Smart Growth became popular—yet it is small enough and cut-off enough from other sprawling metropolises that it is possible to treat it as a microcosm, allowing simultaneous study of both urban and rural areas.

Furthermore, the region had a decided opportunity to embrace Smart Growth. In the late 1990s, the City and County of San Diego both began updating their *general plans*. These plans could have created a framework for dealing with many of the most serious problems facing the region. Indeed, the way the plan updates were started simultaneously created such a rare chance to deal with problems on such a wide scale that it led one of the senior SANDAG staff to claim that "the stars were aligned."

General Plans

General plans, which are also called *comprehensive* or *master plans*, are fairly straightforward documents. They are long-range planning documents that specify how a city or county wants to look in twenty years, maybe thirty or forty if they're more progressive. The plans describe in broad terms where housing, businesses, retail, parks and roads will go and what areas should be protected as open space. The goal of a plan is to make growth more orderly, minimizing negative impacts while encouraging development that increases the tax base and is popular with residents. Each plan spells out the jurisdiction's commitments and can help shape local land and housing markets. Plans are divided into distinct chapters called *elements* such as housing, economic development and circulation (traffic). The requirements for general plans, as well as their legal weight, are spelled out in state law, which creates great variability across the country. General plans are often supported by *community plans* that provide more detail for individual neighborhoods.

Early plans in the United States were usually the product of civic or business groups and gave disproportionate attention to downtowns. The most famous early plans were Chicago's 1909 plan and New York's 1929 plan. Compared to modern plans, early plans were driven by aesthetic principles and focused on making cities look pleasing to the eye. Although business elites occasionally still make plans, local governments write most of them now, and the plans they write are more legalistic and concerned with infrastructure and the timing of its construction.

The element of general plans that acts as a backbone is the *land use element*, which broadly says what will get built where. It is this element that made general plans the perfect partners of Smart Growth. Smart Growth was about where development should go, and these plans spelled out exactly that. The writing of a general plan was an opportunity to commit to Smart Growth like no other.[14]

And, as the San Diego experience shows, the commitments were less than they appeared to be. Despite occasional claims to the contrary, Smart Growth could barely be said to be implemented. Rather, its rhetoric was accepted. This book explains why and ultimately offers suggestions on different ways we can approach the problems of development.

This book has three types of chapters: San Diego history, break-narrative analysis putting San Diego into the context of national

14. When it comes to planning, California is in an odd position. In the 1970s, the state—and San Diego in particular—were leaders in growth management. By the standards of the day, the legal apparatus that was created to support planning, especially for local jurisdictions, was quite strong. This was slowly, haltingly, strengthened in response to the continued outward spread of sprawl. The legal reforms, however, didn't address what, by the dot-com boom, many observers considered to be the main weakness in the public response to urban development: the lack of cooperation between local jurisdictions. As a result, by the rise of Smart Growth, California cities found it difficult to get on the same page, but each had tremendous power to regulate growth within its boundaries. For how other states attempted to implement Smart Growth, see John M. DeGrove, *Planning Policy and Politics: Smart Growth and the States* (Cambridge, MA: Lincoln Institute of Land Policy, 2005).

conflict over land rights and, finally, analysis of the political process. The bulk of the analysis of the legislative process is in the next chapter. The San Diego histories begin in the subsequent chapter with the story of how SANDAG shaped debates about growth. That chapter is followed by two longer histories, first of the City of San Diego's general plan update called the Strategic Framework Element or the City of Villages and then of the County's general plan update, initially called General Plan 2020. The histories will show how Smart Growth could create the illusion of its own success even while it was ground down by daily politics. Break-narrative chapters in these histories will criticize the three major ideologies motivating participation in land use politics, showing how they defined personal interests as the public good. The conclusion brings together these different threads.

CHAPTER ONE
OBSTACLES TO
SUSTAINABLE PLANNING

A s a vision of the future, as a template of what cities could be like, Smart Growth has much to recommend to it. One only has to travel to the cities of Asia or Europe to see that key components can work under certain circumstances. What is questionable is whether such a vision can be implemented through the American system of city planning.

Planners like to portray general plans as very amiable documents, something no right-minded person could object to. After all, general plans are created by planners, working with active citizens, to promote the public good by creating an efficient and beneficial arrangement of land uses. This could be called the nice view of planning, which can be seen in one of the few planning textbooks that discusses writing plans: while Stephanie Kelly notes that, "[p]lanning by its very nature is controversial in the United States," the overall impression of her book—and the profession as a whole—is that the writing of plans is a technical activity under the control of planners and only occasionally corrupted by politics.[1] Not everyone accepts the nice view of planning. The most influential opponents

---

1. Stephanie B. Kelly, *Community Planning: How to Solve Urban and Environmental Problems* (Lanham, MA: Rowman & Littlefield Publishers, Inc., 2004): 56.

are conservatives, especially libertarians and other property rights advocates, who are deeply skeptical of public sector planning. They see Smart Growth as another installment in a long series of foolish liberal meddling in markets and fight it.

The conflict that ensues is but one of the paralyzing forces which makes it so difficult to control land use in the United States. There are many others. This chapter provides an overview of some of the major ones. Individually, each would be fairly easy to address. But taken together, they are like the tiny Lilliputian ropes holding down Gulliver. A few of these problems are distinctive to land use planning, but many of them are inherent in American politics at the local level.

Politics of Planning

As the Greek facades of so many federal buildings in the national capital remind us, the Athenian empire is one of the models for democracy in America. How good of a model it is is questionable: while claiming to represent the *demos*—the people—the Athenian democrats were but a fraction of the population. Women, children and slaves simply didn't count.[2]

In the early years of the American republic, democracy wasn't terribly different. The right to participate in government and public life was jealously held by white property-owning men, with rare exceptions for property-owning women, mainly widows.[3] Women *qua* women were excluded as a matter of course, as were slaves. The poor, lacking property, were seen as not having a stake in the community.

2. Or to be more precise in the case of women and children, they only had rights through a male citizen. Philip Brook Manville, *The Origins of Citizenship in Ancient Athens* (Princeton, NJ: Princeton University Press, 1997): 12.

3. Widows were allowed to vote in several cases in early America, and suffrage was granted to all property-owning women in New Jersey from 1776 to 1807. Alexander Keyssar, *The Right to Vote: The Contested History of Democracy in the United States* (New York: Basic Books, 2000): 6, 54.

The legal barriers to involvement in American public life gradually fell: property qualifications for voting formally ended in the first quarter of the nineteenth century, slavery was banned at the end of the Civil War, discrimination against (white) women voting lost its legal support at the end of World War One, and many of the wide-ranging humiliations of Jim Crow were criminalized by the civil rights legislation of the 1960s. These successes of the American credo are all well-known and are celebrated by cramming them into the brains of school children.[4] Less well-known is that during the ferment of the 1960s, federal laws began including requirements for "maximum feasible participation" in comunity projects. After some initial faltering, it became firmly embedded in local politics.[5]

And yet, after all the progress, if one of the signers of the Declaration of Independence could observe a local government meeting today discussing land use, he would, in many towns, feel at ease. He could chat with the elected officials and discover that they were the property-owning leading citizens, homeowners if not business owners. If the Founding Father mingled with the members of the public sitting in front of the elected officials, he'd discover that they were property owners as well. Thanks to the shifts in international immigration in the 1960s, the minorities present might confound the expectations of 1776, but there wouldn't be enough non-whites to raise concern that they were anything but servants. Indeed, if our time-traveling revolutionaries had any question about the proceedings, it would be a simple, "Why are there so many widows?"

Not all local politics is this way. Participation in other matters appears more open to diversity. For instance, if a neighborhood is

---

4. An excellent book on how history is taught to American children is James W. Loewen, *Lies My Teacher Told Me: Everything Your American History Textbook Got Wrong* (New York: Simon & Schuster, 1996).

5. Jeffrey M. Berry, Kent Portney and Ken Thomson, *The Rebirth of Urban Democracy* (Washington, DC: The Brookings Institute, 1993). The participation law, however, was not followed everywhere. The Daly Administration in Chicago ignored it. Ester R. Fuchs, *Mayors and Money: Fiscal Policy in New York and Chicago* (Chicago: University of Chicago Press, 1992): 263–64, 271.

under immediate threat, perhaps by toxic contamination, participation is broader.[6] And some health and social welfare programs have a distinct client base whose participation is cultivated, or, in the case of parents involved in their children's education, they invite themselves. In short, those who are most directly affected do participate, even if their views do not necessarily carry the day.

Land use is different. Although everyone is affected by how cities and towns are built, not everyone plays a role in designing them. Although it's slowly changing, in many diverse communities, it is as if the older, better educated, white home- and business owners are the only people who have to live with the consequences of urban design. Why there is this divide in participation, which is fundamentally a split between those with property and those without, will be explored later.

What matters here is the consequence of this divide: it distorts our understanding of the negative impacts of growth and eliminates the incentive to confront them. The first effect: if not everyone participates in planning decisions, then their experiences and needs are considered in a clumsy, secondhand way, if at all. Reform efforts might even be justified in the name of the vulnerable populations, but, if they are uninvolved or are unable to sustain their involvement over time, then policies subtly or blatantly shift away from their concerns. As a result, when planners craft visions of ideal cities, inevitably they design cities that are ideal for those with the resources to participate in planning and who demand to be heard.

This political inequality allows metropolitan regions to take the low road on growth. Local jurisdictions, which is where most building authority is vested in the United States, have found it easier to deflect the costs of growth onto marginal populations.[7] As the

6. On local involvement in controversies that revolve around science, see Jason Corburn, *Street Science: Community Knowledge and Environmental Health* (Cambridge, MA: MIT Press, 2005).

7. On the question of who pays the costs of growth, see the work of Harvey Molotch, particularly John Logan and Harvey Molotch, *Urban Fortunes: The Political Economy of Place* (Berkeley: University of California Press, 1987). Incidentally, some states, like

environmental justice movement has argued (mainly in the context of specific undesirable land uses such as nuclear waste facilities), the uneven distribution of the costs and rewards of development eliminates the incentive to deal squarely with the problems of growth. If every local community could resist intrusions successfully, then undesirable uses would become prohibitively expensive and cleaner alternatives would have to be found. But not every community can, so it's easier to use the neighborhoods of the vulnerable as dumping grounds than to figure out an economical way to green industry and transportation. There is one unwanted side effect of growth that is hard to shift onto others—traffic—and it often becomes *the* major local political grievance aired during times of growth.

The Methods of Local Political Madness

The difficulties in making cities more sustainable are not merely a matter of *who* is involved, but also of *how* they go about regulating land. Three facets of planning practices can hinder sustainability: the rituals and incentives of politics discourage leadership from elected officials, the legal system distorts goals and delays implementation, and, finally, the professionalism of planners can become an end in itself. These have all been strongly evident in San Diego and cause damage, to varying degrees, to communities across the country.

Elected Officials

Many elected officials are not—contrary to the public perception—in a position to lead. Their powers are often more circumscribed than people suspect. Indeed, for the mayors of the City of San Diego at the beginning of the case study here, much of their power came from the public assuming that someone who was in effect just another

Oregon and Florida, have begun to curtail home rule as they implement their own growth management programs. This limits local jurisdictions' ability to deflect costs. John M. DeGrove, *Planning Policy and Politics: Smart Growth and the States* (Cambridge, MA: Lincoln Institute of Land Policy, 2005).

councilmember had more power than they did. Further, to lead, an elected official needs followers, and, in many cities, they don't have them. The local party structures are weak, so elected officials take office with few foot soldiers. Instead, they have to, as Ester Fuchs so ably documents in her comparison of New York City and Chicago, perpetually put together temporary coalitions of special interest groups.[8] Instead of leading with a vision, they are too busy being reactive, trying to keep as many demanding groups happy as possible. Fuchs argues that cities with weak political parties have chronic budget problems because elected officials do not have the tools to enforce discipline, but rather they are forced to perpetually attempt to please their backers. Such officials can come across as passive and be the subject of considerable (and not necessarily fair) anger. San Diego is one such city.

This limit on visionary leadership only affects some places, but other limits are shared by all or almost all American cities. Sustainability is by definition, a long-term goal, as it means promoting and maintaining a high quality of life over an indefinite time period. Politicians, however, have much, much shorter time frames to consider. No matter how idealistic they are, they're forced to think in terms of election cycles. This opens up a profound gap between how planners and politicians approach problem-solving. Alan Altshuler's 1965 classic case studies of the Twin Cities lay this out: politicians, given the advantages bestowed by incumbency, often are more concerned with not antagonizing anyone than with promoting an agenda. If they do something, it needs tangible results to show constituents. This makes elected officials ambivalent at best about long-range city planning, for its goals are fundamentally at odds with their own. Planning's emphasis on an orderly built environment decades hence sparks controversy in the present, controversy disproportionate to the good for which elected officials can take credit. To make matters worse, the technical side of planning is

8. Ester R. Fuchs, *Mayors and Money: Fiscal Policy in New York and Chicago* (Chicago: University of Chicago Press, 1992).

expressed through thick documents that are so far removed from practical political matters that elected officials have little incentive to read them. While Altshuler may be overgeneralizing about politicians avoiding controversy—someone elected to a safe district can take more risks and some politicians seek out complicated issues—he is basically right in portraying planning as unglamorous and unrewarding for elected officials.

Altshuler, however, wrote on the cusp of what would, especially in California, become "the quiet revolution" in city planning. By the late 1960s, the environmental damage and infrastructure costs of suburbanization led to increased political support for curtailing the excesses of development. This led to increasing planning regulations at all levels of government, including laws that predicated federal funding on the existence of local plans (written with the previously mentioned "maximum feasible participation" by the public). Between the need to include residents in decisions and the growing complexity of planning rules, planning departments nationwide expanded and became a significant budget item. Politicians started taking long-range land use planning more seriously, to the point that some made careers out of opposition to growth.[9]

For many politicians, however, planning still brings in comparatively few rewards. They have much less to show for a million dollars spent on a general plan update than, say, a new police substation: general plans do not have ribbon-cutting ceremonies; they generate no goodwill from the police officers' union; they don't have walls onto which can be stuck bronze plaques listing all the members of city council; community residents will never walk by them (even if the general plan establishes policies that promote pedestrian-friendly neighborhoods).

One might think that the increased gravity of planning since the time of Altshuler's case studies has, if it hasn't increased its

9. On politicians opposing growth, see Mark Schneider and Paul Teske, "The Antigrowth Entrepreneur: Challenging the 'Equilibrium' of the Growth Machine," *Journal of Politics* 55 (1993): 720–36.

rewards, at least decreased the danger it represents to politicians' careers. After all, planning is now a longstanding function of local government. But planning seems to be even more thankless now: it is much more technical (and more time-consuming), and the rise of pervasive anti-government, pro-market rhetoric ensures that if good comes out of planning, the public will not see it as the product of government foresight but as a miracle of the free market, even if the government subsidies were overwhelming.[10] Indeed, since the Reagan Revolution, for a politician, publicly supporting planning or stronger regulation leads to the risk of being tarnished with the smear "business unfriendly." And just as some politicians make a career out of opposing growth, some conservative elected officials get great mileage, especially in the form of developer campaign contributions, from attacking planning and limits on growth.

Furthermore, politicians have many other issues competing for their attention.[11] These issues can be just as complex as long-range planning, making each a substantial investment of time and energy in its own right. In the first case study of this book, the City of San Diego's general plan update went before city council in a climactic meeting at a rare evening session. The next morning, city council was scheduled to have another meeting. This demonstrates, in a positively mind-numbing way, the time-management issues that face elected officials, for at that morning meeting the agenda included:

10. A telling example of this is the naming of stadiums. While public subsidies are often high, the rights to pick the name go to corporations that give much smaller contributions. Jane Jacobs owes some of the responsibility for reluctance to give government its due. Her justly famous *The Death and Life of Great American Cities* argues that in every dense community there is a vibrant street life trying to get out if only planners stop trying to impose their sense of order. Jacobs, *The Death and Life of Great American Cities* (New York: Random House, 1961).

11. Elected officials in jurisdictions with few people do not necessarily have an overabundance of other political issues, but then the competition for attention is with their day jobs, as elected officials are frequently poorly paid. At the beginning of their political careers especially, some of these part-time officials are rank amateurs and heavily dependent on others for guidance. Term limits help ensure everyone remains an amateur.

adoption of changes to building and fire codes; a
loan for a sludge pump for the Point Loma sewage
treatment plant; the lease of space in the Civic Center
Plaza Building; the installation of additional parking
meters downtown; an agreement with an engineering
firm for sewage and water work; an agreement with
the Metropolitan Water District; a homeless shelter
program for the coming winter; a request from the
Downtown Partnership for additional banners; an
amendment to the council policy on mandatory ethics
training; a street name change request; the purchase
of a property; final parcel maps for two developments;
the vacation of part of a street and another for part
of an alley; an appeal from the Historical Resources
Board; a tentative map for a 456-acre development;
another development on 93 acres; another for 39 acres;
another on 40 acres; approval of a three-story condo;
commendation for a kids safety program; a request
from the city attorney to get a $71,000 loan for a
spouse abuse program; the undergrounding of utility
lines; appointments to the Wetlands Advisory Board;
proclamation of Cabrillo Festival Week; and finally [!!],
an amendment to an element on solid waste disposal.

In addition, the seven public speakers on non-agenda items raised
seven more issues, ranging from canyon restoration projects to a
complaint alleging that the City website was not in compliance with
federal law because it was not fully usable by the blind. With such
a meeting beginning twelve hours after the general plan hearing,
if councilmembers gave their undivided attention to the plan, they
weren't giving it to something else.[12]

12. At its best, a good general plan could make some of these other decisions routine and
thus save time. For that to happen, however, an elected official must have confidence in
the plan, which is unlikely unless they had an active role in shaping it.

In the documentary *Fahrenheit 9/11*, Michael Moore ridiculed members of Congress for not reading the Patriot Act before passing it, but this is not surprising. One former San Diego city council-member estimated that each major issue generates 1,500 pages of paperwork. If the issues are technical or the public correspondence voluminous, there is a temptation to only skim. And if the public correspondence is thin or nonexistent, that suggests that no one else cares anyway. Time is better spent elsewhere.

The staff that assists elected officials faces similar challenges. Except for the highest positions, staff usually focuses upon specific political arenas, but, even within this distribution of labor, aides have many demands on their time, and long-range planning doesn't necessarily fare well in the competition for it. During the San Diego County's general plan update, only Supervisor Slater-Price had her land use aide regularly attend the interest group and steering committee meetings (beginning with the plan's early controversial implosion). The other supervisors got their information about these meetings third hand at best as their own staff had to ask the planners what happened.

Ideally, political staff are experts in their designated fields. But that is not always realistic: youth and idealism are often necessary to generate the enthusiasm required for what can be low-paying and long-houred jobs. Even for staffers who bring experience to the table, each issue is idiosyncratic and takes time to understand. Once a staff person *does* understand their job thoroughly and has built up on the contacts to do it well, they become highly desirable in the private sector, which can offer salaries sufficient to lure them away. This makes staff turnover a problem.

In addition to their personal staff, elected officials have agency staff, commissioners, city managers, chief administrative officers and the like to aid their decision-making. These people, who are supposed to be experts in their own right, make recommendations, write reports condensing information down to critical points, make day-to-day decisions to keep higher-ups from being bogged down in minutiae, etc. But they are not always listened to and sometimes they contradict each other. Indeed, they can have their own agendas and are not always to be trusted: one of the biggest issues in the City of San Diego in the years immediately following the adoption of the City of Villages plan was the extent to which city council could dodge criminal charges for security fraud by pinning the blame on duplicitous staff. Furthermore, if elected officials are critical of agency staff when they bring forth a range of proposals for consideration, staff will eventually get the message that they should only tell their bosses what they want to hear.

The way daily interactions of local politics are organized creates additional obstacles for elected officials. Informal meetings allow people to interact with each other and compromise. The very structure of public hearings, however, discourages give-and-take negotiating. Instead, elected bodies typically follow a variant of the strictures found in *Robert's Rules of Order*—conspicuously not *Robert's Rules of Consensus Building*—that operate more as social control, especially for limiting public input, than as a mechanism for communication. The more strictly those rules are followed, the more each member of the elected body pontificates and speaks to an idealized speaker in the audience and not to each other. In cases where the elected officials have already made up their minds before a meeting starts, the ritual straightjacket of public hearings does minimal damage. But, when new information comes up at a meeting and politicians are forced to make choices on the spot, the artificial rules of discourse they're operating under can isolate them from each other, the momentum of the agenda propelling them forward.

If elected officials try to negotiate outside of public meetings, they face a whole slew of ethical problems, which is why sunshine laws try to keep public business public. But these laws leave elected officials with limited means to deal with complicated controversies other than the classic maneuver of appointing ad hoc committees where the details can be worked out in more informal settings. (These meetings are often difficult for the public to attend even if technically open because they're poorly advertised and take place during the day when most people work.)

At the local level, where partisan divides are not necessarily clear cut, the structure of meetings makes it easier to cast bland "yea" votes than to vote "nay." Having an item on an agenda before an elected body represents considerable preparation. Staff, both political and departmental, have done research; the item may, depending on the jurisdiction, have gone through a de facto dress rehearsal before the relevant subcommittee. Often times, it is easier to take it on faith that all the work has been done properly than to criticize, as voting nay makes one stand out and be forced to defend a position more vigorously. This is particularly true if a matter is seen as specific to another politician's district. All this creates the temptation to say little and cast a yea, and in fact many votes before public bodies are unanimous.[13]

The potential for a herd mentality also undercuts planning by making elected officials reluctant to challenge short-sighted public perceptions. This is especially the case with taxes. Conservatives, beginning with southern California conservatives like Ronald Reagan, have placed hostility to government at the core of their agenda, and nothing symbolizes the evils of government more thoroughly than taxes. When this is taken to an extreme, the corporate body of local government suffers from fiscal anorexia: the fear of taxes, like the fear of calories, overrides common sense and survival instincts. No one wants to be the first to tell people that nothing is for free, that if you're going to press government officials for things like better roads or schools, you have to pay for them. We have the experience of the hapless Democrats under Reagan–Bush to know what happens if someone tries to talk straight about taxes.

Planning is particularly hurt by the hostility towards taxes.

---

13. This is more noticeable on appointed bodies. Elected officials typically go down the line expressing their concerns. Appointed bodies like planning commissions are often more dominated by their outspoken members. Because membership does not require running the gauntlet of electoral campaign publicity, more shy people have seats.

At the state and federal levels, legislators have less of a default to vote yes but instead make decisions based on things like party recommendation, attitude toward the bill author and past votes (i.e., in committees and the other house).

Implementation of plans takes money. In Florida, for instance, the inability to tackle an ineffective tax structure hurt the state's ability to provide promised support for local planning efforts, leading to delays that undercut planning's credibility.[14] Indeed, though it's rarely appreciated, general plans are implicit city budgets. If a jurisdiction has flexibility in its spending, this is okay, but it is easy for plans to become promises to do things for which everyone knows there is no money (or willingness to raise it). Furthermore, since their benefits are not immediate and tangible, planning staff are particularly perceived as expendable when it's time to cut the budget.

If this wasn't bad enough, the legislative process at the local level can add another wrinkle to efforts to pass laws. Local governments often follow a pattern of enacting legislation distinct from state and federal governments. At the state and federal level, non-appropriation bills tend to have an author (also called a sponsor) who introduces the legislation and helps shepherd it through. At the local level, the city staff in the departments that would be affected tend to drive the process. A project to replace aging sewer pipes, for instance, would be nursed through the legislative process by the public works department. This staff-driven approach means that a proposal can move forward without having at least one elected champion if it hits a rough spot. If a controversy erupts, instead of having at least one politician with an incentive to stand in front of cameras to defend the proposal, all the politicians will take on an innocent, shocked expression and start demanding explanations.

In short, final decisions about long-range planning in most local jurisdictions are in the hands of people who may be receiving limited information, may lack the background to judge the quality of that information and may be ambivalent or hostile to planning anyway. They make decisions in hearings in which they have limited opportunities to negotiate or find out additional information. The upshot is that a small group of staff and public committee members

14. John M. DeGrove, *Planning Policy and Politics: Smart Growth and the States* (Cambridge, MA: Lincoln Institute of Land Policy, 2005): ch. 3.

can work on a project literally for years under the illusion that they have the support of elected officials who, focusing on more pressing concerns, have given vague nods of approval. When the project becomes a pressing concern itself, everyone from politicians to citizens groups have intense reactions as they discover their interests threatened.[15] In the end, years of work on a major project like a general plan can be decided by a throw of the dice at the adoption hearing and then risk failure again because the necessary funding is not forthcoming.

But even if elected officials are fully committed to sustainable long-range planning, there is only so much they can do.

Adversarial Legalism

Unlike the powers of the federal and state governments, the powers of cities and counties are not described in the Constitution. While such silence could be interpreted to mean that they are relatively unimportant and should be vested with few powers, tradition has made local control over land use (and education) all but a sacred right.

Likewise, the federal government has the authority to have a strong overarching land use or urban policy but it doesn't use it.[16] Indeed, as critics of American urban growth have pointed out, not having a national policy *is* our national policy. Instead of a coherent approach, the federal government has a patchwork of direct and indirect controls. Some controls are obvious: the federal government intervenes in development to protect endangered species, it controls certain waterways, it owns land, including much of the rural West, and its decisions about where to locate government agencies, like military bases and NASA research centers, can have

15. In the case of especially powerful people, they may have been observing while hoping they do not have to intervene and risk being publicly attacked as a special interest.

16. For a history of the life and ultimate death of an attempt to create a national urban policy during the 1970s, see Sidney Plotkin, *Keep Out: The Struggle for Land Use Control* (Berkeley: University of California Press, 1987).

significant economic impacts. Other federal controls aren't quite as direct but are just as real: the federal government holds the purse strings for the bulk of the country's transportation funding, subsidizes homeownership and is intimately involved in water politics (making the urban West possible). Perhaps most important of all, the federal courts define the legal structure of land as private property.

Aside from nudging by the federal government in the form of money grants and the placement of interstates, however, actual patterns of urban and suburban development are primarily a matter between states and local jurisdictions. Decision-making tends towards the model of the states passing enabling legislation and local jurisdictions making actual decisions. This intense decentralization has one significant strength: it allows for flexibility and innovation. But there's a drawback. Cities and counties are largely left to their own devices, even when there are mandates they technically should be following. This method of having the state and federal governments lay out a broad framework for urban policy but then only providing minimal oversight over local jurisdictions creates a gap in enforcement. Into this gap flow lawyers.

The legal presence in American land use could be good: lawyers could lubricate the machinery of political negotiation by bringing in expertise on the law and mediating between conflicting parties. Unfortunately, what happens instead is that land use lawyers, as a group, act not like oil but glue.

With little assertion of land use authority by the state or the federal government, enforcement often depends upon injured parties suing for remedies. The American court system, however, is slow, expensive and unpredictable, the result of what Robert Kagan calls *adversarial legalism*, in which dueling lawyers debate cases before judges with wide discretionary powers. The system encourages creativity in both arguments and remedies, but it comes at a high cost: uncertainty. A judge's new interpretation of a law can instantly lead to dramatic changes. Entrepreneurial lawyers further add to this instability because even if they lose, they can seek new venues for their cases by appealing decisions and filing new suits in other courts. This process of exhaustively exploring each issue may seem like a good thing—if closure never matters.[17]

Smart Growth, however, faces several points of especial legal friction. This is most obvious when governments try to steer growth away from rural areas.[18] Landowners howl that such efforts violate their property rights. The Fifth Amendment of the Constitution states that private property shall not "be taken for public use, without just compensation." The Supreme Court has long recognized that laws could so constrict the use of property as to effectively take it from the owner (what is called a "regulatory taking"). This requires regulatory relief or compensation to the landowner. Private property rights advocates have long campaigned for a very expansive interpretation of regulatory takings, with some going as far as to argue that *any* decrease in the economic value of property requires compensation. Property rights advocates have had some electoral successes, most notably Oregon's 2004 Measure 37 and Arizona's 2006 Proposition 207, and were active in whipping up the backlash against the Supreme Court's (2005) *Kelo v. New London* decision, which confirmed a very broad understanding of eminent domain, the government power to seize property. The courts have been reluctant to second-guess jurisdictions' land use regulations, but they have affirmed the basically economic nature of property and the federal judiciary has grown increasingly conservative. This has meant considerable grey area, which requires more lawsuits, so planners have to be wary of being sued. This affects planning throughout the United States.

California, however, has several distinctive features that make planning even more difficult. First, state law allows for lawsuits over poorly done environmental impact reports (EIRs), which, under the California Environmental Quality Act (CEQA), are required of major projects. EIRs are public disclosure documents that provide elected officials with analysis that allows them to make informed decisions

17. Robert A. Kagan, *Adversarial Legalism: The American Way of Law* (Cambridge, MA: Harvard University Press, 2001).

18. Anthony Downs, "Smart Growth: Why We Discuss It More Than We Do It," *Journal of the American Planning Association* 71, no. 4 (2005): 367–380.

about developments, ensuring that the desire for growth is balanced by a concern with impacts. In practice, a lawyer can almost always find a plausible error in the analysis or in the procedure for creating the report. As long as they have a sufficient argument to begin a legal process, they can stall the development.

As a result, if a land use project has opponents well-versed in the law, the courts become a tool to slow down and perhaps ultimately thwart it.[19] Ideally, Kagan notes, the threat of litigation would encourage adherence to the law, but the legal system is so open to creative arguments that it can be difficult to gauge what would be a legally safe action. The extra scrutiny lawsuits bring to development proposals can prevent acts of stupidity, but every major development or planning effort can reasonably expect legal trouble during the planning and implementation stages (or in the case of condo construction defects, as the builder's liability approaches expiration). This indiscriminately increases both the time and cost of development, smart, dumb or otherwise. Indeed, as far as developers are concerned, litigation surrounding EIRs has become so inevitable that they routinely include legal fees as a line in their budgets.

EIRs have these effects without necessarily doing anything to protect the environment: all the law requires is that elected officials make decisions with their eyes open and be able to justify the environmental damage a project or a plan they approve entails if mitigation would be too difficult. The reports don't actually stop the damage. Looking back over the time since the state passed CEQA in 1970, probably the only area where the environment is less stressed is exposure to toxins, especially in air pollution, and that is not the result of EIRs as much as deindustrialization, the banning of dangerous chemicals, like lead in gas and paint, and the regime of emissions control (e.g., smog checks).

19. William Fulton, *The Reluctant Metropolis: The Politics of Urban Growth in Los Angeles* (Baltimore: John Hopkins University Press, 2001): 20–21. The reverse is also true: if no one legally savvy cares about what you're doing, you can break the law with impunity. During the time of the major events of this book, the City of San Diego had a reputation for taking a "So sue me" approach.

California may be extreme. In other states, environmental analysis is not necessarily so litigious but the results are not necessarily much better. In mulling over the impacts of such reports in New York City, a CUNY professor raised the question whether the benefits of such reports justified cutting down the trees to print them.[20]

A second distinct feature of Californian politics, one that other states have begun to imitate, also exacerbates adversarial legalism. In California, ballot initiatives are used more frequently and with less flexibility than in other states.[21] Initiatives give people who have lost a decision in front of a judge or an elected body another forum in which they can try to get their way. This reinforces the uncertainty of any seemingly final decision: there's the risk that it'll be reexplored at the ballot box.

The downsides of California initiatives are exacerbated by being inherently nonnegotiable. To be sure, initiatives put on the ballot by elected bodies involve public participation and have some room for give and take. But the wording of privately promoted initiatives can be whatever someone who can afford to have signatures gathered wants them to be. Either way, however, the ballot language is essentially frozen once signature gathering begins. As Peter Schrag has pointed out, this solidity only gets worse if the initiative passes because it takes another ballot measure to modify the original one, unless, of course, it is overturned by a lawsuit.

The dominant style of election campaigning does not help matters. In practice, the notion of elections representing a kind of collective wisdom is true only in the broadest and vaguest sense. Initiative campaigns are fought out through negative television advertising. Rare is the discussion of an initiative focused around accurate descriptions of the initiative's contents or impacts. Instead, debates are reduced to a handful of shock claims. These vary depressingly

20. Tom Angotti, 2004. "Rethinking Environmental Impact Statements," *Gotham Gazette*, (July 2004), http://www.gothamgazette.com/article/landuse/20040720/12/1042.
21. The criticisms of the inflexibility of California initiatives are widely noted by observers of the state's politics but have received one of their best statement in Peter Schrag, *Paradise Lost: California's Experience, America's Future* (New York: The New Press, 1998).

little in light of the initiative's subject matter. No matter what the ballot initiative is supposed to be about, the messages are the same: the initiative is a tax increase; it'll cost billions; it is a Trojan horse that will have huge effects proponents don't mention; the failure to pass the initiative will have devastating results; the initiative includes no accountability measures; the moneys the initiative spent will be subject to annual audits; it'll create more government bureaucracy, etc. It is no surprise when voters respond with confusion, frustration or disgust. Often, they cannot adjudicate between conflicting claims because they rest on how courts will interpret fuzzy wordings and because both sides may be exaggerating, if not outright lying.[22]

So all these features of the legal system—the lawsuits, the endless appeals, the fear of regulatory takings, the ballot initiatives, etc.—what impact do they have? They turn decision-making into something arduous and unpredictable. They concentrate attention on the short-term while paradoxically making the approval process interminable. Instead of conflict being mediated, it is dealt with through chronic temporizing while the power of small but legally savvy sophisticated groups is greatly magnified.

Planners Themselves
Readers at this point may begin to see the likely fate of a general plan in a jurisdiction whose population is not homogenous.[23] It'll be written by a faction of the upper middle class and represent their interests. It'll fly under the radar for some time, but the closer it is to adoption, the more it will be struck by powerful and random

22. I once had the slightly comic experience of trying to volunteer repeatedly for a campaign against a particularly poorly worded initiative. The person locally responsible for the "no" campaign was a paid consultant who couldn't figure out what to do with a volunteer. The San Diego "no" campaign amounted to misleading tv ads clearly intended to scare without giving viewers the slightest inkling what the proposition was about.
23. Some jurisdictions, especially smaller suburbs with high rates of homeownership and few opportunities for additional development, can adopt general plans quickly and with little controversy.

crosscurrents blown by the parts of the upper middle class whose views were neglected in the process of developing the plan. Especially when there is no consensus about how a city or region should grow and thus there is more need for a plan, this can quickly degenerate into what, for want of a better term, could be called a *death spiral*. This is the time when lawmaking gets compared to sausage-making: broad principles, idealism, the larger context, concern for the future—they are all chucked overboard as personalities, short-term political calculations, Machiavellian maneuvering and face-saving come to the fore. Generosity among participants fades, and technical matters and expediency trump the big picture. All that matters is finding the least damaging political closure.[24] When it comes to a plan that has been touted to be Smart Growth, that means continuing to claim it is so while retreating from the bold steps understood to be necessary to implement it.

In theory, the planning profession would help jurisdictions stay on course, stay focused on the greater good, ensuring that something worthwhile survives the political storms. Unfortunately, however, planning can instead sometimes simply help provide an illusion of progress.

Planning is, above all, a profession. That creates needs among planners that have nothing to do with the stated goals of the field:

> Planners and their professional body need the government as an employer and to legitimise their claim to professionalism (and associated status and benefits). Part of the requirements of professionalism are neutrality and expert status. So planners, through their professional status, are unlikely to take political stances or perspectives that are overtly anti-status quo.[25]

---

24. This does not appear to happen that frequently in Sacramento, perhaps because so many of the bills are so modest in nature. It most assuredly happens at the federal level. Death spirals, however, have gotten uglier as increased polarization makes it harder to reach the point where people are so exhausted that they're willing to compromise.

25. Philip Allmendinger, *Planning Theory* (New York: Palgrave, 2002): 22.

And this dependence of planners on government is within a very specific context: global capitalism. As Marxists emphasize, planning is limited by the capitalist ideology sanctifying private property and by the disciplinary power of markets.[26] They argue that capitalist states need planners to legitimate and execute development, but effective regulation of growth could threaten the ability to generate profits and tax revenues. This creates a love–hate relationship in which the state embraces planners while at the same time rendering them mostly harmless.[27]

Attempting to be impartial experts about development while the market is widely seen as the appropriate guide for growth puts planners in an awkward situation. On one hand, the profession has embraced Smart Growth, which, because it is so controversial, requires substantial political support to implement. On the other hand, the planning profession has the tools for neither mass mobilization nor for self-defense against politically motivated attacks. Instead of confronting this head-on, it is often easier for individual planners to embrace the profession's insistence on neutrality.[28]

Although planners are reluctant to recognize it, planning is perhaps unique among professions in the United States in the extent to which some people *really* hate it.[29] For reasons ranging from ideol-

26. David Harvey, *The Urbanization of Capital* (Baltimore: John Hopkins University Press, 1985). See also Jill Grant, "Canada's Experience in Planning for Sustainable Development," in *Towards Sustainable Cities: East Asian, North American and European Perspectives on Managing Urban Regions*, ed. Andre Sorensen, Peter J. Marcotullio, and Jill Grant, 147–160 (Hampshire, England and Burlington, VT: Ashgate Publishing, 2004): 156.

27. Michael Dear and Allen J. Scott, eds., *Urbanization and Urban Planning in Capital Society* (London and New York: Methuen, 1981). Many of these limitations are imposed upon planners through the enabling laws that tell them what they should be doing, laws that would look very different if written by planners. If Karl Marx were alive, he'd probably say that planners make plans, but not under conditions of their own choosing.

28. See Charles Hoch, *What Planners Do: Power, Politics, and Persuasion* (Chicago: Planners Press, 1994).

29. On the incredible political resistance planning encounters, see John M. DeGrove, *Planning Policy and Politics: Smart Growth and the States* (Cambridge, MA: Lincoln Institute of Land Policy, 2005). On how planners refuse to see the inherent opposition

ogy to desire to increase investments to exasperation with red tape, property owners see nothing nice about planning. They already have plans of their own for their land, often money-making plans which may be thwarted by the jurisdiction's official plan.[30] Thus, they see the regulation of land as an anathema and act accordingly. Some have substantial access to wealth and use it to support their preferred political candidates, meaning that a planner's boss might fundamentally hold their goals in contempt.

This points to a fundamental challenge, if not contradiction, in planning: if there was a consensus of what needed to be done, there would be little need for plans. Writing a general plan is a political conflict in which certain viewpoints are backed by the prestige of the planning profession, others backed by money and many others excluded. A plan envisions a rational order, an order that the more genteel property owners try to impose upon their brethren whose love of profit outweighs concerns for the impacts of their developments. This allows for a blunter description of a plan: a plan is an act of power. Or, as is often the case in the United States, a plan is a fantasy of power because private property rights are so strongly respected and plans are so flexible that someone with money can create political pressure to have them changed or ignored.

Rarely, planners will explicitly embrace politics. This was first done in the 1960s as a conscious rejection of the then dominant *rational-comprehensive planning* paradigm and its claim to impartial expertise, which was criticized as a cover for promoting elite interests. Equity and advocacy planners made it their goal to support poorer communities, who had the least resources to plan for themselves.[31] Institutional support for this approach to plan-

---

between their views and landowners, see Frank Popper, "What's the Hidden Factor in Land Use Regulation?" *Planning* 37, no. 11 (1978): 4–6. It is probably the three best pages on planning ever written.

30. See also Yonn Dierwechter, *Urban Growth Management and Its Discontents: Promises, Practices, and Geopolitics in U.S. City-Regions* (New York: Palgrave Macmillan, 2009): 52.

31. A famous early statement of this position is Paul Davidoff, "Advocacy and Pluralism in Planning," *Journal of the American Institute of Planners* 31, no. 4 (1965): 331–338.

ning has been limited, and its marginal status outside of academia is a testament to the extent to which more conservative approaches shape the field.

Some planners have tried to sidestep the dilemmas of politics by embracing what is called *communicative planning*, which recasts planners as expert negotiators, facilitators who merely mediate conflicting views and try to help people reach a consensus. It's a clever approach. One of the main criticisms lodged against it is that it simply accepts institutional power arrangements, and the story of San Diego County in Part III of this book will show why someone might say that.

As a profession, planning has turned partially inward and has conformed to expectations of what a profession is. That means developing a set of stances and practices similar to other professions. Planners dress in particular ways, use specialized language and claim to have expert knowledge and procedures.[32] They follow specific educational and career paths and pay dues to professional organizations, which have local chapters and national offices. They attend conferences, those choreographed displays of science (presentations) and status (award banquets with foods that radiate as much bourgeois pretension as consistent with the hotel's profit margin). On this broad level, planning is quite similar to any other profession.

But do the problems of urban sustainability really require cadres of middle-class experts to solve? Take the classic approach to planning. It's a series of distinct steps: defining a problem or mission; establishing a vision; formulating specific goals, policies and standards; collecting data; creating a series of alternatives;

The rhetoric of planners helping those with the least resources comes from Norman Krumholz's tenure in the 1970s as the planning director in Cleveland, one of the few moments when planners had the institutional backing to promote the welfare of disadvantaged residents.

32. Eliot Freidson, *Professionalism Reborn: Theory, Prophecy and Policy* (Chicago: University of Chicago Press, 1994).

modeling their potential impacts and then presenting them to decision-makers, who pick the one that best suits their priorities. The resulting choice is then the official plan. It is then implemented and monitored.[33] This approach contains much accumulated wisdom, and significant delays in the San Diego planning case studies resulted from deviations from it. Yet, fundamentally, there isn't a necessary connection between following this path and improving cities and regions. This approach to planning boils down to two steps. First, establish the proper schema of appropriate categories by pinpointing types of land uses, hierarchies of roads, functions of communities and the like. Second, hold the built environment to that idealized structure. This creates an appearance of order, but this approach is hardly ever held accountable to whether it accomplishes its aims, like reducing traffic congestion or increasing housing affordability.

In other words, planning can become an end unto itself, an exercise in wishful categorization. Erving Goffman noted this shift in evaluating professionals long ago: "the professional takes the stand that the service he performs is not to be judged by the results it achieves but by the degree by which available occupational skills have been proficiently applied ... "[34] Courts have come to accept this standard of professional conduct: it doesn't matter whether the patient died. What matters is whether any other doctor would have done the same thing.

In planning, the risk is that the practices of naming and imposing order either (a) focus solely on immediate concerns at the expense of long-term needs or (b) turn into empty rituals that create a reassuring sense of order, like the environmental impact reports mentioned earlier that categorize possible damage but do

33. For a summary of different typologies of plan writing, see Lewis Hopkins, *Urban Development: The Logic of Making Plans* (Washington, DC: Island Press, 2001): 190 and see also Stephanie B. Kelly, *Community Planning: How to Solve Urban and Environmental Problems* (Lanham, MA: Rowman & Littlefield Publishers, Inc., 2004): xv.
34. Erving Goffman, *The Presentation of Self in Everyday Life* (New York: Anchor Books, 1959): 220–21.

not actually protect against it.³⁵

Another example from California state law: jurisdictions are required to provide adequate affordable housing (§65583 et seq). Jurisdictions prove they are complying with state law by demonstrating that they have zoned sufficient land for multifamily housing. Nothing guarantees that the land will be built upon or that the housing will be affordable. Indeed, before the real estate market began to collapse in 2006, high-end developments were the only multifamily projects built privately in many areas of California. There was no real connection between the law and the cost of housing for families of limited means—yet even the most exclusive jurisdictions went through this process of proclaiming a commitment to affordable housing.³⁶

While speculating that perhaps planners just avoid politically charged terms, two researchers studying general plans concluded that "the explicit inclusion of the concept [of 'sustainability'] has no effect on how well plans actually promote sustainability principles." While supportive of sustainability, the researchers also recognized that their study "supports the frequent criticism that the sustainable development concept is superficial, lacks political commitment, and cannot serve as an influential basis for policy development."³⁷ Likewise, scholars reviewing Smart Growth in general plans from Georgia and Kentucky noted that actual policies in the plans were short of what could be expected for documents claiming to express support for such a comprehensive ideal, and in fact some of what they saw "suggests the use of symbolic language

35. Anecdotally, it seems that the closer a planner is to a particular empty ritual, the more critical they are of it, up to the point where they become responsible for making sure that the said ritual goes smoothly. An excellent work on how governments need to be able to observe order is James Scott, *Seeing like a State: How Certain Schemes to Improve the Human Condition Have Failed* (New Haven: Yale University Press, 1998).
36. A strengthening of this law will be discussed briefly in the County case study.
37. Philip R. Berke and Maria Manta Conroy, "Are We Planning for Sustainable Development? An Evaluation of 30 Comprehensive Plans," *Journal of the American Planning Association* 66, no. 1 (2000): 30.

as cover."[38] Other research is also modest in its assessment of initiatives to manage growth: Jerry Anthony saw the impact of the ten state-level programs as "weak" because many of the urban densities declined despite policies to encourage the opposite; Kee Warner and Harvey Molotch concluded that local growth management programs do not affect the rate of growth as intended (although they positively impact its quality).[39]

As mentioned earlier, Smart Growth has a symbiotic relationship with general plans: because it is so focused on *where* growth goes and that's exactly what general plans designate, at first blush Smart Growth needs general plans. This is not a coincidence: Smart Growth is the product of general plan thinking: it is an ingenious attempt to minimize the harm of growth while using only the restricted tools available to the planning profession. Likewise, the planning profession needs Smart Growth or something like it to justify its existence if it is going to be anything more than the rubber-stamping of forms developers submit. There might be other ways to encourage smarter growth, ways completely unrelated to the regulation of building, but they're beyond the ken of the planning profession, a point to be returned to later.

The limitations of planning as a profession—its practice of imposing order by naming and its attempt to regulate property when free markets are hegemonic—create the conditions where it is possible to generate a formal but hollow commitment to sustainability. This has long been the case in American city planning. San Diego is typical. Before the 1960s, local planning was quite weak. The City of San Diego was by no means unique in having a planning department that consisted of a planning director and an office assistant. Plans, however, were still written, establishing a long tradition of plans

---

38. Lin Ye, Sumedha Mandpe and Peter B. Meyer, "What is Smart Growth—Really?" *Journal of Planning Literature* 19, no. 3 (2005): 312.

39. Jerry Anthony, 2004. "Do State Growth Management Regulations Reduce Sprawl?" *Urban Affairs Review* 39, no. 3 (2004): 391; Kee Warner and Harvey Molotch, *Building Rules: How Local Controls Shape Community Environments and Economies* (Boulder, Colorado, Westview Press, 2000).

being little more than thought experiments, leading to a curious mixture of big promises and low expectations.

Today, plans in many states carry more legal weight. But they can be written by community members and endorsed by elected officials, and yet be little more than words in a parallel universe to the actual business of development because the words are disconnected to the day-to-day business of government. The opposite can also happen: the rhetoric of planning can allow planners or elected officials to act in bad faith, promising more support than they intend to give. Either way, naming and categorizing is mistaken for the potential for on-the-ground change.

The emphasis on physical form in Smart Growth rhetoric encourages such fallacious thinking. There's a tendency for Smart Growth advocates to read off proof of sustainable development from the physical structures in a building project. Outward signs, like a mix of uses that should *in theory* encourage walking, are taken for evidence that *in fact* the Smart Growth principles lowered a development project's impact on the physical environment.

All of this plays out as a story: a plan will get written, promise Smart Growth, be given awards, and have its greatness confirmed by visiting planners who see in pilot projects positive proof of Smart Growth.[40]

The San Diego experience, however, shows how misleading official pronouncements and hasty evaluations—what Robert Bruegmann calls the *tourist-eye*—can be.[41] There are numerous

40. Economic pressure on university presses increasingly encourages attention to sales numbers, discouraging books on single cities (other than Los Angeles, Chicago and New York) and instead encouraging books that have case studies from different regions of the country because of the implied national market. But the more cities covered the more likely the author's understanding of them is superficial.

41. Optimism is not required for breezy statements about San Diego. Richard Hogan, who focused on the northern suburbs, reached some conclusions similar to this book's, but his work was based on sporadic presence in the region and contained a number of factual errors and omissions. Most curious, for example, is the explanation for the "creation" of SANDAG, an organization discussed in the next chapter (see his p. 41). Hogan appears to

examples of this. Peter Calthorpe's *The Next American Metropolis* included a case study of Rio Vista West, a development in Mission Valley, which still exists in basically the same form. Located near the San Diego River, the development mixes housing, a small mall and a trolley stop. Calthorpe noted that it "is a good example of the hybrid planning which must find ways to combine the sometimes contradictory needs of transit and the pedestrian with the realities of modern auto use and retail development criteria." The project, however, remains an isolated bubble within Mission Valley's notorious sprawl: developers at virtually every other trolley station turned their buildings away from the rail line or otherwise disregarded it, leaving the trolley without the ridership to justify frequent service. The Rio Vista West development itself is bisected by a four-lane street and its major retail component is indistinguishable from any other big-box-anchored strip mall development. Calthorpe also discussed San Diego's transit-oriented development (TOD) guidelines, claiming that its "exhaustive input and education process proved successful in both tailoring the guidelines to the unique qualities of San Diego and allowing people to understand the changes that were proposed." TOD guidelines ended up playing a role in the City of San Diego's general plan update, albeit a totally negative one, as will be seen.[42]

Periodically, San Diego is praised for its moves towards Smart Growth or a national website will link to an out-of-context local newspaper article proclaiming progress on the same. In a survey of successful projects, www.smartgrowth.org included Liberty Station, a local infill redevelopment of a military base, gushing praise for its

---

be implying that a locally famous 1974 planning document called *Temporary Paradise?* and a 1972 Comprehensive Planning Organization (CPO) report on affordable housing somehow led to SANDAG's creation. In fact, the 1980 emergence of SANDAG was merely a renaming of CPO, which had been around since the 1960s. Hogan, *The Failure of Planning: Permitting Sprawl in San Diego Suburbs, 1970–1999* (Columbus: Ohio State University Press, 2003): 41.

42. Peter Calthorpe, *The Next American Metropolis: Ecology, Community, and the American Dream* (New York: Princeton Architectural Press, 1993): 131, 142.

community involvement and mixed uses.[43] Nothing on the website indicated the controversy or alienation this project generated, for its critics alleged it was a corrupted giveaway as the original plan was revised time and again to the benefit of the developer.[44] And the development still feels profoundly auto-dominated.

The planning and development website of Planetizen used to display an article from the *San Diego Union-Tribune* about a downtown plan passed in 2006. The article, whose headline was changed from "Council Approves Downtown Strategy" to "San Diego Adopts Smart Growth Plan For Downtown," didn't give much context for an outside audience about the extent of the controversies over the downtown plan or its lingering problems. (In perfect Californian fashion, it was of course sued over its environmental impact report.)

Another example: Michael Neuman claimed that:

> The 1992 New Jersey State Plan and San Diego's Regional Growth Management Strategy provided new visions for their jurisdictions and new models for state and regional planning. These two plans also redefined the relations between planning and governance... These two new plans held out the promise that planning, by redesigning governing institutions, could be a path to real democratic reform.[45]

As will be discussed briefly in the next chapter, San Diego's Regional Growth Management Strategy was a nonevent. If anything,

43. http://www.smartgrowth.org/library/articles.asp?art'2178&res'800. Accessed July 10, 2006.

44. A good overview of the criticisms can be found in Steven P. Erie, Vladimir Kogan and Scott Mackenzie, *Paradise Plundered: Fiscal Crisis and the Governance Failures in San Diego* (Palo Alto: Stanford University Press, 2011).

45. Michael Neuman, "Does Planning Need the Plan?" *Journal of the American Planning Association* 64, no. 2 (1998): 208–220. While this quote is wishful thinking, Neuman would go on to write one of the more hard-nosed articles on the limits of planning. Neuman, "The Compact City Fallacy," *Journal of Planning Education and Research* 25 (2005): 11–26.

it was a classic example of local jurisdictions pretending to cooperate while committing themselves to as little as possible.

Of the two plans that are at the center of this book, one won its awards: the City of San Diego's Strategic Framework Element won accolades from the local chapter of the Urban Land Institute, the state chapter of the American Planning Association and the California League of Cities—the last an award for its public outreach, the area where the plan was most criticized by local residents. Furthermore, the alleged success of the plan helped propel the city planning director into the same position in Los Angeles.

This is not to say that the planners or their allies were happy with what happened to the City's plan. During lunch of the second day of the city council's adoption hearing, a small meeting was held at SANDAG. With a number of the plan's biggest advocates in attendance, disappointment about what was happening in the council chambers all but overwhelmed the meeting's official agenda. People spoke candidly about what went wrong and then put on brave faces when they went back to defend the plan before council. The final City of Villages plan bears no scars visible to outsiders. Nothing in the document indicates that it is anything other than good planning.

CHAPTER TWO
SANDAG'S CRYSTAL BALL

Since its inception, advocates for Smart Growth have argued that American cities need regional governments to deal with problems—like traffic congestion and air pollution—that spill across jurisdictional borders.[1] What these observers really mean is that they need stronger regional governments. Many areas in fact have a government body called a Council of Governments or COG.

San Diego is no exception. It has the San Diego Association of Governments, whose acronym, SANDAG, while not as clever as the heart of Texas's HOTCOG, *is* relatively pleasing compared to Los Angeles's SCAG, the Bay Area's ABAG or what San Diego itself narrowly avoided in the 1970s, SANCOG. And SANDAG is certainly more informative than the Five County Association of Governments, which is only outdone in uselessness by the Six County Association of Governments. (Both are in Utah.)

SANDAG *could* be a decisive force in San Diego politics: its board of directors has long included a County supervisor and either the mayor or a councilmember from all eighteen cities in the region (with the belated additions of a second place at the table for both the County and the City, in recognition of their importance). The board also has a handful of nonvoting advisory members, including

1. E.g., Peter Calthorpe and William Fulton, *The Regional City: Planning for the End of Sprawl* (Washington, DC: Island Press, 2001).

the Port Authority, the City of Tijuana, and, in recognition of the strong military presence in the area, a liaison from the Department of Defense. In short, SANDAG's board includes the major governmental players in the region. They *could* conspire to make San Diego better. Yet SANDAG has gone the way of most COGs.

Created in response to federal laws of the 1960s, COGs are an ethereal layer of government between the state and local jurisdictions and are often unknown outside of activist circles.[2] For many of them, one of their main sources of power comes from being designated the local Metropolitan Planning Organization (MPO), which means that they distribute federal transportation moneys. While control over that hefty purse could be a potent source of power, the political structure of COGs ensures that it is not used as such. Instead of defining the limits and powers of their member cities, as the federal government has increasingly done since the Civil War amendments to the Constitution, COGs act more like the national government under the Articles of Confederation: they are the product of smaller political units jealous of their powers. Local jurisdictions structure COGs to require a high degree of consensus and are reluctant to give COGs much power of enforcement.[3] William Fulton's observation about the Los Angeles COG could be applied to COGs more generally: "Throughout its entire history, SCAG's real purpose has been to protect the local governments in Southern California from the creation of something worse"—with worse being defined as something imposed by the state or federal government that would coerce them into actually dealing with region-wide problems.[4]

---

2. On the creation of COGs, Charles Hoch, *What Planners Do: Power, Politics, and Persuasion* (Chicago: Planners Press, 1994): 34.

3. Robert W. Burchell, Anthony Downs, Barbara McCann and Sahan Mukherji, *Sprawl Costs: Economic Impacts of Unchecked Development* (Washington, DC: Island Press, 2005): 169–70.

4. William Fulton, *The Reluctant Metropolis: The Politics of Urban Growth in Los Angeles* (Baltimore: John Hopkins University Press, 2001): 155. Elsewhere, Fulton talks about the weakness of COGs and the potential power of MPOs. He sees SANDAG as an exception to the disorganized powerlessness typical of COGs, but that should be seen as more

SANDAG often labors in obscurity: the local jurisdictions receive a lot more attention from just about everyone. Indeed, elected officials of jurisdictions that are represented on the SANDAG board don't necessarily pay much attention to SANDAG either. This is not simply cynicism towards government but rather a recognition, perhaps unduly pessimistic, of what SANDAG can and cannot do. Compared to local jurisdictions, SANDAG simply doesn't have much power. Most notably, it lacks control over land use, without which it has limited ability to compel adherence to its ideas.

For much of the early period of the time covered by this book, SANDAG's weakness was underscored by a threat of dissolution: Steve Peace, a state assemblymember (D–Chula Vista), promoted legislation that would have combined SANDAG with other local agencies, most notably the Port District and the two transit districts, to create a more unified decision-making structure for the region. The uncertainty surrounding SANDAG's future raised the question of whether to replace the retiring executive director, since the new person might be without a job within a few years. Peace's vision of integrated decision-making, however, was diluted down to several pieces of spin-off legislation and a study of the feasability of regional government.

Despite its weakness, in the late 1990s, SANDAG tried to play a role in the local Smart Growth efforts. The first way was unhampered by its lack of land use power.

The Population Estimates

SANDAG had the power, through its extensive research arm, to shape how people—expert and lay—understood local issues. The staff tackled region-wide problems with volumes of reports and demographic estimates that profoundly shaped the discourses on

---

a statement about the other COGs in California than an endorsement of SANDAG. William Fulton, *Guide to California Planning,* 2nd ed. (Point Arena, CA: Solano Press. Books, 1999): 95–96.

47

growth. Indeed, it is hard to overestimate the impact of SANDAG on this score.

The two demographic estimates mentioned in the introduction were SANDAG's Series 8 Forecast, completed in 1995, and its 2020 estimates, which were released three years later. Series 8 was where, as described at the beginning of the book, SANDAG's projections first ran out of land to house everyone anticipated to live in the region (by 2015). The land shortage was papered over, and thanks to a severe recession, the projections received little attention. The 2020 forecast was tougher to ignore because it was released as the economy was heating up. That made the gap between the growing population and the supply of land more real. The gap would become ground zero for some of the most important political debates in San Diego.

When it came time for SANDAG to project where in the region the excess population would live, staff followed Smart Growth principles. They linked the surplus people to a map developed for the Regional Growth Management Strategy in the early nineties. The map was called the Land Use Distribution Element, a functional and banal name that turned into an eyebrow-raising acronym: LUDE (pronounced "lewd").

The idea behind LUDE was to funnel growth into clusters of higher density development that were accessible by mass transit, that is, the previously mentioned transit-oriented development or TOD approach. TODs were seen as a way of injecting islands of pedestrian-friendly development into seas of sprawl, islands that would be connected together by transit lines, creating "pearls on a string" as advocates liked to call them.

With the assistance of planners in the local jurisdictions, SANDAG staff developed a map for LUDE by adding density to approximately 150 real and potential transit centers throughout the urbanized parts of the county. Around each transit center, they hypothetically changed single-family housing zoning to multifamily housing and made commercial areas mixed use.[5] To be sure, no

---

5. *Mixed use* means combining different functions of buildings in the same area. One

local jurisdiction had yet committed themselves to such increased residential housing densities, so the new map simply showed that it was in fact possible to fit the excess population into the region according to Smart Growth principles. This gave SANDAG staff confidence that they had a possible solution to one of the toughest challenges facing the region.

Staff made a case for their ideas in many meetings and reports. One of the first reports was ostensibly a description of four possible land use strategies the region could adopt.[6] The scenario painted in the least flattering light was the status quo approach, which would chew up the remaining developable land in the region at an extraordinary rate. It was sprawl, pure and simple. The scenarios got better until the fourth and most intensive one, which was based on the staff's LUDE map. The report favored this final Smart Growth-based approach, which aimed to pull half of the growth anticipated in the County's general plan for rural areas and put it into the cities.

The report walked the thin line between being emphatic and being gingerly, stressing the high costs of doing nothing while emphasizing the modesty of what had to be done. The report went to great lengths to assuage fears of higher densities:

> Any density increases implied by the Land Use Distribution Element alternatives are both modest and appropriate for urban areas. They do not call for high-rise apartment buildings or extremely dense development. They do not fill the older sections of our cities with high-density multifamily structures.

---

of the original goals of zoning was to prohibit such mixing, as it might mean a tenement beside a plush department store or a polluting factory beside a school. Smart Growth attempts to change this hostility because a mix of uses is necessary to make walking and mass transit practical. When Smart Growth advocates think of mixed use, their vision is not of unsightly businesses invading residential areas but a mom-and-pop store with the owners living above it.

6. See San Diego Association of Governments, *2020 Cities/County Forecast: Land Use Alternatives* (San Diego, 1998).

They do make more land available for multifamily and
mixed use near transit, but mostly at densities that are
already in each plan.

The report called into question the densities for single-family
detached housing, noting that "our current plans call for future
residents to live at a density less than half of what we live in today."[7]
In other words, existing plans anticipated continuing the nationwide trend towards lower densities. If this could be reversed, the
problem of not having enough housing for everyone could be solved.
At least for 2020.

The campaign for the Smart Growth option had in fact begun
before that report was released. In July 1998, the SANDAG Board of
Directors adopted the region-wide forecasts, which spelled out in
broad brushstrokes how San Diego would grow from 2.8 million to 3.8
million by 2020. The initial report was merely fourteen pages of tables,
which had a total of only three complete sentences. Nonetheless, the
forecast had already begun to draw media attention: a front-page *San
Diego Union-Tribune* article the preceding September had discussed
a draft of the report, quoting a City of San Diego councilmember
as saying, "It's definitely a wake-up call."[8] An editorial in the same
paper a week later proclaimed an inchoate version of what was to
be a common refrain: a million more people would be here by 2020
and San Diegans had to plan properly to accommodate them, lest
the quality of life deteriorate.[9] While advocates for planning always

7. San Diego Association of Governments, *2020 Cities/County Forecast: Land Use
Alternatives* (San Diego, 1998): 3. One of the reasons for the lower planned densities was
that some of the open land was geographically constrained, which limited the housing
that could be built.

On the national density trends, see William Fulton, Rolf Pendall, Mai Nguyen and
Alicia Harrison, *Who Sprawls the Most? How Growth Patterns Differ across the U.S.*
(Washington, DC: The Brookings Institution, 2001).

8. The councilmember was quoted in Lori Weisberg's September 28, 1997 piece in the *San
Diego Union-Tribune* entitled "County's Growth Measured in Millions."

9. One spin that the October 5, 1997 editorial put on the forecast never resonated, namely

emphasized San Diego's distinctive characteristics—the wonderful climate encourages immigration, there was little land—the rhetoric about the need to prepare for demographic growth could as have easily come from Orlando or Chicago or Boston, though there was neither much awareness of what was happening in other cities nor many calls to look at population growth as a national issue.[10]

SANDAG's use of the "million more" refrain—one City of San Diego planner described their message as "The people are coming! The people are coming!"—continued its long tradition of acting as both a Paul Revere and a Thomas Paine of growth, for it had long argued that growth was inevitable and had to be faced through collective action. Indeed, this rhetoric was older than SANDAG itself.

Long before SANDAG was an independent organization or even called SANDAG, County planners were already crafting similar language. In 1960, the County developed a preliminary statement of alternatives for a regional plan. It presented a stark contrast. Either San Diego could become a "sea of roofs" or have greenbelts. The first option was a planner's nightmare:

> [d]eliberate repetition here of the unbridled urban sprawl, monotony and congestion which have all but ruined many metropolitan areas... [a]n ultimate population of 5,000,000 or more... [l]oss of attractive natural features of San Diego County... [l]arge expansion of the number of freeways beyond those now in the planning stage, and the probability of serious traffic congestion...

that since the much of the growth was coming from the Hispanic population, increasing their education levels should be a priority so that they could take the positions of power their numbers represented.

10. The discussion of other cities is based on their websites, which are no longer in existence: Boston's www.metrofuture.org, Chicago's www.goto2040.org and Orlando's myregion.ord. On the last also see Jonathan Barnett, "Alternative Futures for the Seven-county Orlando Region," in *Smart Growth in a Changing World*, ed. Jonathan Barnett, 61–75 (Chicago: Planners Press, 2007).

The greenbelts approach envisioned a:

> [d]eliberate refusal to repeat here the unbridled sprawl…
> [a]n ultimate population well under 5,000,000…
> [r]etention of most of the attractive natural features of
> San Diego County… [l]ittle expansion of the freeway
> system beyond those now in the planning stage, and
> little probability of serious traffic congestion… no
> 'leap-frogging' of new subdivisions into rural areas.[11]

There is no doubt that the greenbelt alternative appealed to the writers of the report. The sea of roofs, however, was a prescient description of what was to happen over the next forty years.

The planners of the 1960s saw San Diego at a crossroads, and their rhetoric echoed down the decades:

> The responsibility to make such a decision [about the
> future of the region] is ours. It is not inevitable that
> all the mistakes which have been made elsewhere be
> duplicated here. True, you "can't stop progress", but
> progress can be defined, and any type of change not
> considered to be progress can be discouraged. The
> attractive features which brought most of us to San
> Diego can be retained.

> The time for such a decision is now. San Diego County
> has its first million people, and the vanguard of the
> second million is arriving daily. That first million
> was accommodated without too much disruption of
> our landscape or way of life. All around us, however,

11. San Diego County Planning Department, *San Diego County Regional Plan: Objectives and Policies: Preliminary Statement of Alternates, Development Pattern* (San Diego, 1960–65). No page numbers.

are warning signs of trouble ahead. The assimilation of our second million people largely will determine our pattern of development. This is the eleventh hour. There is still time for agreement on what the San Diego County of the future will be like, but that time is running out fast.[12]

The 2020 forecast version of this call to action added several wrinkles that became factoids in the debate on the future of San Diego: 60 percent of the growth would be from natural increase, not immigration (which had historically been the main source of local population growth); the population would be older and more ethnically diverse; housing costs would rise faster than incomes; and, as other SANDAG reports indicated, traffic would be worse.

Of these claims, the most rhetorically powerful was that 60 percent of the growth was internal or "our children" to use the preferred phrase.[13] This alleged fact about the future growth became a tool to bludgeon critics of growth. It had two implications. First, since the people who lived in the region were responsible for more than half of the growth, policies designed to discourage immigration into the region wouldn't work. Second, since they were their children, presumably current residents would feel a greater moral responsibility for the new people than if they were somebody else's kids. By stressing a concern with family and not the wider community, however, such rhetoric reinforced the individualistic outlook that made it so difficult to deal with growth at all, and at least some staff developed misgivings about it.

---

12. San Diego County Planning Department, *San Diego County Regional Plan: Objectives and Policies: Preliminary Statement of Alternates, Development Pattern* (San Diego, 1960–65).

13. In meetings and in the press, this 60 percent statistic had a way of growing by rounding up: the 60 percent became two-thirds, which became 70 percent. In the original *2020 Regionwide Forecast*, natural increase was estimated to be 61 percent of population growth from 1995 to 2020. In a November 3, 1999 *San Diego Union-Tribune* article by Mark Arner, SANDAG staff was quoted as saying that it was two-thirds of the growth.

Those who supported good planning at the City of San Diego embraced this rhetoric wholeheartedly—only to find themselves accidentally undermined by SANDAG. The County was much less cooperative. Indeed, one of the greatest mistakes of its plan update would be spurred by a hostile reaction to the population figures in the SANDAG 2020 estimate.

But before we can get to the stories of those plans, we'll first have a preview of what can happen with general plans because SANDAG itself wrote one. It represented the organization's second major attempt to influence growth.

REGION 2020

The 1980s was a time of tremendous growth for the region, and this rapid growth was widely perceived, especially by environmentalists, as jeopardizing San Diego's quality of life. Great political battles raged over what to do, culminating in a series of ballot propositions during the 1988 general election. Only the seemingly weakest initiative, the Regional Planning and Growth Control Measure, passed.

This initiative, often just called Proposition C, mandated the creation of a regional board that "shall have the authority to require that the County and the cities adopt the necessary legislation to implement the regional growth management plan."[14] The initiative described the seven elements the regional plan should have and capped population growth in each city to 75 percent of what SANDAG demographers projected.

The Regional Growth Management Strategy (RGMS) that the initiative called for was passed by the SANDAG Board of Directors in January 1993. It was more notable for its attempt to think regionally than its contents: while general plans can run into the hundreds of pages, this plan was less than seventy pages, with considerable

14. San Diego Association of Governments, *Regional Growth Management Strategy* (San Diego, 1993): 121.

white space, and mainly listed recommendations. Each jurisdiction had to self-certify they were following it, which didn't require any hard negotiating, so the plan allowed jurisdictions to be like toddlers engaged in parallel play: pretending to do the same thing but not really interacting. It is debatable whether the initiative could be said to be implemented as SANDAG did not compel jurisdictions to follow the plan, as ballot language required.[15]

In the late nineties, SANDAG began revising the RGMS, calling the new iteration REGION2020. The motivation for revising the plan came from several sources. First, the RGMS had received little attention because of the recession. Second, the underlying problems—sprawl and the lack of housing in general plans—continued. Third, SANDAG planning could only be effective as a perpetual activity. Since SANDAG had no authority over land use, its long-range plan carried little weight and did not guide development. Instead, planning at SANDAG only had influence by creating a forum for encouraging planners and politicians to think about the regional consequences of their actions. For this to succeed, there had to always be something new to work on. This meant REGION2020 looked more like an educational effort on the principles of Smart Growth than a full-blown plan.

A major goal of REGION2020 was to get the local jurisdictions to sign a resolution of Smart Growth principles, which meant adopting some or all of a host of ideas: refocus growth into urban areas and away from open space, promote walking and mass transit, encourage a job/housing balance, widen choices of housing tenure, provide adequate infrastructure to Smart Growth Focus Areas, and "[r]econcile local plans with the regional forecast agreed upon by SANDAG"—that is, add enough housing to the jurisdictions to

---

15. Innes et al. describes in detail the process of creating the plan, albeit in a polllyannish tone. While cognizant of the criticisms of the plan as ineffectual (borne out by subsequent events), the Innes case study takes an upbeat tone by evaluating the plan in terms of increased communication between jurisdictions. Judith Innes, Judith Gruber, Michael Neuman and Robert Thompson, *Coordinating Growth and Environmental Management through Consensus Building* (Berkeley: California Policy Seminar, 1994): appendix three.

solve the housing capacity problem in the 2020 forecast.[16] SANDAG staff went out to the cities' elected officials and tried to sell them on Smart Growth. In the end, the cities formally supported the SANDAG resolution, but the complaints and reluctance of elected officials said much more than their ultimate endorsement.[17]

REGION2020 culminated in SANDAG's biannual regional summit, in which SANDAG recognized the commitments individual cities made to Smart Growth (by adopting a resolution of support). The summit, held in March 2002, was mainly platitudes—two platitudes to be exact: we need more money and we need to cooperate. Higher levels of government were roundly blamed for their role in the region's problems. No one, in a room of eight hundred people, including many of the region's elected officials, took any responsibility for San Diego's problems or offered a serious proposal to generate money locally. Other than a loud allergic reaction to developer-friendly County Supervisor Bill Horn, who had been reelected earlier in the week, and several attacks on the local political structures, the summit was a polite, feel-good affair. Afterward, an environmentalist suggested that all that was missing was closing with everyone singing "Kumbaya."[18]

16. San Diego Association of Governments, REGION2020: *Smart Growth Definition, Principles, and Designations* (San Diego, n.d.).

17. For instance, after a joint SANDAG–Metropolitan Transit System presentation that made the case for a new bus system to a suburban city council, I rode down an elevator with several councilmembers. One contemptuously bet another that the transit authority staff person probably drove to the meeting. (He did.)

18. The results of REGION2020 paralleled Amy Helling's conclusions about VISION 2020, an attempt to reconsider growth in Atlanta. Helling argues that visioning there was not connected to development in any substantial way. Contrary to the expectations of some of the participants, no real plan was created, and this lack of results was in part permissible because there was no urgency "since consequences that are severe, but very distant in time did not lead to compromise." She quotes a participant as saying, "This process has given the false impression to the public that something is being done, when in fact, all that has resulted… has been the agreement that we need to continue to have more meetings." Amy Helling, "Collaborative Visioning: Proceed with Caution!" *Journal of the American Planning Association* 64, no. 3 (1998): 335–349. The Atlanta experience is

Ironically, the only people who ponied up money were the people blamed for not doing so. The California Department of Transportation, known as Caltrans—or to critics who associated it with mindless highway construction, "Car Trance"—was officially shifting towards a "multimodal transportation system" that did not rely solely on automobiles. To encourage SANDAG's Smart Growth efforts, a Caltrans representative announced at the summit that the agency was contributing a million dollars to REGION2020.

The SANDAG summit, then, was a starting point, not an end point. It marked the transformation of REGION2020 into the Regional Comprehensive Plan (RCP), which was to be an eighteen-month effort to create a genuine general plan for the region. Necessity forced the RCP to be modest: the short time frame, complete with public participation, required cobbling the plan together from existing plans (for transportation, for instance, or open space). The plan was like its predecessors: it encouraged dialogue between jurisdictions, but much of the dialogue was local elected officials and planners pleading for incentives and not mandates, or "carrots not sticks" as they put it. In other words, they wanted to be bribed, not be held accountable.

But it didn't matter that much: the two most significant general plans for the region—for the City and County of San Diego—were already well underway and had generated intense internal dynamics that made them immune to new SANDAG visions, but, as will become clear, SANDAG played a role in the plan updates, a role that staff would rue.

---

also discussed in John M. DeGrove, *Planning Policy and Politics: Smart Growth and the States* (Cambridge, MA: Lincoln Institute of Land Policy, 2005): 231–32.

PART II
PLANNERS AS
PHILOSOPHER-KINGS
THE RISE AND SPRAWL OF
THE CITY OF SAN DIEGO

Probably the most cussed and discussed people in city government today are the planners.

—Peter Kaye, *San Diego Union*, May 5, 1963

CHAPTER THREE
THE DEATH AND LIFE OF
SAN DIEGO PLANNING

In the late 1980s, the City of San Diego faced a choice. It was time to hire a new planning director. There were two finalists. They offered quite different approaches to planning. One, Mike Stepner, had been a planner with the City since 1971 and stressed the role of local communities in planning. Bob Spaulding was the planning director of Scottsdale, Arizona. He considered developers to be the customers of planning and saw his mission as providing them with good customer service.[1]

Like other cities in California and the Southwest, San Diego at the time was in the midst of another of its booms, a boom intensified by the money pouring into the region from the Reagan military build up. The population increased 27 percent over the 1980s,

---

1. The best history of San Diego growth issues before the 1980s is Abraham Shragge, "Boosters and Bluejackets: The Civic Culture of Militarism in San Diego, California, 1900–1945." PhD diss., University of California, San Diego, 1998. Shragge mainly focuses on the Chamber of Commerce's city-building strategy of luring the military into building bases throughout the region as a way to overcome geographical barriers that made the area implausible for large-scale development. For a history of San Diego politics between Shragge and the beginning of the time period here, see Mike Davis, Mayhew, Kelly and Jim Miller, *Under the Perfect Sun: The San Diego Tourists Never See* (New York: The New Press, 2003).

going from a little less then 900,000 people to 1.1 million by the end of the decade.[2] The growth was so dramatic and the negative consequences so evident that growth was a central topic in local politics. There was a steady stream of ordinances and ballot initiatives that tried to limit or steer or otherwise minimize the impacts of the new development.[3] Twenty years of mayors—Pete Wilson (R, 1971–1983), Roger Hedgecock (R, 1983–85), and Maureen O'Connor (D, 1985–1992)—explicitly embraced growth management.

And yet, when it came time to pick a new planning director, instead of choosing the planner who had significant experience with the City's growth management plans, city council picked the pro-development candidate, Bob Spaulding. Events would prove this decision to be as bad as it was counterintuitive.

At first, the problems were what was to be expected when a new boss, with a new philosophy, took over a department and attempted to steer it in a direction that many of the established employees considered wrongheaded. More an administrator by temperament than a planner wanting to improve the city, Spaulding focused on facilitating development and bringing in new computer technology, not on seeking community input. As the planning department began withdrawing from the communities and morale sank, the turnover rate rose (though it was officially blamed on low pay).[4]

Then Spaulding had a series of interactions with a woman in the planning department that he called a consensual affair and she called sexual harassment. She said it caused her too much stress to work. The city manager's office and the planning department agreed to an almost $100,000 settlement, divided into five payments just below the $20,000 threshold for reporting the money to city

2. Philip Pryde, *San Diego: An Introduction*, 3rd ed. (Dubuque, IA: Kendall/Hunt Publishing, 1992).

3. Nico Calavita, "Growth Machines and Ballot Box Planning: The San Diego Case," *Journal of Urban Affairs* 14, no. 1 (1992): 1–24; Roger W. Caves, *Land Use Planning: The Ballot Box Revolution* (Newbury Park, CA: Sage Publications, 1992).

4. Leonard Bernstein, "City Planner Seeks Morale Cure, is Caught in Cross-fire Public Service," *Los Angeles Times* (San Diego County Edition), December 2, 1989: 1.

council. In early 1991, news of the deal became public. The scandal forced Spaulding to resign, leaving him entangled in lawsuits with the planner and the City.

The scandal could not have come at a worse time for the planning department. The nation was slipping into a recession and San Diego's dependence on defense spending meant that the end of the Cold War cut heavily into the number of middle-class jobs. As had been the pattern in the city since World War II, when the economy soured, the efforts to manage growth were replaced by conservative attacks on planning as red tape interfering with the recovery.[5] The hostility towards planning in the early nineties, however, was intensified by a decade of Reagan–Bush rhetoric critical of government and the widespread sense that the collapse of European communism vindicated free markets. Soon, the city would have a new mayor, Susan Golding (1992–2000), who was nothing if not business friendly.

In July 1991, before Golding was even elected, city council slashed $3 million from the planning department's budget, cutting dozens of positions (with the hope of reabsorbing the personnel into other departments).[6] Then, six months later, city council, on the initiative of Councilmember Ron Roberts, placed the planning department under the operational control of the city manager. This action was a significant symbolic demotion. In the 1960s, developers, frustrated by the planning department's (ultimately unsuccessful) resistance to their covering Mission Valley with pell-mell growth, repeatedly attempted to cut the planning department's special relationship to city council because they believed that if the planners had to report to the city manager they would be more docile. After the Spaulding scandal, council no longer saw planning as central to policy-making.

5. Parke Troutman, "A Growth Machine's Plan B: Legitimating Development When the Value-free Growth Ideology is Under Fire," *Journal Of Urban Affairs* 26 , no. 5 (2004): 611–622.

6. Leonard Bernstein, "Newest City Planners Didn't Plan on Being Laid Off," *Los Angeles Times* (San Diego County edition), July 18, 1991.

It was just another administrative function.[7]

An oft used metaphor to describe this action was that council wanted to "wash its hands" of the planning department. This cleansing action, however, required a high capacity for irony: not only was the planning department penalized by reducing it to an administrative function because of its planning director, who, in opposition to many staff, treated it as an administrative function, it was put under the control of the office that had arranged secret payments in the first place—hardly a way to make sure such abuse didn't happen again.

To salt the wounds, Jack McGrory, the new city manager, was hostile to planning. In an interview conducted for UCSD-TV, he described his attitude towards planners: "One of the things that I felt I had to do in the first couple of years was break their independent culture and make them more part of a team." His approach was to disperse planners to other departments. He also attacked one of the main accomplishments in the City's planning efforts when he went after the city's contributions to its housing trust fund to help balance the budget.[8]

The planning department died slowly as it slipped down the administrative hierarchy during reorganizations. Supporters of planning proclaimed each demotion to be the death of the department. But it did not truly die until Jack McGrory opted to leave vacant the director position after Spaulding's replacement left in September 1996.

McGrory denied that this was an attack on planning. He claimed that all kinds of planning was continuing at the City and that his critics were making too much of the semantic shift in the department

7. At least one other city's planning department wrecked on the tension between a special executive position and administrative duties: Seattle's short-lived executive planning agency's status as a long-term planning unit alienated others in city government and hastened its demise. Linda C. Dalton, "Politics and Planning Agency Performance: Lessons from Seattle," *Journal of the American Planning Association* 51, no. 2 (1985): 189–99.

8. Michael Granberry, "Budget Cuts May Hit Housing Fund Hard Government," *Los Angeles Times* (San Diego County edition), June 13, 1992.

name from "planning" to "development." They suffered, he claimed, from "an acute sense of paranoia." But his views were clear: in the same interview he questioned his critics' mental balance, he said, "I see the traditional type of planning the city has done has gone the way of the horse and buggy."[9] In the next budget prepared by the city manager's office (beginning July 1997), "long range planning" was nowhere to be found (but there's more to the story).

Only a Flesh Wound

Jack McGrory was partially right when he claimed that planning continued at the City: while he was destroying planning's institutional base, planning-related activities continued. Yet budgetary neglect, changes in administrative personnel and inconstant political support left many efforts aborted or ineffectual. The transit-oriented development guidelines city council adopted had minimal impact. Mayor Golding's Livable Neighborhoods and the Renaissance Commission were to revitalize existing communities but fizzled out. The dean of the short-lived University of California, San Diego School of Architecture drew acclaim for her plan linking Mission Bay and San Diego Bay, but that plan was soon forgotten.

Only the Multi-Species Conservation Program (MSCP), an ambitious effort to protect threatened and endangered species while allowing development to go forward, had some success.[10] Implementing

9. McGrory was quoted in Roger Showley's October 6, 1996 piece in the *San Diego Union-Tribune*. When asked by Showley in 2012 about McGrory's views on planning, Bill Fulton, who had just become the City of San Diego's planning director, replied, "I'm glad the city manager of Paris didn't have that attitude in 1400." (*San Diego Union-Tribune*, September 2.)
10. More information on the MSCP can be found in Allison Rolfe, *Mapping the MSCP Process: Habitat Conservation Planning in the San Diego Region* (master's thesis, San Diego State University, 2000) and Gene Bunnell, *Making Places Special: Stories of Real Places Made Better by Planning* (Chicago: Planners Press, 2002): 485–493. Details of similar programs in the LA area can be found in William Fulton, *The Reluctant Metropolis:*

the City's portion of the MSCP, however, exacerbated an underlying problem: the general plan was years overdue for an update, and its failure to say anything about the tens of thousands of acres affected by the MSCP was just one more entry on its list of shortcomings.

San Diego's general plan had last been overhauled in 1979, when it implemented a nationally recognized system of dividing the city into tiers to focus growth. While refinements had been made over the years, the plan was reaching its expiration date. The maps of the general plan and the individual community plans were so outdated that they complicated evaluating development proposals. More importantly, the tier system had been concerned with making outward growth orderly. The city was, however, running out of vacant land, rendering the plan obsolete. Future growth, if it was to occur, would be more infill in existing communities than outward expansion.

There was no comprehensive plan for how to face this challenge. Indeed, the city had been without an effective approach to funding infrastructure in existing communities for over fifteen years. When the City was formulating its tier system in the late 1970s, it was based on the assumption that real estate taxes would fund infrastructure in the inner tier of older communities. Right before the plan could be finished, however, Californians passed Proposition 13, which dramatically limited real estate taxes.[11] The City charged ahead with the tier system without revising its funding strategy, guaranteeing serious infrastructure problems in existing communities.

The problems with the general plan were only symptomatic

The Politics of Urban Growth in Los Angeles (Baltimore: John Hopkins University Press, 2001), ch. 8; Stephanie Pincetl, *Transforming California: A Political History of Land Use and Development* (Baltimore: John Hopkins University Press, 1999).

11. Proposition 13 had several features that severely limited taxes. First, real estate taxes were rolled back to one percent of the value of a property when it was last sold, with only a two-percent increase per year for inflation allowed. This meant that property owners who held the same property for decades would pay very modest taxes. Second, new taxes required a vote of the people, who often voted no.

of the low regard held for planning at the City. At least that was the view of those who had spent their professional lives promoting good planning in San Diego. Mainly Anglo planners, architects and political aides in their forties and fifties, they campaigned for the return of planning—both as a vision and an institution—to the City. Although they began even before Jack McGrory reorganized the planning department into thin air, his de facto elimination of the planning director position spurred them to redouble their efforts.

Conditions were ripe for planning's rebound. First, the embarrassing Spaulding scandal was four years (one term of office on city council) in the past. Second, Jack McGrory would soon be under a cloud for his endorsement of a disastrous contract with the Chargers professional football franchise.[12] Third, as a practical matter, the destruction of the planning department did not exempt the City from state planning mandates, and the City ordinances requiring that the general plan be examined every five years were still on the books. Fourth, while "business friendly" was still the watchword, the economy was changing dramatically: the recession was giving way to the dot-com boom, leading to renewed concern about the consequences of growth and to renewed interest in using planning to control them. Fifth, everybody was doing it: the economic boom was national and it was giving planning, under the guise of Smart Growth, a tremendous boost.

San Diego advocates for planning spoke at luncheons and argued

---

12. The first provision of the contract that exploded politically was the locally infamous "ticket guarantee:" for ten years, the City had to buy all the unsold tickets for ten home games a year. After the new contract was signed, the Chargers went to the bottom of the league. Attendance plummeted, putting the City in the position of giving the team back their stadium rent. The second major damaging provision was a clause that allowed the Chargers to periodically shop their team around to see if another city would give them a better offer.

In early 2004, it became known that when McGrory was the city manager, the City had begun to underfund its pension system to pay for Golding's monumental projects, and former city manager belatedly received more flak (such as Don Bauder's piece in *CityBeat* on March 10, 2004).

their case in private. The Council of Design Professionals—a coalition of the local chapters of organizations like the American Institute of Architects, the American Planning Association and the Urban Land Institute (a realtor organization)—lobbied for planning to be returned to the immediate control of city council and for the restoration of the position of planning director. The highly respected League of Women Voters, while unable to reach a consensus on whether city council or the manager should control the planning department, advocated that planning should be resurrected. Citizens Coordinated for Century Three (C3), the one good government group that participated in the Council of Design Professionals, renewed its efforts to have the ideas of the 1974 visionary plan *Temporary Paradise?* implemented.

To address the issue of the status of planning at the City, an unofficial working group, dubbed "Where's Planning?" and led by assistant city manager Kurt Chilcott, began meeting twice monthly in 1996. While one participant compared it to going to the same meeting over and over again, out of this group came the idea for a general plan update. The approach to be taken was no means original. A description of Canadian planning at the time is apt:

> Many communities have engaged in a process called 'visioning' in recent years. This process involves extensive public participation to create a vision statement setting out the community's hopes for its future. Most of these visions reflect a cultural consensus: people want dynamic, vibrant, diverse, and successful cities. The vision statement then directs the strategic plan for the community... detailed neighbourhood plans provide guidance for local land use decisions.[13]

The San Diego plan advocates did not draw inspiration from

13. Jill Grant, "Canada's Experience in Planning for Sustainable Development," in *Towards Sustainable Cities: East Asian, North American and European Perspectives on Managing Urban Regions*, ed. Andre Sorensen, Peter J. Marcotullio, and Jill Grant, 147–160 (Hampshire, England and Burlington, VT: Ashgate Publishing, 2004): 155.

the work of Canadians. Their model was much closer to home. Los Angeles began its plan update with a "strategic element" to guide the updating the rest of the plan. Writing a similar element was to be a vehicle for bringing planning in San Diego back from the dead.

The plan advocates had allies. Some community group members, considering the 1979 general plan a technical document lacking vision, had wanted to revisit it since its adoption. They too pressed for an update. Mayor Golding had roots in a community planning group herself and was seen by some as sympathetic to their views (but note the quote below).

The driving force for the plan update on city council, however, was Byron Wear, who represented the beach communities and part of downtown. Elected in November 1995, he had a predilection for huge, controversial land use initiatives, including the redevelopment of the Naval Training Center (Liberty Station) and efforts to strengthen regional government for San Diego. He was in a position to push for the general plan update because he chaired city council's land use and housing committee.

The green light for updating the general plan was given on February 12, 1997 at a joint meeting of that committee and the planning commission. The purpose of the meeting was to flesh out a list of planning priorities for the City. Each councilmember and commissioner came up with two lists, an "A" list of items that could be prioritized and a "B" list of items that would have to wait. The general plan update ended up in a unique category, what Wear jokingly dubbed the "A minus" list: they had neither the staff nor the resources to do it immediately, so they would try to fund it for the next fiscal year.

Wear's then chief of staff Kay Carter described the process of getting the plan update in the budget as thus:

> From a political standpoint, a lot of the council thought it was about as interesting as watching the grass grow. Mayor Golding—we sorta hounded her to get on board with this. I think she had been burned a couple of times

by these issues. To her credit, she reluctantly agreed to provide for it.[14]

Money was found for fiscal year 1998, the same year the planning department disappeared from the budget. It was a paltry sum: the original request for the first year was only $129,000.[15] There was debate about whether anything could be accomplished with such a small appropriation. Planning staff, taking advantage of the anticipated low cost of a strategic framework element, convinced Mayor Golding that they could start small and grow. They had little choice: word was that the "tenth floor"—as city council was referred to in insider parlance—would not support spending a million dollars on the plan update. The $129,000 was a toehold.

How exactly the toehold would turn into a general plan update after the framework element was adopted was not extensively discussed: this first element would only take a year to eighteen months, so what to do next could be decided during the next budget cycle. It took, however, several years just to get a strategic framework element started.

Six months after the initial appropriation for the plan, there was a changing of the guard: Jack McGrory resigned as city manager. The same month, Mayor Susan Golding appointed an architect in the "Where's Planning?" group—Mark Steele—to be the chair of the planning commission. The chief opponent of planning was out, and both council and the planning commission had members committed to the plan update.

The Structure of the Plan

The planning commissioners, city councilmembers and staff spent the ensuing months developing a structure for the general plan update process. It was deeply affected by the initial budget constraints. Not

14. Interview with author, December 27, 2001.
15. San Diego City Manager, *Proposed Annual Budget: Policy Budget, Fiscal Year 1998.* No. 1 (San Diego, 1997): 91.

only was the minimalist approach of adding one new element to the general plan and then updating the others turned into a virtue, outside consultants were ruled out. This saved considerable money. It meant, however, that the city had to rely on its own resources, which limited access to other viewpoints or to people with extensive experience working on general plans. (Michael Stepner, who had stayed with the City despite not being made planning director in the 1980s, left during the ramping up to the plan update.)

To compensate for the limited money, planners relied on the resources of other City departments. This increased communication across the City's bureaucracy. It also had the deliberate effect of allowing planners to hide the cost of the update by scattering expenses throughout the City budget. Plan advocates would later claim to have done a lean update. In truth, it would be all but impossible to calculate how much was spent.

The plan update was designed with three main components: staff work, public outreach and committees. The way the committees were organized profoundly affected the course the plan update would take.

The Public Face

The public face of the Strategic Framework Element planning process was a forty-member citizens advisory committee. In city planning, such committees often required considerable staff time to manage but were seen as worth it in terms of increased legitimacy and new ideas. They had been used nationwide for decades to help steer a wide variety of land use projects, especially ambitious ones. Indeed, often a motivation for such a committee was the hope that having involved well-known and institutionally connected private citizens, usually local activists and business leaders and sometimes luminaries, would help draw attention to the effort.

San Diego's Strategic Framework Element's advisory committee, called the Combined Citizens Committee because it was made up of four subcommittees, was unusual. An overriding goal in selecting committee members was the desire to avoid "the usual suspects" as it was frequently put. That is, San Diego's civic elite was perceived to be a small, inbred group, and unless an effort was made to get fresh faces, the Combined Citizens Committee would have the same people who were on every other planning committee in the region (for water quality, traffic, housing and the like). To get a committee innovative enough for the radical new direction of the plan ("grow up, not out"), the plan advocates wanted to avoid people who would come to the table with entrenched positions. The selection process sought people who could put aside their affiliations and look at the city as a whole. As a result, no interest group was formally represented.

Each of the four subcommittees had a planning commissioner, who would provide expertise but not serve as the chair. Of the 50 persons who ultimately served on the committee who weren't planning commissioners, 13 were women. Four represented community planning groups; 5 more, community-based organizations. At least 23 had careers dependent on growth: developers (5), architects and planning consultants (9), bankers (3), and realtors (2) as well as one employee each from an insurance company, a utility and two public–private organizations.

Officially, the Combined Citizens Committee was appointed by Mayor Golding in the fall of 1999. A description of the committee meant for public consumption implied that the full committee was created and the subsequent subcommittees were structured around the issues the public said they were most concerned about.[16] This was backwards and elided a lot of behind-the-scenes preparation for the plan update. The idea for a citizens advisory committee was endorsed by council's land use and housing committee in October 1997, two years before the mayor's appointments. In early 1998, the subcommittees were given their names and the steering committee (to be discussed shortly) had interviewed possible chairs. Although council district offices put forward names to make sure that their areas were represented, the committee membership in the main

16. City of San Diego Planning Department, *City of Villages: A Commitment to Public Involvement* (San Diego, 2002): 19.

grew by accretion along the strands of the networks of the people who originally pushed for the general plan update, creating a group whose worldviews were mostly compatible with theirs.

Participants in the plan update process developed radically different understandings of what this committee did. Critics of the Strategic Framework Element viewed it as a front for staff, a way for them to claim public participation when they in fact controlled the plan update process. Staff, on the other hand, saw the committee as the driving force behind the more ambitious Smart Growth ideas, pushing them further than they had anticipated going.

The Stealth Committees

In addition to the Combined Citizens Committee, the general plan update had another guiding committee, the steering committee. Many of the people involved in the plan update but not working for the City were unaware of its existence. This obscure committee in fact met fifty times, more than any other group working on the plan. There was no conscious effort to hide the doings of this committee—references to it can be found in documents written for the public—but there was no effort to advertise it either: its meetings were not open to the public, and staff presentations to the public didn't mention it.

Officially, the committee began with three members: the city manager, the chair of the land use and housing committee (Councilmember Wear), and the chair of the planning commission (Commissioner Steele). Sometimes their staff or representatives from the mayor's office were present as well. The chairs of the Combined Citizens Committee's subcommittees and the chair of city council's public safety and neighborhood services were also eventually invited to join.

The purpose of this committee was to structure the process and provide guidance. It was not to do any planning per se. Since it met behind closed doors and left little of a paper trail, what it did is a matter of speculation. In the technical sense of planning—establishing standards, doodling on maps—the committee might have avoided planning. Indeed, in an interview for this book, one of the early committee members spoke of it as of little consequence and was unaware that the meetings had a formal name. On the other hand, the steering committee met regularly throughout the entire update, years after the basic structure of the process had been established. This makes it hard to imagine that the political side of the general plan was not a topic of conversation.[17]

The same could be said of the Smart Growth Implementation Committee. It was created by Mayor Golding's successor after she was termed out in the year 2000. Supposedly little related to the plan update was discussed at its meetings, even though the plan was one of the City's main tools for promoting Smart Growth. It met in private, however, so it's impossible to be certain.

Private Faces of the Plan

In addition to stealth committees of unknown magnitude, the City's general plan update had a nebulous private face as well. The plan was the product of a dense network of advocates, including administrators, politicians, staff and private land use professionals. Some of their connections went back many years. Others were of much more recent vintage: a critical node in the network was the redevelopment of the Naval Training Center, then still in progress. It was in the district of Councilmember Byron Wear, and one of the consultants on the project was Mark Steele. A key planner at the City on that project was Gail Goldberg, who was one of the first

---

17. In (legal) theory, there should have been a paper trail allowing for the reconstruction of such events because the offices of outgoing elected officials were supposed to turn over everything but personal documents to the city clerk's office. When I interviewed Kay Carter in Byron Wear's office, she made me copies of all sorts of documents from various filing cabinets, but, after Wear was termed out, I went to city clerk's office to get access to all the contents of those filing cabinets. The clerk gave me two boxes of materials to look through—everything Wear's office had given them for eight years in office. This defies credulity. The situation with Mayor Golding's office was virtually identical.

two staff assigned to the plan update.

Goldberg, who shortly became the planning director, had a network of professional ties to consultants, architects and others linked to development. Some became members of the Combined Citizens Committee and otherwise donated their time and resources to the plan update, partially making up for the lack of consultants. These professionals, some of whom had pushed for the general plan update, had a kind of *quid pro quo*: they provided expertise for free and in return received an understanding of the City's future intentions.[18]

This tripartite planning process for the Strategic Framework Element—public, stealth and private—was not merely a result of the budgetary constraints. It was also shaped by attitudes towards public participation.

Planners as Philosopher-kings

The City's plan update was informed by a very specific philosophy of public participation, a philosophy that appeared promising and daring in the beginning but slowly unraveled. It was like a Greek tragedy: the plan advocates knew exactly what they wanted to avoid and yet ended up doing it.

In looking back on San Diego's history, the planners recognized in the public a deep streak of distrust towards their profession. Most emphatically, conservatives in 1965 forced the City's first real general plan onto the ballot and were able to defeat it because of a single reference to urban renewal, a program in which local jurisdictions seized private property for redevelopment. But there was no shortage of community/staff conflicts in more recent

18. This sentence has evoked strong contradictory responses from participants who read drafts. It has been suggested that I was naive for not drawing attention to the way these consultants would receive business as a result of the general plan update and that I was cynical for impugning their motives and ignoring their years of civic volunteer work.

74

memory. The City had a reputation, largely deserved, for being unresponsive, a situation common in local government.[19] The complaint was one found in a study of local governments across the United States:

> Participants repeatedly claimed that the actual pro-
> cedures used to involve them in government were a
> sham, designed only to fulfill an agency's obligation
> under its public participation requirement. Much
> of the criticism centered on the symbolic nature
> of public hearings, a common technique of citizen
> participation. A hearing can easily be turned into
> a "dog and pony show," where officials dutifully
> present a plan, listen attentively to suggestions and
> complaints by those who attend, and then go ahead
> and carry out the plan exactly as they intended to
> do in the first place.[20]

In San Diego, the feeling that participation was a farce repeatedly created enormous friction, a friction exacerbated by City departments not always talking to each other.

To counteract this profound suspicion, staff took the approach that if they were to treat the public as equals, they could develop trust. They hoped that if they showed the public the population projections for San Diego and let people work out the implications for themselves, they would come to the same conclusions as the planners, namely that the consequences of trying to stop the growth were worse than the growth itself. The public would see that the best approach was to prepare for the growth. At this point, discussion would naturally turn towards the Strategic

19. Fear of special interest groups has led to government in California being *designed* to be unresponsive. Peter Schrag, *Paradise Lost: California's Experience, America's Future* (New York: The New Press, 1998).

20. Jeffrey M. Berry, Kent Portney and Ken Thomson, *The Rebirth of Urban Democracy* (Washington, DC: The Brookings Institute, 1993): 37.

Framework Element. The underlying idea was simple: if the planners trusted the public, the public would slowly learn to trust them. This approach did, in fact, appear quite successful in focus groups.

In a broad sense, some of the advocates felt that the purpose of the plan update wasn't so much to update the plan—they thought that the current general plan was full of sound planning principles even if it was dated in the particulars—but to generate support for planning. As Planning Commissioner Mark Steele put it:

> Five people could have gone into a dark room at the beginning in 1997 and laid out this same plan. But it wouldn't have been a doable plan because there weren't enough people involved in it to actually make it happen. And so in my own estimation, in many regards the plan is a little bit academic—you need the plan now to have the legislative ability to enforce things and so forth and so on. But Smart Growth is happening in San Diego because of the process, not because of the plan, but because of the process. [four sentences deleted]
>
> While an enlightened few could have come up with that idea in the beginning it took a couple... three years to get enough people involved in enough levels particularly the planning commission, city council, community groups, the mayor—all these people to where everybody says, "Yeah, that's a good idea." Hopefully everybody imagines that they thought of it because it makes it an even stronger idea.[21]

Although it did not become obvious for some time, this dipped into the deepest well of contradiction: like much enthusiasm for public participation, it was predicated on the assumption that

21. Interview with author, September 12, 2001.

"the public" would reach the same conclusion as themselves. This is probably the original sin of all advocates of democracy, but, in late-1990s city planning, this was particularly seductive: Smart Growth, by offering everyone something in the abstract and appearing capable of handling long-term needs, was—for at least several years—self-evidently common-sensical and necessary. No one was offering serious alternatives, and it was an oft-repeated phrase that "we can't just keep doing the same thing."

How public input was treated exacerbated the contradiction between wanting other people's input and having a preconceived outcome in mind. The public was treated like the members of the Combined Citizens Committee—that is, as individual residents and not representatives of groups. Residents were simply a source of ideas. All ideas were worth considering; it didn't matter who uttered them. They didn't carry more weight if the person represented an interest group. The planners would decide which ideas were good and bad. An organized effort to protest the direction of the plan couldn't fit into this very well. Since all special interest representatives, *qua* special interest representatives, were barred from the Combined Citizens Committee, those who felt left out couldn't claim that they had been excluded from the committee, as no other group was represented either.

This meant that while the plan advocates wanted to create trust, the venues for public participation they created offered only a mimetic equality. The public could imitate and follow in the footsteps of the planners, but there was no mechanism for handling serious disagreement, no way to give potential critics enough sense of control that they felt a sense of ownership. Instead, the process was constructed in such a way that critics were permanently on the outside where they were never obligated to compromise: giving them anything less than everything they wanted would appear like a cynical attempt at appeasement.

Over time the limitations of this approach would become apparent. While the plan was able to proceed for many years without serious opposition, it was unable to get buy-in from anyone not involved in the beginning. Enthusiasm, yes; support, no. The plan belonged to those who started it, and members of the public eventually sensed this. When they became unhappy with what they saw, they had no meaningful way to participate in the process. In the end, their only alternative was to crash the party.

CHAPTER FOUR
TWO YEARS OF FALSE QUIET

While planners were quietly spending 1998 preparing for the plan update, SANDAG released its estimates of a million more people in the region by 2020. At a 2001 breakfast speaking engagement, planner Gail Goldberg said that the estimates had been "a stunning revelation." The immediate effect was to delay public outreach until SANDAG had finished the rest of their analysis. More broadly, the plan became, to use the language of an early draft, "based upon" the SANDAG estimates.

SANDAG projected that the City of San Diego would need 50,000 more housing units than in its current plan to be able to accommodate its share of the million more people expected to live in the region by 2020. Overcoming this shortfall morphed into the justification for the plan update. The need was so obvious that apparently none of the plan advocates voiced doubts about the wisdom of increasing the city's housing capacity. It was simply a moral duty to prepare for the inevitable growth: in the late 1990s, the cost of housing was increasing rapidly and ignoring the question of how to respond to the shrinking supply of available land would only make the situation worse.[1]

1. The dot-com boom created new jobs by the thousands in San Diego, but housing construction lagged behind, especially for condominiums. Vacancy rates plummeted; rents soared as the only new housing was luxury housing or projects built specifically as affordable housing (e.g., built by nonprofits). The reason for the unresponsive building

Despite having similar housing shortfalls, no other local jurisdiction understood the SANDAG numbers as an obligation to prepare for more people. And the plan advocates knew to expect resistance within the City of San Diego as well. As they did with other sources of conflict, their approach was to sidestep potential opposition, as an interview excerpt demonstrates:

> AUTHOR: And a large part of what you're doing is trying to find room for more housing… other jurisdictions in the county are less enthusiastic about trying to accommodate the SANDAG numbers. Was it pretty… from what you said it sounds like it was pretty much clear from the get-go that the City was going to try to…

> PLAN ADVOCATE [interrupting]: We never asked that question. We were very careful. We knew that it was the responsible thing to do.[2] We knew that the quality of life here would be better if we did plan for it. So we never bothered to ask people whether we should accept… accept these numbers or not. Instead, our approach has been it's probably better to plan for population growth because we know it's going to happen. It may happen in ten years; it may happen in twenty years; it may be thirty years out that we actually get these numbers, but it's going to happen. We're talking about natural increase—people here having children—so that kinda changes the discussion too. We're not just talking about people moving here.

market was hotly contested. On the right, regulation—especially the rules governing construction defect litigation—was blamed. On the left, developers were criticized for concentrating on the most profitable markets, and landlords were criticized for taking advantage of the situation by raising rents dramatically but not investing their super-profits into maintaining their properties.

2. Several words have been deleted from this quote to modestly smooth it out and to maintain anonymity.

AUTHOR: And, did city council, did they take the same attitude initially that "well, we'll find some way to do this?"

PLAN ADVOCATE: That's exactly what I mean when we didn't ask that question. [laughs]

For several years, this linking of the general plan update to the SANDAG figures went uncontested. The ambition to do so made the City of San Diego the boldest leader in Smart Growth in the region—until it undermined the update process.

The General Plan Update Goes Public

In 1999, the effort to create the Strategic Framework Element began in earnest, over four years after the plan advocates began promoting the idea, and two-and-a-half years after it was declared an "A minus" priority. In June and August, staff conducted the first two phases of what would ultimately be five phases of public outreach.

Each phase included five geographically dispersed meetings. Planners had several motivations for this approach. First, to meet with each of the community planning groups individually would have been too time-intensive. Second, the planners felt that if they organized meetings by the local planning areas, people would attend not as residents of San Diego as a whole but as residents of the immediate neighborhood, complete with knee-jerk reactions and pet peeves.

Staff organized the meetings around an orderly progression of points they wished to cover: they had a message to present and they wanted feedback. In the early phases of meetings, staff encouraged dialogue between attendees, believing that if people worked out the issues of growth among themselves, they would be more convinced than if planners pontificated from on high. Negotiation and mediation—the bedrock of committee meetings in which people represented interests—played no part.

How staff interpreted public comments were evident in the pamphlet written to describe the Phase I meetings. Residents' positive impressions of San Diego were reduced to bullet points, such as:

Like: Coastline; rural areas like San Pasqual areas; Mission Trails Park; climate; community identity; Balboa Park and free parking; liberal way of life; variety of parks; sports teams; arts; La Jolla Playhouse; character of older neighborhoods; proximity to Mexico; safety; improvements to freeways; strong downtown and small communities; optimism; spirit of entrepreneurship.

No sense of who spoke was left. Comments floated freely. From this impressionistic sweep of public opinion, staff could take what they wanted.

December 1999–June 2000: Citizen Committee Meetings

After the initial two rounds of public meetings, the focus shifted to the Combined Citizens Committee and its subcommittees. During this time, the subcommittees worked on the "core values" and policy recommendations that would inform the general plan update. With a few exceptions, what was decided upon could have come straight from a 1960s general plan: walkable neighborhoods, respect for the environment, regional cooperation, etc. Only a few key points, like an emphasis on connections with Latin America and concerns about housing affordability, were in any way distinct to San Diego. It was an exercise that had been repeated hundreds of times in hundreds of places with similar results.

The flurry of meetings cumulated in two afternoon workshops of the Combined Citizens Committee in June 2000. Their purpose was to select a growth strategy for accommodating the additional housing anticipated to be necessary by 2020. Given that it was only a question of when the growth would occur, slowing the growth was not taken seriously. The committee quickly rejected spreading the additional housing evenly throughout the city. On the surface, such an approach was appealing. The density increases would be slight: an area with ten dwelling units per acre might need twelve units. But it meant invading single-family neighborhoods with multifamily housing, which would be politically unpopular, and it was unrealistic: spreading the density evenly throughout the city would require demolishing and rebuilding all the housing stock to make it slightly denser. Barring an atomic explosion or spectacular earthquake, that was unlikely to happen.

If stopping the growth and spreading it out evenly were not options, then the question was what was the best approach to concentrate the growth. One approach would have been to follow SANDAG's population modeling in which excess population was assigned to *Smart Growth Focus Areas* (i.e., around transit). Another approach would have concentrated the extra population entirely in downtown. A third approach would have focused the growth in downtown and in the subregional centers.[3]

The approach that was selected by the end of the workshops put some growth in downtown and the subregional centers but went one step further. In each community, there was—or at least potentially was—a "village" or walkable mixed-use core. Much of the future growth would be concentrated in these villages.

This approach was called the *City of Villages*, a name that seemed designed to alleviate fears of the potential inhuman scale of large urban development. It had a nice ring to it and in fact had been used repeatedly elsewhere: Sydney, Australia; Unley and Plymouth, England; and Concord, New Hampshire.[4] In the United States the

3. The planners also mentioned annexation, but it had a host of political and practical difficulties and wasn't considered as a full-blown alternate like the others.

4. For an analysis of the "urban village" concept (in the British context) and its appealing and oxymoronic qualities, see Bridget Franklin and Malcom Tait, "Constructing an

phrase was popular as a developer slogan in the late 1980s.[5]

In San Diego, the City of Villages concept proved extraordinarily popular. It appeared to offer everything. By focusing growth in the villages, single-family neighborhoods—and the people voting in upcoming elections—would be spared the consequences of growth in their immediate neighborhoods. By encouraging the construction of condominiums and apartments, it could increase the stock of affordable housing. The increased densities would make mass transit more viable, minimizing the traffic that accompanied new growth. The plan would also reduce the pressure to build homes in the backcountry and thus help preserve the environment. Furthermore, the additional growth would be accompanied by infrastructure, which hadn't always happened in the past, meaning that the communities would be upgraded and actually improved by growth. In short, everybody would get something out of the City of Villages. Indeed, the Smart Growth allure gave the plan a hypnotic effect: all but the harshest opponents admitted they liked the concept before they proceeded to criticize its implementation.

When asked in an interview if the choice of the City of Villages was pre-ordained, Mark Steele of the planning commission explained:

> I mean it's so obvious. I think that that's why it's been so successful. It's not changing anything really. It's just focusing and controlling things... You couldn't just suddenly decide... like the one thing that said, "Let's put all the density downtown." Well, how do you get people to do that? In building a city it's not like there's a king somewhere that says, "I will build 50,000... 150,000 housing units in this one area. So it is!" It just doesn't work that way.[6]

Image: The Urban Village Concept in the UK," *Planning Theory* 1, no. 3 (2002): 250–272.

5. Robert Beauregard, *Voices of Decline: The Postwar Fate of US Cities* (Cambridge, MA: Blackwell Publishers, 1993): 234–35.

6. Interview with author, September 12, 2001.

Transit First

The appeal of the City of Villages was intensified by a project being prepared concurrently by the Metropolitan Transit District Board (MTDB). MTDB, which ran the largest transit agency in the county, was working on a plan called Transit First, which was hoped to radically increase the viability of mass transit in the region. On the face of it, the suggestion of a widely used mass transit system in southern California lacked plausibility. MTDB's charismatic consultant Alan Hoffman, however, framed Transit First in aggressively pragmatic terms. His presentations were quite conscious of public agencies' concerns about cost and of potential riders' choice of driving a car if mass transit was unappealing.

The new approach centered on a fleet of *flex-trolleys*, rubber-wheeled trolleys that alternated between having their own right-of-ways and driving amidst auto traffic. While technically buses, Hoffman argued against calling them such because they had a slew of advantages—from technologies built into the vehicles themselves to a comprehensive network of transfer points—that provided a trolley-like riding experience. Besides, he noted, the public hated anything called a bus.

Transit First and the City of Villages needed each other. Transit First had limited potential without the densities promised in the City of Villages, and the traffic of the City of Villages would be a nightmare without improved transit. The two planning projects, while coordinated at the staff level, ran on parallel tracks. As the City of Villages approached adoption, the awkward question arose, "What would happen if the City adopted the City of Villages but then the money for Transit First fell through?" It was never satisfactorily answered.

The Rest of 2000

At the end of August 2000, the planning department conducted its third wave of public outreach. In addition to providing a platform for MTDB and SANDAG to present their ongoing projects to the public, the City planners wanted reactions to the selection of the City of Villages strategy and on the plan's vision statement and core values. In both cases, the basic decisions had been made, and staff was looking for feedback or refinements. In other words, they were test-marketing. This began a shift towards selling a particular brand of plan update to the public.

Who would ultimately make a decision about the City of Villages was changing, however. Four of the eight city council seats were up for election, and none had incumbents running (thanks largely to the effect of a term limits law enacted in the early nineties). Three of the four council candidates who won did so handily in the general election. The fourth, Scott Peters, representing part of the northern suburbs, won a much closer race. Peters and Toni Atkins—newly elected from a district representing neighborhoods north and east of downtown—were both Democrats who took a keen interest in the City of Villages.

Mayor Susan Golding was also termed out. The list of candidates for mayor on the primary ballot was extensive, but only establishment Republicans were in serious consideration. The frontrunner was County Supervisor Ron Roberts, the same man who, as a city councilmember, helped put the planning department under the control of the city manager, which had been the first step in its demise during the 1990s. Roberts had run for mayor in 1992, coming in third in the primary.

In the 2000 primary, he won almost 26 percent of the vote, significantly ahead of any other candidate but well below the 50 percent threshold to win the election outright. In the run-off in November, he faced Dick Murphy, a judge and former councilmember who had squeaked by the third-place candidate by 166 votes.

Both Murphy and Roberts, like the other major candidates, had endorsed Smart Growth ideas as a way of dealing with the city's problems. Ron Roberts had founded a short-lived group known as the Smart Growth Coalition. Murphy's campaign slogan was "A candidate with 20/20 vision," which was in part seen as an allusion to the year 2020 endpoint for the general plan update.

The press coverage was favorable to Murphy. The *San Diego Union-Tribune* portrayed Roberts as abrasive, and, after rides on the Padres baseball team's private planes came to light in September, the newspaper questioned his ability to represent the interests of the City in the ongoing problems with building the team a new stadium. Murphy was portrayed as level-headed and the right man for the job.[7]

Although some environmentalists didn't feel that either candidate had much to offer, Murphy won the endorsement of the Sierra Club. This made additional headlines as Roberts blamed his not getting the endorsement on Carolyn Chase, the co-chair of the Sierra Club's local political committee. Chase denied the charge in a letter to the editor to the *San Diego Union-Tribune*.[8] On the same day, the paper also published a letter from another environmentalist, Lori Saldaña, claiming that Chase had "been actively fund raising and volunteering for Murphy and lobbying on his behalf within the Sierra Club" and suggested that she not accept any appointments from Murphy if he won.

In the end, Murphy again squeaked by, this time getting 51.67 percent of the ballots cast (203,048 versus 189,939 votes). Events would suggest that he might not have been the right man for the particular set of challenges he would face. Indeed, as is clear from his

---

7. For samples of the press coverage, see Philip LaVelle's *San Diego Union-Tribune* pieces on September 18 and 20, 2000 as well as the *San Diego Union-Tribune* editorial September 10.

8. Roberts's sense that Carolyn Chase was responsible for his not getting the Sierra Club's endorsement probably stemmed from one incident. The Sierra Club was one of the hosts of a debate between Roberts and Murphy. Chase moderated. For much of the night, the two men's positions were all but indistinguishable as they fell over each other portraying themselves as environmentalists. At one point, however, the candidates were asked whether they supported a proposal to open a road through a particular piece of sensitive habitat. Roberts answered first and equivocated. Chase replied, "Wrong answer." Murphy then proceeded to espouse the environmentalist position.

Chase's version of the debate in her column in the *San Diego Daily Transcript* (September 8, 2010) makes no mention of the road closing and does not positively endorse either candidate. The letters to the editor about the Sierra Club's endorsement—by Saldaña and Chase—can be found in the October 21, 2000 edition of the *San Diego Union-Tribune*.

2011 autobiography, Murphy had, up to that point, led a charmed public life and had little experience in dealing with failure, experience he would desperately need when his methodical agenda was swamped by crises.

But 2001 began with optimism. City council had many fresh faces—five of the nine members were new—and the mayor had clear priorities and significant goodwill. Things also were looking up for planning: shortly after Murphy and the new councilmembers were sworn in, the city manager split the Department of Planning and Development Review into two departments, thus giving planning its entirely own spot on the city's organizational chart for the first time in almost a decade. Gail Goldberg was named director.

———————

At the same time Dick Murphy and four new councilmembers were elected in the November 2000, another councilmember, Juan Vargas, won a seat in the state assembly. His chief of staff, Ralph Inzunza, handily won the February 2001 special election to replace him.

In January, Valerie Stallings, who represented part of the beach communities as well as the suburban areas just north of Interstate 8, pleaded guilty to two misdemeanors and resigned. She had been under a cloud since April when the weekly *San Diego Reader* reported that she had bought shares of a company belonging to the owner of the Padres baseball team at the initial offering price—an offer not made to the public—and then within a month sold them for a huge gain.[9]

Her seat was vacant until an April special election. The contest pitted County Supervisor Ron Roberts's chief of staff against environmentalist/surf-shop co-owner Donna Frye. It was a classic fight between money versus grassroots, and the grassroots won with 52.25 percent of the vote. Frye was sworn in on June 12, giving

9. Matt Potter, "City Lights: Feathering the Nest," *San Diego Weekly Reader*, April 6, 2000.

the famously conservative San Diego a Democratic majority on its city council.

Despite having seven new members in half a year, city council still had many who were committed, to varying degrees, to the Strategic Framework Element. Scott Peters and the new mayor saw the plan as a tool for fulfilling campaign promises. Toni Atkins, representing much of inner-city San Diego, was also supportive but very concerned with the infrastructure shortfall. Ralph Inzunza himself was a past member of the Combined Citizens Committee. Byron Wear would not be termed out of office until 2002. The plan, then, had a core of five likely "yea" votes—enough to carry council—if it were done in a satisfactory fashion.

Of the new councilmembers, one was outspoken against the plan, as she was outspoken against many other things: Donna Frye, who began her elected career with what one observer dubbed a "vote 'no' on everything" approach. She quickly took the role of populist and watchdog and subjected many projects to much more scrutiny than they would have received otherwise. This made her a black sheep on a council where conflict avoidance and compromise were paramount.

The Plan Finishes Out the Year

After the City of Villages was picked as the strategy for the element, the Combined Citizens Committee met less frequently for the rest of 2000. Then it was reorganized and new members brought onboard, as some of the original members, who had been told they would be needed only for a year, said that they did not have the time to serve any longer.

Simultaneously, the committee and the planning department realized that the subcommittees had served their purpose. In the case of the public facilities subcommittee, for example, they came to see that the question was not documenting the facilities shortfall—a fairly straightforward process—but finding the billions of dollars to cover it. Thus, new members with new areas of expertise were brought in and the subcommittees were restructured: *public outreach* (self-explanatory), *pilot villages* (to establish the selection procedure for three test villages), *action plan* (to write a manual on the first five years of implementing the plan) and *facilities financing* (to perform a miracle).

CHAPTER FIVE
COMMUNITY PLANNING AND
RUMBLES OF TROUBLE

P ublic meetings for the Strategic Framework Element were so
tightly scripted as to be lifeless: what happened before the
planning commission, the land use and housing committee
of city council, the full city council and the Combined Citizens
Committee was all choreographed in advance with little anticipation of negotiation. First was an overview by staff, accompanied by
PowerPoint slides. Then, if it was a council meeting, chairs of the
subcommittees of the Combined Citizens Committee gave updates—
an approach taken because the planners felt it would be tougher
for city council to be mean to members of a citizen committee
than to staff. Then the planning commissioners or councilmembers went down their ranks, responding with their concerns or
ideas. Spontaneous interaction was so rare and changes from the
preceding meetings so minute that little ever happened at any City
of Villages meeting. The exception was the Community Planners
Committee, a monthly meeting of representatives, often the chairs,
of the community planning groups.

Planning groups were institutionalized throughout the country
in the 1960s in response to increasing federal mandates for public
participation and to increasing concern about the legitimacy of
planning efforts, which was being called into question after urban

renewal left entire neighborhoods destroyed.[1] Such groups—in San Diego and elsewhere—represented either one community or a cluster of nearby communities. These groups had three main functions: to review local land use proposals, to provide input on changes to the municipal code and to write and update community plans, the local versions of the general plan. Each group, which typically had twelve to twenty members, was the first body that heard significant land use proposals affecting its area—and which proposals required their input was a source of tension: the groups wanted a say in as many as possible because they feared insensitive projects; developers wanted their input minimized to save money and time and to avoid NIMBY (Not In My Backyard) reactions. The groups' advisory recommendations were forwarded to the planning commission and, if need be, city council. Because they represented the local knowledge about land use and the politically organized sentiment of the community, their views were taken seriously.

Although group members were often confident of their ability to represent their communities, planning groups had serious problems. Their voluntary status, long hours and technical nature tended to limit participation to those with significant personal resources. In practical terms, the groups were often dominated by Anglo, upper middle-class, middle-age or retired, homeowning men. In San Diego, the young, minorities, renters, and those lacking extensive education were effectively disenfranchised at this critical, entry level of government (though nationwide the picture was more complicated).[2]

People with lower status not only played a smaller role in planning groups, they were frequently the target of them. This was most obvious in discussions of homelessness: the impression the planning groups often gave was that the problem of homelessness was not that residents abandoned some of their neighbors to sleep in the streets but that those unkempt people had the audacity to

1. Douglas Harman, *Citizen Involvement in Urban Planning: The San Diego Experiment* (San Diego: Public Affairs Research Institute, San Diego State College, 1968).
2. On national variations, see Jeffrey M. Berry, Kent Portney and Ken Thomson, *The Rebirth of Urban Democracy* (Washington, DC: The Brookings Institute, 1993).

be visible within the boundaries of the community planning area.

Planning group members tended to focus on how development proposals impacted the quality of life and their investments in homes and businesses. If their major investments were in commercial or industrial lands or in undeveloped property, then they might be willing to sacrifice some community character to make money. Or, as was more often the case, if their investments were just in their homes, then they saw development, especially if it meant more traffic or multifamily rentals, as a threat. Those who saw their role defensively understand planning from what Jill Grant in her research on Nova Scotia dubbed the "plan as shield" perspective: they saw their community plan as

> a shield that they wield to defend their neighborhoods from enemy incursions... Those who view the plans as armour reiterate plan policies self-righteously in public meetings. They feel betrayed and wounded when they lose a battle.[3]

But either as home- or business owners, they viewed renters—much of the population in larger cities—with indifference at best, with irritation and dread of outsiders at worst.[4]

As the Strategic Framework Element turned into a plan to find room for 50,000 more housing units, city staff had doubts about the involvement of planning groups and wanted to sidestep them as much as possible. Involving them, however, was unavoidable: in 1975, city council passed two policies related to public input. The first said that the City was to conduct a "comprehensive review and revision" of the general plan "with citizen participation." The second policy

3. Jill Grant, *The Drama of Democracy: Contention and Dispute in Community Planning* (Toronto: University of Toronto Press, 1994): 7.
4. For a Twin Cities case study of this dynamic, see Edward Goetz and Mara Sidney, "Revenge of the Property Owners: Community Development and the Politics of Property," *Journal of Urban Affairs* 16, no. 4 (1994): 319–334.

established the Community Planners Committee (CPC) and tasked it with "participating in an advisory capacity in the comprehensive review of the General Plan."[5] Indeed, the CPC was to be "a nucleus committee" for the five-year revision of the general plan, though both the 1979 plan update and the Strategic Framework Element established entirely different citizens committees.

The first involvement of the CPC in the Strategic Framework Element was a September 1997 resolution supporting a plan update, as long as the "committee formed to work on this plan include[d] representation from the Community Planning Committee and other community representatives." This happened. The CPC, as a whole, however, did not become involved in earnest until three years later. At its October 2000 meeting, staff explained the status of the plan and then returned to the monthly meetings continuously for over a year. (Staff also maintained extensive contact with individual members and planning groups.)

The newly elected Mayor Murphy attended the January 2001 CPC meeting, promising to go to all the community planning groups. He did so, after a fashion: he made appearances at a number of staff's spring Phase IV meetings, which were organized as joint meetings of the planning groups, typically with three groups per session.

The Phase IV meetings were much more focused than their predecessors. The goal was to receive input on where to put the villages in each community planning area, input staff used to develop a map of transit corridors and potential villages. The subsequent map had approximately three villages in each planning area. The largest village was the almost two-square mile retail area in Mission Valley. Most other villages were much smaller, some only several dozen acres.

For many people, the reason for the map was unclear. While it was easy to get the impression that it showed planned village sites, the map, as staff explained it, simply designated all the potential

5. City council policies 600–07 and 600–09.

villages to be analyzed in the environmental impact report (EIR). By state law, every major development required an EIR to evaluate its impacts (as well as those of several, potentially less intense, alternate versions). To avoid being accused of not analyzing all significant consequences, which would give opponents of a project an excuse for starting a lawsuit, staff wanted to include every potential village: adding a village later would mean going back and redoing part of the analysis. Staff explained this to assure the public that the map showed the range of possibilities and was not an indicator of their intentions. This downplaying of the map was the first use of what would become an increasingly common tactic, namely, trying to defuse resistance by delaying controversial decisions, preferably until after the Strategic Framework Element had been adopted.

The first opportunity the CPC had to discuss the map was its June 2001 meeting. With hindsight, it was the beginning of the Strategic Framework Element's unraveling. It signaled the classic first stage of a land use political crisis: critics, not sure what they were up against but suspicious, claimed that they needed more time to consider the proposal—time used to mobilize opposition.

At the beginning of the meeting, Planning Director Gail Goldberg said that they had originally hoped to get CPC approval of the map of potential villages that night, at least for the purpose of doing the environmental analysis. Staff, however, had heard "loud and clear" that people wanted more time. Staff had consulted with the mayor, who felt that community input was more important than "artificial deadlines we had all set for ourselves." As the CPC members went down the line giving their feedback on the City of Villages planning process, they uniformly said they had not yet digested the map of potential villages and were unprepared to give feedback. Some commented on the anxieties residents had about the map: one mentioned that she had been getting phone calls about a rumor that there would be densities of one-hundred dwelling units per acre in her community. The committee passed a motion saying that they would discuss the City of Villages in August, which was normally one of their two months of the year off.

July 2001

In a discussion of urban planning in Norway, Terje Holsen notes, "It is not too brave a prediction to say that municipalities themselves are likely to claim that their efforts to involve the public is [sic] better than those affected by the planning would feel it is."[6] By the end of June, this was becoming evident in San Diego. Perceptions of what was happening with the City of Villages were starting to diverge radically.

The July edition of an online periodical called the *Planning Report* had a brief interview with Gail Goldberg with the headline "San Diego's planning director is overcoming native NIMBYism." She repeated her story of the focus groups, in which the public realized that stopping growth was impossible and instead of fighting it, people had begun to work to prepare for it. Goldberg described the outreach meetings as if those in attendance represented the collective will of San Diego. She also said council would be adopting the plan in the fall.

On July 19, 2001, the planning commission held a joint hearing with city council's land use and housing committee. During public testimony, a handful of people, mainly from North Park, gave one of the first bursts of organized opposition to the City of Villages. Their community, an older neighborhood northeast of downtown, could not, they argued, handle the proposed densities on the village map. They wanted the process slowed down to reconsider.

Councilmember Scott Peters, representing the northern coastal suburbs, was displeased with (a) staff saying that the estimated date for the council vote on the plan adoption was being pushed back three or four months, into early 2002, and (b) the calls from North Park to go slow. He noted that:

---

6. Terje Holsen, "Public Participation—For What Reasons?" in *Compact Cities and Sustainable Urban Development*, ed. Gert de Roo and Donald Miller, 217–226 (Hampshire, England and Burlington, VT: Ashgate Publishing, 2000): 221.

I guess that what I want to say is that I'm still excited about the Strategic Framework. I think it's the key to the quality of life for the future of San Diego. I'm very grateful to all the people who've put in time on this.

But I'm sick to my stomach about the timing. And I think we do a disservice to the people who've put in so much time by just continually talking about delaying approval. And maybe it's because I come from a different perspective, but in district one, stuff is happening now, all the time. And I need this stuff to be able to assure that's done right…

We're in irons. The sails are flat. I don't think were moving. Where's the urgency? We have a transportation crisis *now*. I talk to people who leave all the time from San Diego because they can't get around, at least in the north. We have a housing crisis *now*. We need a street design manual *now*. How hard is that?

Councilmember Toni Atkins gently rebuked Peters for underestimating the severity of the infrastructure problems that the older communities faced.

The next day, another front opened on what was becoming a little planning war. State law spelled out the procedures for a jurisdiction to certify an EIR for a project. One of the initial steps was that the lead agency hold a public meeting to take comments on the scope of the possible impacts they should study.

At this "Notice of Preparation" meeting, Tom Mullaney, who had co-chaired the city's strongest attempted (but unsuccessful) slow-growth ballot initiative in the 1980s, stood up and challenged the premises of the plan update, calling the SANDAG population projections "phony."

He represented an environmental organization called the Friends of San Diego (in part inspired by the 1000 Friends of Oregon).

Founded the preceding August and officially registered in October with Mullaney and Carolyn Chase as officers, this group, which shared an office with Mullaney's mortgage brokerage, dabbled in many planning issues but only found its focus in its challenge to the City of Villages EIR. Its opposition to the Strategic Framework Element ran parallel to that of the community planning groups.

The CPC meeting the week after the EIR meeting was relatively mild. Many fundamental doubts were raised, however, especially by representatives of the older communities. Guy Preuss, who served on the Combined Citizens Committee, called the above quoted speech by Councilmember Peters "inane" and wanted to know, "Who the hell told us that we have to do this [take the additional population]?" Other committee members expressed concern that the City of Villages map, while allegedly tentative, could force them to do things they didn't like: "Maps," one warned, "have a way of becoming reality." They feared getting the density without the infrastructure—again. They were worried that transit would either not be there or would be put in the wrong place because Metropolitan Transit District Board was too inflexible.

Summer to Fall: Criticisms Mount

In August, the committees of the plan did not meet—save for the CPC—as people took their summer vacations. Staff, however, continued to go out to individual community planning groups to get their input on the map of potential villages. Enthusiasm for the ideas in the City of Villages was beginning to be tempered by people's realization that some of the increased density had to go near where they lived. Staff found itself trying to sell the plan while simultaneously soliciting feedback on what would make it acceptable. Questions, however, were becoming more pointed.

The August meeting of the CPC was low key. Gail Goldberg filled in for the project manager. She began apologetically, noting that staff was trying to establish a new relationship of trust with the communities and the process was going to be painful on both sides. Goldberg clarified the meaning of the map and the vote that staff hoped the CPC would make in support of the City of Villages. She downplayed the significance of the Strategic Framework Element per se, arguing that the real decisions would be made later, at the community plan level. If a community did not wish to have increased density, they would lose nothing by accepting an environmental analysis map with increased density. They would get their chance to decide how to implement the plan locally down the road when their community plans were updated—a claim that was met with skepticism. The tone of the meaning, however, was set by a presentation by Alan Hoffman, whose can-do pragmatism shifted the discussion onto more positive terrain as he made the case that a reliable mass transit network for San Diego was within reach.

The September meeting, which was the supposed end of the CPC's involvement, was the opposite of the August meeting. During public comment, Tom Mullaney stressed the importance of the "quality of life"—a phrase usually implying that newcomers were a threat—and Tom Story, of the mayor's office, assured the committee that his boss would only support density increases in communities that wanted them.

Staff came to the meeting with a several-page motion that they wanted approved. The CPC members rejected it as too long. After vigorous criticism of the plan and the update process, they approved a motion that simply gave the go-ahead to do the environmental analysis and to endorse the City of Villages as the way of adding 50,000 housing units to the general plan.

Two days later, the Combined Citizens Committee held its monthly meeting. After working for almost two years, fatigue had set in and attendance was low. In what must have been a recognition of this, the meetings were no longer held in a large room in Balboa Park but in the same building as the planning department, in a room that could barely hold the committee if all the members showed up. (At the January 2002 meeting, Goldberg noted, "We have more staff than committee members. This is not good.")

Poor attendance led to a highly informal meeting. It turned into a discussion of what had gone wrong with the CPC. Staff was frustrated. The committee members made personal attacks and said things that were "cruel" and "horrible." What was especially galling was the suggestion by the City Heights representative that he and Guy Preuss be paid a dollar a month for six months to get the plan back on track—a complete dismissal of staff's professionalism. Staff was upset with the CPC's chair for allowing such caustic theatrics. Members of the Combined Citizens Committee made suggestions on what else staff could have done, and staff kept responding, "We did that!"

CHAPTER SIX
THE AMERICAN DREAM
AS A POWER TRIP

The households that are caught up in this urban housing process are consciously or unconsciously competing for relative positions in a dynamic social landscape in which there are big financial gainers and big losers. Like the day bugs and the night bugs that live off of the same food source—the winners and losers are in serious competition, but because they are unaware of the existence of the other and do not know of the incompatibility of their goals of mutual prosperity, open conflict seldom occurs. But one group of households makes significant equity gains and those gains are at the expense of others who slip behind.

—John S. Adams (1984) "The Meaning of Housing in America"

Kids don't vote.

—*The Wire*, season four

E nvironmentalists have long criticized American housing as unsustainable. They have focused on one aspect of the American Dream: large lots that surround the home. It makes each house take up so much space that everything is at a distance from everything else, making cars necessary for any trip more ambitious than visiting neighbors. That is, large lots *are* sprawl. Shrinking the lots around homes, however, is a narrow and unimaginative understanding of sustainability.[1]

The American Dream appears unsustainable in other ways, ways that are hard to see because its emotional pull is so strong and it feels so natural. Yet, if one steps back from the intense emotions evoked by notions of "Home sweet home," the Dream begins to look curious. Frequently homeownership is not simply shelter infused with emotions and status. It is *an investment strategy*. That is, the belief that houses are not simply a roof and walls but are an important avenue of acquiring wealth. Although they would risk looks askance during the Great Recession, realtors have long said and are starting to say again that homes are a good investment: not only do owners avoid throwing away money on rent, their homes are a hedge against inflation. Homeownership is so central to financial success that to have never owned your own home is a mark of economic failure. This is where the problem lies.

That this might be bunk was inconceivable when the Strategic Framework Element was started. In the wake of the housing industry's meltdown in 2006–08, which took a chunk of the global economy with it, it is partially recognized today—but only partially. In another five or ten years, it will be forgotten and realtors will be able to keep a straight face when they talk about the investment potential of homes. Why will this happen? Despite all the criticisms of the housing market that have emerged over the last decade, housing is still viewed through the rosy lens of the American Dream. The subprime fiasco can be dismissed as the result of greed and corruption. There's little interest in taking a hard look at the Dream, only

1. On the emotional side of the American Dream, see Janet M. Fitchen, "When Toxic Chemicals Pollute Residential Environments: The Cultural Meanings of Home and Homeownership," *Human Organization* 48, no. 4 (1985): 313–324. A quasi-existential analysis of homeownership can be found in Robert M. Rakoff, "Ideology in Everyday Life: The Meaning of the House," *Politics and Society* 7, no. 1 (1977): 85–104. For an excellent book on the lawn in American culture, see Theodore Steinberg, *American Green: The Obsessive Quest for the Perfect Lawn* (New York: W. W. Norton, 2006).

a desire to get it working again. Add some safety features to the mortgage industry, let the failed loans clear through the banking system and off we go again.[2]

What should most give pause to advocates of the financial advantages of homeownership is a paradox observed by John Dean at the end of World War II: a house is the only commodity that we expect to be worth more the longer we use it. Of course, a few commodities come to be seen as desirable precisely for their age, and they are vaulted into the lucrative categories of *art* and *antique*. It's understood, however, that mundane commodities—clothes, computers, most cars—will slowly decrease in value even if we maintain them well. Yet homes are expected to not only be used intensively for years but be worth more for it. Except for highly particular circumstances, like aging shade trees and homes that take on the quality of antiques (like a Craftsman or Queen Anne's Revival), this doesn't make much sense. It isn't accepted worldwide: indeed, in Japan, many of the connotations of permanence and security that Americans associate with homes are associated with the land. It is understood that the home itself needs to be periodically torn down and rebuilt.[3]

The curiousness of the American view can be seen by looking at one of the main alleged benefits of homeownership: it's a "hedge against inflation." True, a home will not disappear in the event of the value of the dollar going south, but the notion that a home should rise in value is tenuous. Rising in value is quite an accomplishment

2. Arthur C. Nelson argues, based on survey data, that Generation Y (whose formative experiences with homeownership took place during the final stages of the housing bubble and then its implosion) have more doubts about homes as an investment vehicle. If members of that generation can hold to such views despite what could be strong temptations to abandon them, the effects on housing markets could be profound. Nelson, *Reshaping Metropolitan America: Development Trends and Opportunities to 2030* (Washington, DC: Island Press, 2013): 45.

3. John P. Dean, *Homeownership: Is It Sound?* (New York and London: Harpers & Brothers, 1945). On Japan, see Richard Ronald, "Property, Consumption and Investment—Meaning and Context: The Economic Significance of Home Ownership in Divergent Socio-economic Conditions," online working paper (Department of Environment, Faculty of Human Development, Kobe University, Kobe-shi, Japan, n.d.).

for a commodity that, sweat equity aside, just sits there. A company's stock price can be driven up by productivity gains or market expansion, but a house does nothing to generate wealth. It provides shelter. So why should a home increase in value, year after year?

There are several positive ways that homes can increase in value. The first is that the surrounding uses could become more desirable to potential buyers. The rundown house across the street could be restored, a new school could be built within walking distance, a new office complex nearby could suddenly have hundreds of families looking for homes in the immediate vicinity, an influx of hipsters and artists could give a neighborhood new charm. That is, the opportunities on adjacent lands can push up the desirability of a parcel. It is for reasons like this that any hundred square feet of Manhattan are worth so much more than any similarly sized lot of random mountainside in the Rockies. This goes hand in hand with another way that houses can become valuable, namely to have the rest of the economy grow, which would lead to higher salaries for home buyers. The more wealth an economy creates, the smaller portion of household wealth would be needed to be spent on housing (though this savings could be swallowed by, say, rising standards in living quarters). A similar effect to rising incomes could be created by subsidies for the purchase of homes. Lowering the interest rates purchasers have to pay on loans could have the same result. All of these things happened for the quarter century after World War II. That's the happier story, basically a story of economic growth.

Other dynamics can lead to darker stories of rising home prices. Most notably, one is to have first-time buyers go further and further in debt to get into the game. That makes available more money to pour into the system. There are, of course, limits to this. People can only borrow so much money. Then the rise in home prices stalls and goes into reverse. This too has happened in postwar America. Curiously, whenever this happens, people forget about the decline in housing prices when they start to rise again, and renters again will feel the pressure to get in while they still can. Andro Linklater, in his history of the rise of private ownership of land, quotes an observer from 1836 sounding all the world like someone in any recent housing bubble: "Who ever heard of a man buying and selling a farm at the same or a lessened price?"[4]

That run-ups in the housing market depend on more and more people pouring more and more money into an essentially unchanging commodity suggests an uncomfortable analogy: the American Dream bears the marks of a Ponzi scheme. In that con game, an *artiste* like Charles Ponzi promises people enormous returns on investments and at first delivers them. But it's a sham. No money is invested. Instead the con artist uses money from later investors to pay off early ones, skimming off a considerable portion for personal gain in the process. To delay running out of money, the con artist recruits more and more people into the scheme. This works as long as the number of new investors exponentially increases. That of course can't happen indefinitely and eventually the whole thing crashes.

That the American housing market for the last decade looks a lot like a Ponzi scheme should not be particularly controversial. Billions upon billions of dollars flowed into housing markets with little change in the actual homes to justify the subsequent inflation, and, when the market collapsed, millions of people were left holding the bag. Recognizing a Ponzi scheme streak in housing markets can explain why mortgage brokers felt the need to loosen their standards, ultimately accepting "liars loans" in which they did not verify income or assets: they needed more warm bodies to keep pumping up the prices. This led to more and more creative accounting and deception to make people eligible for home loans, making the system more and more vulnerable. As soon as it became difficult to recruit people for increasingly exotic and strained mortgage instruments, the whole thing imploded in a matter of months. Many people could probably see and accept the parallels between the bust of the housing bubble and a Ponzi scheme.[5]

4. Andro Linklater, *Owning the Earth: A Transforming History of Land Ownership* (New York: Bloomsbury, 2013): 222–23.

5. See for instance ibid., 350–1, 366. The economist Hymn Minsky, whose reputation has grown tremendously since the housing bubble collapse, sees "Ponzi financing" as one

To suggest that a Ponzi-like dynamic is inherent in longer waves of housing prices, to suggest that the shenanigans of subprime mortgages were not that anomalous or even the cause of the market meltdown, is much more controversial but deserves consideration because it can explain some troubling features of housing markets and encourage us to develop more ways to provide shelter for future generations. We should recognize that if we continue on as we have, the housing market will continue to spike and bust again and again, with people each time just as dumbfounded by what happened.

What makes the comparison of the American Dream of home-ownership and Ponzi schemes plausible is the result not of the house itself but from the land underneath it. Political economists have long struggled to make sense of the unique economic characteristics of land. Two in particular are of note here: one piece of land cannot be substituted for another and the supply of land is essentially finite.[6] This creates dynamics quite different from the classic relationships between supply and demand in which increases in demand will lead to more production. Land can be used more intensively by building taller buildings and land further out can be brought within a region's economy (e.g., building roads into the countryside). But, on the whole, it is difficult to produce housing in response to increased need (especially when regulations slow the development process). This can make housing markets act as

---

of the three basic states of investment along with hedge and speculative financing. He argues that markets (including housing) are prone to crashes because periods of stability lull people's sense of risk until they take on investments dangerous enough to crash. Hyman P. Minsky, *Stabilizing an Unstable Economy* (New York: McGraw Hill, 1986, 2008). Minsky's growing reputation is discussed in John Cassidy, *How Markets Fail: The Logic of Economic Calamities* (New York: Picador, 2010).

6. John Logan and Harvey Molotch, *Urban Fortunes: The Political Economy of Place* (Berkeley: University of California Press, 1987): 23–27.

Social Security has also been compared to a Ponzi scheme. See Eric Laursen, *The People's Pension: The Struggle to Defend Social Security Since Reagan* (Oakland, CA: AK Press, 2012):, 279-81. Chapter 17 has a good discussion of intergenerational equity.

if there is a monopoly even when ownership is finely distributed among homeowners and small business owners. Modest increases in demand can quickly outstrip supply, leading to bidding wars for an effectively finite supply of homes. As a result, homes will increase dramatically in price without having changed in any way. This can only be sustained as long as more people pour money into the home market. (For a contrasting example, modern agriculture tends towards instability because there is the strong incentive for each farmer to overproduce.[7] This leads to very different dynamics.)

Housing does not have to experience Ponzi-like bubbles. If housing prices increase very slowly, then new buyers won't pay much more than the sellers. There is much to be said in favor of such scenarios, but, when that's the case, the American Dream *as an investment strategy* works poorly, perhaps gaining owners little more than their imputed rent: the sellers lock up their wealth in a financial vehicle that makes them little money. Indeed, if maintenance, taxes and lost opportunities are taken into account, they might lose out financially and the benefits of homeownership are more intangible (e.g., a sense of security, pride, the pleasure of "piddling around" the house)—benefits that are no less important to people for the inability to attach a dollar sign to them. In many parts of the country, including urban San Diego, prices, however, are rarely stable but instead are in a perpetual state of rising or falling. When that happens quickly, like in California from the turn of the century to 2006, the Ponzi scheme comparison is strongly suggestive: investors are making money hand over fist, hoping to not be the last people to buy before the crash of home prices.

This leads to an interesting question: who loses during a crash?[8]

---

7. Paul K. Conkin, *A Revolution Down on the Farm: The Transformation of American Agriculture Since 1929* (Lexington, KY: The University Press of Kentucky, 2008).

8. The "eating their young" phrase in this context comes from Jens Ladefoged Mortensen and Leonard Seabrooke, "Egalitarian Politics in Property Booms and Busts: Housing as a Social Right or Means to Wealth in Australia and Denmark," in *The Politics of Housing Booms and Busts*, ed. Herman M. Schwartz and Leonard Seabrooke, 122–145 (New York: Palgrave Macmillan, 2009): 137.

If the Dream is to be sweet for someone, it has to be bitter for someone else. Who is left with a sour taste in their mouth? Who buys houses at inflated cost?[9] The loser in this scheme isn't random. A description from the Australian experience by the brilliant housing sociologist Jim Kemeny is apt:

> In effect, the capital gains of one set of owner-occu-
> piers are being paid for by another set of owner-
> occupiers paying greatly inflated prices for old houses.
> A cross-subsidisation therefore takes place between
> different groups of owner-occupiers. In practice, the
> burden of carrying the full weight of market pric-
> ing of old houses falls on the shoulders of first-time
> or recently established buyers who buy the oldest
> houses (where the difference between the purchase
> price paid and the original construction cost plus the
> value of any capitalised improvements is the greatest)
> and who have little or no capital gain from previous
> housing to transfer.[10]

9. This section especially touches upon a large body of literature coming out of the United Kingdom and to a lesser extent, Australia and New Zealand. Starting in the 1960s, it was suggested that relations to housing tenure create housing classes akin to occupation classes. Peter Saunders, *Social Theory and the Urban Question.* 2nd ed. (London: Hutchinson Education, 1986). The notion of housing classes came under fire for failing to distinguish between the social positions of different kinds of owners. Ray Forrest, "The Meaning of the Home," *Environment and Planning D* 1 (1983): 205–216; David C. Thorns, "The Implications of Differential Rates of Capital Gains from Owner–occupation for the Formation and Development of Housing Classes," *International Journal of Urban and Regional Research* 5 (1980): 205–30. Such criticisms should not be used to discredit the emphasis on housing as a major fault line but rather spur more thorough research.

10. Jim Kemeny, *The Great Australian Nightmare* (Melbourne: Georgian House, 1983): 25. It should be noted that this can be quite different from bubbles in other investments, like stocks, where buyers and sellers are less likely to be differentiated by age (in part because of higher turn-over in the instruments they own).

To simplify, this means that someone has to pay for the increased values of homes, and this is largely a generational shift of wealth from younger to older—and possibly, from immigrants to citizens.[11] This suggests that US housing markets are addicted to large-scale international immigration.[12]

As Kemeny argues, this intergenerational shift has profound consequences. Research on relative poverty suggests that with steady housing costs, people who have kids (that is, most people) will experience a double peak and double trough of prosperity and (relative) poverty.[13] Young couples are comparatively affluent because of their few expenses.[14] Children, however, use considerable resources, limiting what is available for other needs. Once the children are adults, however, a couple's expenses plunge and they have more discretionary income. Retirement diminishes this. Kemeny notes that:

> [t]he overall effect of owner-occupation on the family cycle of relative poverty is… dramatic. It replaces a cycle of two peaks and two troughs with a cycle consisting of one long and deep trough of poverty stretching from the first formation of the household through the childbearing and to the near end of the childrearing years, followed by one heightened peak

11. The relationship between immigrants and housing is an intriguing one. If the arguments of this chapter are correct, then international immigration could very well play a key role in creating upward pressure on American housing prices.

12. Keep in mind that the issue is the cost of the homes, not homeownership rates per se. Myers argues that rising home prices and ownership rates were positively correlated nationally in the 1990s because the increases prices created an investment incentive (while decreasing home prices makes ownership look less appealing). Dowell Myers, *Advances in Homeownership across the States and Generations: Continued Gains for the Elderly and Stagnation among the Young*. Note 08, (Fannie Mae Foundation Census, 2001).

13. Jim Kemeny, *The Great Australian Nightmare* (Melbourne: Georgian House, 1983): 78.

14. See also Michael Stone, *Shelter Poverty: New Ideas on Housing Affordability* (Philadelphia: Temple University Press, 1993).

of prosperity in the post-childbearing years which becomes a relatively shallow trough of poverty in old age.[15]

At best, this is simply backwards: it puts the brunt of the expense of housing on people at a time when they really need the money for raising children. If this happens on a modest scale, this is obnoxious—a kind of fiscal hazing—but not necessarily earth shaking. There are other intergenerational transfers of wealth, like education spending, that muddy the issue enough that there isn't an overall obvious direction.

Under conditions of population growth and a finite supply of land, however, this can careen wildly out of control. It can become a form of age-based domination. While the existence of hostility like racism, class inequalities and sexism are widely recognized, the idea of one generation benefitting at the expense of another is counterintuitive because love of family members is expected to ensure intergenerational reciprocity.[16] The reality of generational selfishness can be seen through one major example: the national debt. Before the rise of the Tea Party, the way Democrats and Republicans worked out political compromises and avoided having the constituents of either party make sacrifices was by having subsequent generations pay. Low taxes kept Republicans happy and large programs kept the Democrats happy.[17]

15. Jim Kemeny, *The Great Australian Nightmare* (Melbourne: Georgian House, 1983): 80. Kemeny further argues that this distinctive distribution of relative poverty across the life span profoundly affects people's willingness to be taxed to support the welfare state. For a discussion of this issue, see Herman M. Schwartz and Leonard Seabrooke, eds., Introd. to *The Politics of Housing Booms and Busts* (New York: Palgrave Macmillan, 2009): 11–13.
16. On intergenerational economics see Nancy Folbre, *Who Pays for the Kids? Gender and the Structure of Constraint* (New York: Routledge, 1994).
17. David Brady, 1994. "Is Disorder Institutional?" in *The New American Political (dis) order*, ed. Robert Dahl, 39–47 (Berkeley: Institute of Government Studies Press, 1994): 42. Or, as a legislator in Jim Mills's history of 1960s Sacramento politics put it, the way to get reelected is to vote for every appropriations and against every tax increase. James R. Mills, *A Disorderly House: The Brown–Unruh Years in Sacramento* (Berkeley: Heyday Books, 1987).

Similarly, during housing booms, older Americans are able to use their monopoly position in the housing market to extract a premium from younger generations, who suffer for it: the enormous transfer of wealth must be paid. Younger Americans double-up, reduce spending in other areas of their lives, work full-time while attending school, and delay having children.[18] Sometimes, they will even engage in a miniature act of intergenerational revenge: they'll move back in with their parents.[19]

If this weren't bad enough, homeowners as a class are extremely confident about their moral worth as they are modeling good citizenship.[20] They are advancing along the socially acceptable life course; their willingness to better themselves by owning property and committing to a neighborhood are marks of maturity. Ownership is likewise long been believed to promote a sensible attachment to the social order and inoculate people from dangerous, unAmerican ideas like communism. In contrast, renters are seen as a threat. They "don't have a stake in the community" because they are more likely to move from place to place. Supposedly this lack of connection encourages antisocial behavior and complacency about neighbor-

18. This leads to the great conceptual defect of Obamacare: the mandate to buy health insurance presumes that the problem with rising healthcare costs is that younger, healthier Americans, who often face significant college debt and weak job markets, aren't doing enough to subsidize those who are older and sicker.

19. See Tamara Draut, *Why America's 20- and 30- Somethings Can't Get Ahead* (New York: Doubleday, 2006). The emphasis on owning single-family detached homes also has had profound implications for gender relations. See also Dolores Hayden, *Redesigning the American Dream: Gender, Housing, and Family Life*, 2nd ed. (New York: W. W. Norton, 2002).

20. An excellent history of evolving notions of American citizenship is Michael Schudson, *The Good Citizen: A History of American Civic Life* (New York: Martin Kessler Books, 1998). The notion of renting and homeownership as forming an appropriate life cycle is from Constance Perin, *Everything in Its Place: Social Order and Land Use in America* (Princeton, NJ: Princeton University Press, 1977): ch. 2. On the historical relationship between property and community, see Gregory S. Alexander, *Commodity & Propriety: Competing Visions of Property in American Legal Thought, 1776–1970* (Chicago & London: University of Chicago Press, 1997).

hood decay. Often, since those who can buy do so, renters are often the economically disadvantaged members of the community and potentially of different social or ethnic backgrounds from homeowners. These differences lead them to be seen as a threat to the homogeneity of a neighborhood and a potential tax burden to boot.

Despite its antiquity and its appeal to common sense, the heady brew of homeownership and democracy does not bear up to close inspection. This is most obvious when it comes to the allegedly distinctively American quality of this Norman Rockwell view of local politics and homeownership. There is also an Australian Dream, a Canadian Dream, and New Zealand Dream, and, to a lesser extent, a British Dream.[21]

It's important to see this commonly shared dream for what it is. It is a status system. It creates a pecking order, justifies people's places within it and encourages a particular distribution of resources.[22] To wit, the Dream defines democracy in such a way as to encourage participation in local government by its adherents and makes it more difficult for others to participate.

Renting and owning are often seen as the only possible relationships a person can have with their shelter. In a series of arguments refined over several decades, Jim Kemeny has argued that this is a profoundly misleading understanding of the role of housing in modern states. He argues that homeownership is financially appealing, not because of its innate qualities, but because governments subsidize it and putatively constrain other forms of housing tenure. The division of obligations and responsibilities in renting are often taken as natural in the United States, but in fact renters in some

21. On the UK and Australia, see Jim Kemeny, *The Myth of Home Ownership: Private Versus Public Choices in Housing Tenure* (London: Routledge & Kegan Paul, 1981) and Kemeny, *The Great Australian Nightmare* (Melbourne: Georgian House, 1983). For Canada, see Richard Harris, *Creeping Conformity: How Canada Became Suburban, 1900-1960* (Toronto: University of Toronto Press, 2004).

22. This formulation of a status system is heavily influenced by Omi and Winant's notions of *racial project* and *racial formation*. Michael Omi and Howard Winant, *Racial Formation in the United States: From the 1960s to the 1990s*, 2nd ed. (New York: Routledge, 1994).

countries are given more rights normally associated with owning, like lifetime security of tenure and more rights to modify the interiors of where they live. Owning is in fact an expensive housing option and its high cost begets an even higher cost: the interest on mortgages. Every owner in effect pays the original owner once for the house and pays for the privilege of doing so by paying the bank a second time. An alternative is *cost-basis housing*, in which a public or nonprofit corporation owns housing without attempting financial gain.[23] The residents have many if not all the rights of owners, save the ability to sell at a profit. And the housing corporation charges a rent that covers its costs and a portion of all the outstanding mortgages (much like a homeowner association fee). As the corporation's housing stock matures, a smaller and smaller portion of its homes have mortgages, meaning that less money is being paid out and that savings is passed along to residents. This is like what happens when an individual owner's housing costs go down after paying off their mortgage: all they have to pay is upkeep and taxes. When new people move in, they don't have to pay the mortgage again. Over time, cost-basis housing becomes increasingly cheap. Eventually, the ownership option becomes competitively disadvantaged, triggering, Kemeny argues, attacks from homeowners, like when Thatcher began selling off council housing.

This points to an important feature of the American Dream: once a home is bought, no matter how naively, the new owner is committed to the maintenance of the Dream. The home is for many people the largest investment they make in their lives and threats to it have dire financial implications. This is enough to propel them into local land use politics. Homeownership then becomes a powerful conservative force in local government: its advocates have a strong incentive to be involved, they can easily make networks as their

23. This is not to be confused with *affordable housing*, the American term for subsidized housing for the residual population that cannot be housed by for-profit ventures. Cost-basis housing can work for all socioeconomic classes, though it would need subsides at first to level the playing field with subsidized individual homeownership.

neighbors are potential allies, they have a lot of resources and their ideology is seen as common sense.

A belief of many homeowners, one that guides their participation in politics, is that increases in the density of housing will decrease the value of their homes. Unless it is replacing an unpopular or unsightly existing land use, most new developments in existing neighborhoods can expect at least a modicum of resistance from nearby homeowners.[24] The sophistication of the resistance is a largely function of the social class of the residents. Upper middle class homeowners, many of whom are professionals themselves, are able to ward off most undesirable uses. Poorer neighborhoods are less able to put up resistance to lower-status land uses, like affordable housing and waste transfer stations.

Homeowner activism has two interrelated negative effects. Insofar as it limits the supply of housing, it drives up the cost of housing for others, to the financial benefit of those who already own homes. This puts such activism in a negative light: while claiming to represent the community as a whole, homeowners are in fact a privileged faction of it. When they participate in land use politics, they engage in mortal combat with the other propertied factions—landowners and developers.[25] What happens to renters is but collateral damage.

Perhaps the most enduring effect of the homeowner participation in local politics is to orient city planning to their own needs, which are more long-term than speculators' but far short of those of future generations.[26] Indeed, on a day-to-day basis, much city planning is focused on the tool that most benefits homeowners: zoning. At face value, zoning is merely the most specific policy tool for determining

---

24. Katie Williams, "Does Intensifying Cities Make Them More Sustainable?" in *Achieving Sustainable Urban Form*, ed. Katie Williams, Elizabeth Burton, and Mike Jencks, 30–45 (London and New York: E & FN Spon, 2000).

25. See Sidney Plotkin, *Keep Out: The Struggle for Land Use Control* (Berkeley: University of California Press, 1987).

26. One of the few groups to explicitly associate land they own with future generations are family farmers who hope that their children will take over their operations.

the location, purpose and dimensions of buildings.[27] Its often highly technical language, however, obscures the origins of zoning and its continued purpose: exclusion of land uses and persons considered a threat to homeowners and other property owners.

Zoning, it could be argued, was conceived in the same spirit as eugenics. Both were products of the early twentieth century, a time of backlash against high levels of international immigration on one hand and a belief in Progress on the other. Eugenics and zoning had the same goal—maintain racial purity—and took a similar approach: the application of rational principles. Eugenics used control over genes to maintain the purity of the master race; zoning used and continues to use physical separation. The landmark 1926 Supreme Court case *Village of Euclid v. Ambler Realty Co.*, which affirmed the constitutionality of zoning, sounds like eugenics in its concern about health and invasion when it declared that apartments in single-family neighborhoods very often were "a mere parasite."[28] In the South, the racial nature of zoning was open until a 1917 Supreme Court ruling said that explicit discrimination was going too far (because it violated the rights of white property owners wanting to sell to blacks). This forced racialized land use policy underground.[29] Afterward, southern cities merely fell into line with the rest of the country in crafting ordinances in which particular land uses like apartments or laundries became the understood technical language for indicating stigmatized groups.[30] The stated goal in city after city was the same:

27. Christine M. Boyer, *Dreaming the Rational City: The Myth of American City Planning* (Cambridge, MA: MIT Press, 1986).

28. 272 U.S. 365 (1926) (USSC+).

29. Christopher Silver, "The Racial Origins of Zoning in American Cities," in *Urban Planning and the African American Community: In the Shadows*, ed. June Manning Thomas and Marsha Ritzdorf, 23–42 (Thousand Oaks, CA: Sage Publications, 1997): 30–31. On the creation of condos as a legal category in the US, see Daniel Lauber, "Condominium Conversions: A Reform in Need of Reform," in *Land Reform, American Style*, ed. Charles Geisler and Frank Popper, 273–301 (Totowa, NJ: Rowman & Allanhead, 1984).

30. Kenneth Baar, "The National Movement to Halt the Spread of Multifamily Housing, 1890–1926," *Journal of American Planning Association* 58, no. 1 (1992): 39–48.

protect single-family detached houses from obnoxious uses.

Over the years, the emphasis in exclusionary zoning has shifted to requiring each home be on a large lot.[31] This drives up the cost of the resulting homes, creating a financial barrier to lower classes. As one of the San Diego County community planning group chairs once put it, small lots in his area would "lead to a ghetto."

In short, local city politics is dominated by a very particular special interest group. Like a massive star that bends light towards it, homeowners are the center of gravity of urban land use politics. They don't always win—not by a long shot—but they focus debate on the future towards the impacts on themselves, often at the expense of discussion of the effects on renters and subsequent generations. Mike Davis describes this in Los Angeles:

> It is symptomatic of the current distribution of power (favoring both capital *and* the residential upper-middle classes) that the appalling destruction and misery within Los Angeles's inner city areas... became the great non-issues during the 1970s, while the impact of growth upon affluent neighborhoods occupied center-stage.[32]

And homeownership can be an erratic force in politics: its financial commitment to rising home values requires additional growth, yet having the growth too close to home is perceived to damage it. This leads to support for Smart Growth in the abstract but opposition within the homeowner's own neighborhood, a phenomenon observed nationally and which strongly impacted the outcome of the City of Villages general plan update.[33]

---

31. Charles Monroe Haar, *Suburbs under Siege: Race, Space, and Audacious Judges* (Princeton, NJ: Princeton University Press, 1996). Given California real estate prices, what counts as a large lot is much smaller than most of the rest of the country.

32. Mike Davis, *City of Quartz*, (New York: Vintage Books, 1994): 212.

33. Anthony Downs, "Smart Growth: Why We Discuss It More Than We Do It," *Journal of the American Planning Association* 71, no. 4 (2005): 367–380.

CHAPTER SEVEN

TURNING TOWARDS THE

HOME STRETCH

D
uring the first two-thirds of 2001, public participation in the City of Villages took many forms: the Phase IV meetings, the lengthy dialogue with the Community Planners Committee, the input on what the environmental impact report should cover as well as the intense rounds of meetings with individual community planning groups. Then, the general plan update laid dormant, at least as far as outsiders were concerned. The project, however, was proceeding apace.

The planning department hired the firm of Kelling, Northcross & Nobriga to prepare a facilities financing report. According to the City's own estimates, the communities were over two billion dollars behind in infrastructure.[1] The consultants were brought in to find

---

1. Kelling, Northcross & Nobriga, *Facilities Financing Study for the Finance Citizen Committee* (San Diego, February 12, 2002). The infrastructure shortfall estimates could have been made controversial. The most commonly cited figure was $2.5 billion. Planners calculated the cost of all the unbuilt infrastructure in the community plans to be $2.4 billion, with $854 million having funding identified. This approach was dubious, however, in that the City of Villages implied updating all the (sometimes quite dated) community plans, which meant new sets of infrastructure priorities. It also ignored needs, like water and sewer, that other agencies provided, needs that sometimes had independent revenue streams and other times would compete with the plan for general fund money.

strategies to pay for this shortfall—but not the cost of the City of Villages itself, which had not been calculated. The consultants first compared San Diego's revenue streams to similar cities and then calculated how much money specific tax and fee hikes could generate.

Their findings became central to the plan update's rhetoric. San Diego's fiscal conservatism had put the City on the low end for many taxes and fees. To make matters worse, the report said, the formulas for distributing state revenues that were locked into place by the Proposition 13 regime left San Diego worse off compared to other major California cities: it received back only 17 percent of the property tax it sent to Sacramento while cities like Fresno got back 24.6 percent and Los Angeles 28.9 percent.

San Diego had no direct control over how the state legislature distributed revenues, but it could raise a number of local taxes and fees and remain below the state average. The consultants and the finance subcommittee of the Combined Citizens Committee worked to develop a range of options, from instituting a trash-collection fee to making the entire city an assessment district. The goal was to collect the approximately $90–100 million a year believed necessary to cover the shortfall. The subcommittee, however, was acutely aware that the political climate made *any* tax or fee increases highly unpopular.

A Looming Problem

When the plan advocates hitched their efforts to SANDAG's estimate of a million more people in the region by 2020, they had unwittingly hitched it to a falling star. As 2001 came to an end, the star began its descent.

In the late 1990s, SANDAG used figures provided by the State Department of Finance to calculate that the region's population was approximately 2.9 million. The initial census 2000 figures, however, showed that it was closer to 2.8 million. This information, as well as the discovery that Latina birthrates had fallen much faster than anticipated, was included in SANDAG's next forecasting cycle. By the end of 2001, the initial 2030 estimates became available. Their projected population for the City of San Diego for 2020 was lower than in the previous forecasts. Accordingly, on December 20, 2001, Gail Goldberg sent out a letter to the members of Combined Citizens Committee telling them that instead of trying to accommodate an additional 50,000 housing units, the City of Villages would only need to find room for 17,000 more units. After this, staff justified the plan more in terms of quality of life issues than the need to accommodate new growth.

This decision raises the question: why didn't the City simply extend the end point of the plan to 2030 or 2040 instead of reducing the number of additional housing units it would attempt to accommodate? Other cities, typically ones with a stronger commitment to planning than San Diego (e.g., Santa Barbara or Portland) used thirty- or forty-year time frames. The hope might have been that cutting back on the additional housing would lessen the mounting resistance to the City of Villages. If so, it failed. It did more to highlight the instability of attaching the general plan update to demographic forecasts constantly under revision.

The New Year

As 2002 began, the Combined Citizens Committee started wrapping up its original mission, but more still needed to be done. A selection process and criteria for picking the pilot villages had to be created and a five-year implementation plan written. The facilities financing subcommittee had to turn the consultants' ideas into a credible financing strategy. The last subcommittee had the most work to do: public outreach.

The Strategic Framework Element's final year was marked by a dysfunctional relationship between the planning staff and the public. Despite the considerable appeal of the City of Villages, the community planning groups were getting squeamish. And more of the general public had begun to find out about the plan. Like the planning groups, they found the concept alluring but didn't like how they thought it would be implemented in their communities.

The planning department sailed into these tricky winds with a poorly rigged ship. They were dishonest with themselves about what they were doing and thus could not adequately respond to criticisms without revealing a profound contradiction in their own thinking: planning staff insisted that the plan was a grassroots effort while treating the adoption of the plan as an effort in salesmanship.

One of the few occasions where this came close to the surface was the January 2002 meeting of the Combined Citizens Committee. One staff person explained how the planning department had to make it clear that the plan was "people driven" and not "City driven." The next staff person to present mentioned one of the techniques they were using to get the word out about the plan was "ghosting" letters to the editor to the *San Diego Union-Tribune*. Then the committee and staff discussed how to "sell" the plan. No one commented on the glaring contradiction in selling a people-driven plan. The staff person insisting that the plan was not City-driven pointed to the way every map and every document related to the plan update had been revised in light of public feedback. But those changes had been filtered through staff. There was no give and take, a situation intensified by the external pressure to hurry up and finish the City of Villages. (As will be seen in the next case study, negotiation takes a *long* time.)

Staff also saw the hundreds of public meetings that they held as proof of public participation, but the public wouldn't have agreed. Although staff's willingness to hold many, many meetings in communities pointed to their dedication, they also considered as public the meetings held downtown during work hours. For people who had to work, these simply were not an option. For those who could show up, the organization of the meetings was discouraging. When the City of Villages went before city council or the planning commission, other items were on the agenda as well. Unless the plan was declared *time certain*, it was impossible to tell when it would be discussed.

People had to wait hours, not knowing when their chance to speak at the podium for three minutes would come.

The Breakdown of Trust

Planning staff was in an increasingly difficult situation. On one hand, residents wanted the plan update process slowed down so their concerns could be addressed—and sometimes addressing their concerns would mean abandoning the key ideas behind the City of Villages. On the other hand, some on city council were pushing to get the plan adopted as soon as possible.

To complicate this further, the plan had, to use a phrase coined by Dutch researchers, begun to "cast a shadow:"[2] developers had begun lobbying for their projects, not on their consistency with community plans, but on their consistency with the City of Villages concept. This played well with staff and the planning commission but not with community groups. The planning commission was also pushing developers to add more residential density to their projects. While building at lower densities precluded building desperately needed housing, the increase in density was going ahead without a way of addressing the already existing shortfalls in infrastructure. This alarmed community activists. Planning group members saw it as proof that their worst nightmare—more density without adequate facilities—was coming true.

In January 2002, the relationship between CPC and the city planning department turned towards open antagonism. Since its adoption in the late 1990s, the City was trying to make regular updates to its Land Development Code. In the second update, adopted back in December 2000 and January 2001, city council voted to make two zoning overlays apply to more of the city. The zoning overlays dealt with parking near transit stops and with tandem parking.

2. H. Mastop and A. Faludi. "Evaluation of Strategic Plans: The Performance Principle," *Environment and Planning B* 24 (1997): 828.

The tandem parking regulation allowed projects to count one extra-long parking space as two spaces instead of one, meaning they could meet parking requirements with less land. This had a "wink, wink" quality because it was common knowledge that people were reluctant to park in tandem, as the second vehicle blocked in the first. In other words, giving credit for tandem parking allowed developers to meet code without providing enough parking. Similarly, the transit overlay zone allowed a 15 percent relaxation of parking standards for development projects near transit. The idea was that with transit available, fewer parking spaces were necessary (and having fewer parking spaces allowed for more density, making transit more practical). Parking in San Diego's older communities, however, was already scarce, so it was unlikely that the CPC would be enthusiastic about these changes.

The real problem, though, was that someone forgot to tell the planning groups and the CPC that the parking requirements in their communities were being lowered. The CPC found out shortly before its January 2002 meeting—that is, a year after it happened and five months after it went into effect. One of the areas affected was Clairemont Mesa, whose representative on the CPC, Dave Potter, was its chair. He wrote a motion questioning the legality of the City action and calling for the adoption process to be redone. It passed 18–0–4, a no-confidence vote against how the City handled public input. (Two years later, city council largely rescinded the lower parking standards.)

The Salesmanship Begins in Earnest

February marked the beginning of a presentation blitz that slowed only at the end of spring. Staff went out to dozens of groups, from the Sierra Club to the Society of Marketing Professionals to college classes. Staff also conducted the fifth and final round of public meetings.

The first Phase V meeting took place in the suburban north. It went remarkably well. People were excited about the possibilities and appeared willing to pay the cost of covering the multibillion dollar infrastructure shortfall (even though the shortfall was mostly in communities far to the south) because they were told that it would only cost them $75 a year. The atmosphere was not even dampened by many of the people finding out, halfway through the meeting, that a number of them had $60 tickets on their windshields because they had parked illegally in the too small library parking lot.

The other four meetings, however, went downhill. Staff was increasingly on the defensive and visibly tired. Questions grew sharper; personalities in the audience, odder and more troublesome. Instead of the meetings drawing their audience from one-fifth of the city as intended, people came disproportionately from the immediate vicinity and were there not to discuss the City of Villages but to complain about some local development project they didn't like.

The Environmental Impact Report

Since the City of Villages did not involve any actual building, it had a *program-level* EIR, which provided a broad-brush analysis of potential impacts. It was to be followed by an additional EIR for each community plan update and then again for each specific development deemed to have potential significant impacts. Consistent with the desire to minimize the significance of the Strategic Framework Element, the City chose to push as much of the analysis as possible into the later EIRs.

On January 12, 2002, the massive draft EIR (DEIR) was posted on the City's webpage and then, shortly thereafter, made available at local libraries. State law gave people forty-five days to comment, and the City was required to respond in writing to each comment. All the comments and responses went into an appendix in the final EIR, which had to be certified by both the planning commission and city council.

Some of the most extensive criticism of the EIR came from the

Friends of San Diego and from Dave Potter of the CPC. They took different public stances: Potter, himself a planner retired from the City, wanted the City of Villages to be right by his sights; the Friends believed that if the environmental analysis were done properly, it would show that the costs of growth were higher and thus bolster their slow-growth views. Nonetheless, Potter and Mullaney reached similar conclusions. While their arguments were generally quite technical (as was everything else about EIRs), they could be reduced to two overarching claims: the analysis in the EIR was not thorough and too much analysis was improperly delayed until subsequent EIRs.

One of the major faults of the EIR, they claimed, was that it did not even analyze the right thing. According to state law, an EIR must do "ground to plan" analysis as well as "plan to plan" analysis. That is, it must compare the proposed project to the existing plan as well as current conditions. The City did not do both of these. The environmental analysis concentrated just on the 17,000 to 37,000 additional housing units of the City of Villages. It should have also examined the impacts of building all the other housing in the plan and thus provide a complete picture of growth's impacts on San Diego by the year 2020.

Regardless of the accuracy of these criticisms, the EIR was marked by impatience, a cavalier attitude about getting sued and a desire to be cheap. The EIR's traffic modeling epitomized the latter two points. According to the Smart Growth and New Urbanism, the City of Villages should have substantially reduced the number of additional auto trips by encouraging walking and transit riding. The City's existing traffic modeling, however, was built around the logic of car driving. Since the modeling could not see Smart Growth, it could not register its improvements. But instead of taking the time and money to develop more sophisticated traffic modeling, planners went ahead with the current system. It concluded, perhaps unfairly, that the villages led to only a six-percent reduction in traffic over what would occur if the growth occurred in sprawl patterns, meaning that traffic would on the whole be much worse than it was at the time the EIR was being written, regardless of what kind of growth San Diego experienced. This put staff in the position of advocating a plan that their own analysis appeared to show was overrated.

The EIR gave critics of the plan something to hold onto. They had been defending their own communities in isolation, responding to local concerns. The EIR became a rallying point around which they could find common ground. It became a way of showing that the problems of the plan update were systemic. As Tom Mullaney of the Friends of San Diego put it, the flagrantly low quality of the EIR was "throwing down the gauntlet."

In the face of criticism of its EIR, the city planning department had two basic options: appease people by doing the analysis they wanted (assuming they really wanted it done and weren't just trying to stall a project they didn't like) or defend what they had already done. The City could have also mixed the two approaches in a divide-and-conquer strategy. The City's lawyers, however, said that the EIR was legal, so the planning staff took the second approach and tried to persuade people that what they had done was adequate. They also extended the EIR process to give people more time to provide input and feel comfortable with the document that was being produced. Alienation from the City of Villages—despite its inherent appeal—was too extensive for that to matter.

No Longer in a Bubble

One of the dilemmas faced by the Combined Citizens Committee was the result of Proposition 13. The finance subcommittee had to advise the planning department and city council whether to propose *general* taxes, which required a simple majority in a public vote, or *specific-purpose* taxes, which had to win a two-thirds majority. While general purpose taxes were, statistically speaking, much easier to pass, San Diego voters were perceived to be so leery of the City and of taxes that they would not support a blank-check tax. Based on the success of a huge 1998 school bond measure, it was believed that taxes had the best chance if voters in each neighborhood knew that they would receive specific local benefits. Thus, a specific-purpose tax would generate more support, but the big unknown was whether it was enough support to reach the two-thirds bar.

At the beginning of the twenty-first century, the City of San Diego had a hotel tax of 10.5 percent, which was comparatively low, as the leaders of the local tourism industry preferred to keep it. Concerned that the City might raise it, Doug Manchester, a local hotel developer, engineered the San Diego Taxpayer Protection Act. This ballot initiative—designated Proposition E—would have required that all City tax increases meet the two-thirds majority requirement.

City council was unhappy with this: raising money to fund local government was tough enough without a developer playing on antitax sentiment to protect his own bottom line. To defeat Manchester, council put an initiative on the ballot (Proposition F). It required that any measure that mandated a two-thirds threshold in future elections must itself pass by two-thirds. Furthermore, the council initiative would be effective immediately, affecting other measures on the ballot. Since few initiatives ever garnered the two-thirds required to pass, it would likely kill the hotel developer's initiative.

In the March primary, the strategy appeared to work. While Proposition E won 54.4 percent of the vote (out of 162,843 votes), Prop F's 50.3 percent was enough to kill it. The proponents of the Prop E cried foul and the Howard Jarvis Taxpayers Association sued the City.[3]

3. This section was largely based on a series of articles by David Hicks (*San Diego Daily Transcript*) and Ray Huard (*San Diego Union-Tribune*). See Hicks's articles "San Diego Rules Committee Scraps Hotel-tax Increase," October 5, 2001; "With Deadline Looming, Proposals Being Finalized for March Vote," October 22; "City Continues to Struggle with Hotel Room Tax Issue," November 5; "City Moves to Guard Tax Base against Manchester Initiative," November 7; "Strange Pair of Initiatives," November 19 as well as "Legal Battle Looms over City Tax Proposition," March 12, 2002. Huard's pieces are "San Diego Eyes Boost in Hotel Tax," September 27, 2001; "Committee Would Kill Tax-limiting Measure," November 8; "S.D. Council to Offer Rival Ballot Proposal," November 20 and "City Loses Court Ruling on Tax Vote," August 9, 2002.

Into the Storm

Legislation can suffer many different fates. If there's a consensus about the need for a bill and everyone agrees on the particulars, adoption can be anticlimactic. City council might not even discuss the matter but merely pass it without comment. Sometimes, the mere hint of controversy is enough to shelve a bill. In between those two extremes are various kinds of jockeying as side deals are made to craft the necessary majority for passage. This can get ugly.

Sometimes, especially when there is a recognized need for a project but strongly different views on its content and the pace of adoption, the legislative process can turn into what was earlier called a death spiral. That is, a controversial project moves within sight of being adopted but with powerful groups having significant objections to its current form. The proponents are put in the position of being forced to make rapid compromises and can get so caught up in the process of negotiation that they lose sight of their principles. This can happen for different reasons: they're spending more time negotiating with opponents than talking with their own organizations, they lack the time to appreciate the long-term implications of what they're agreeing to, they become pessimistic about their ability to get anything more, they're losing political support or they suffer from burn out. And critical power brokers might want to kill the program or simply don't understand it. This all works to make the adoption process erratic. No one wants it this way: proponents want the measure passed intact; opponents don't want it to pass at all, and elected officials prefer everything worked out before it reaches them.

Perhaps because the underlying concept is so vague, local government programs to promote sustainability, either in the name of good planning or environmental protection, seem particularly susceptible to death spirals. Requirements for such programs are often handed down by state or federal mandate, sometimes as a precondition for specific funding. This means that there might not have been a groundswell of interest in starting the adoption process in the first place. Some members of the community or elected body might even be downright unenthusiastic or resent being forced to follow the state or federal law, especially if funding is not included or if the result will be more regulation of local business. These people may want to take the adoption process slowly, either to kill it or force negotiations to continue until they're satisfied. On the other hand, sustainability or planning advocates are urging the project to go forward. And external forces, like public pressure or deadlines, might compel the adoption process to go forward despite objections. In the ensuing death spiral, it becomes difficult, if not impossible, to keep everyone happy, and all these conflicting elected officials and special interest groups go to great lengths to avoid being unhappy. What happens, then, is an unpredictable storm.

The City of Villages was heading into one of these legislative tornados.

As the finishing touches were being put on the City of Villages, attention shifted towards the planning commission and city council, the two entities that had to approve it. All along, they had gotten at least quarterly updates, usually at joint workshops of the commission and council's land use and housing committee, but the guidance they provided had been in the form of individual comments, not motions, so how each body as a whole stood was uncertain.

The last joint workshop was on April 3, 2002. Councilmembers began staking out their positions on the plan update, and they were becoming more critical. Donna Frye was concerned about current development projects masquerading as the City of Villages. Brian Maienschein said that given how impacted the streets in Mira Mesa were, he'd laugh if it weren't so sad that they were trying to put two-thousand additional units in that community, the third most of any area after downtown and Mission Valley. He pressed staff hard on what exactly the proposed density increases meant. The villages were supposed to be hypothetical, awaiting for the community plan updates, yet staff was treating them as real. "Am I supposed to believe these numbers or not?" he bluntly asked. George Stevens, who had been on the land use and housing committee for years, said he didn't recognize many of the names on the Combined Citizens Committee and thus was concerned that his district was under-represented. He asked whether the Combined Citizens Committee could be augmented, and staff, probably surprised to be asked such a question since the committee had already met fourteen of its fifteen times, gracefully said yes. Stevens then launched his oft-made attack on taking resources from his district—library and park maintenance moneys and street sweepers were again his main examples—and using them to cover operating expenses in the newer communities. Scott Peters again expressed his impatience at the update's slow pace. The recurrent theme of all the councilmembers and the planning commissioners, as well as members of the public who spoke, was the question, "How are we going to pay for all of this?"

At the end of the month, the full council was updated on the City of Villages. It must have been tedious for the members of council on the land use and housing committee because the update was almost identical to the one they received twenty-six days earlier. More of interest were the two new planning commissioners voted in: Mark Steele and Carolyn Chase.

Mark Steele's first term on the planning commission had expired the preceding June. Mayor Murphy had wanted to make a fresh selection for his first appointments but reappointed Steele when another vacancy appeared. Councilmember Frye questioned Steele's ability to serve on the planning commission because his architectural firm was involved in so many projects and he would have to recuse himself too many times to be effective.

Carolyn Chase was in many ways Steele's opposite. While Steele was part of the local establishment, Chase was an activist, most heavily involved in environmental issues, and she had few quibbles about blasting the said establishment. But her support of Murphy during his mayoral campaign had increased his credibility. While Steele had been involved with the City of Villages from the beginning, Chase had only participated in the two workshops in 2000 where the City of Villages strategy was picked. She reflected on the planning process in her July 16, 2000 *Daily Transcript* column. Her words were prophetic:

> Other benefits to slowing growth are: reduction in tax and infrastructure burdens, less traffic, less water and sewer problems, well, just less. In this case, less is more. And let's not forget that straight line forecasts have a tendency to go up and down. Commitments in "up" times are not always sustainable in the "down" ones. When I raised the issue that the "slow growth" alternative should be given comparative treatment with other alternatives, staff later came to reassure me that all the alternatives would be equally evaluated in the Environmental Impact Report. What I'm suggesting is that it should be given equal consideration in the public process as well. Without it, they are setting themselves up for a "backlash." They are not going to be able to "sneak" density in around the City.

The plan update process had been taking so long that it ran into council's annual June budget hearings, pushing the estimated adoption back to August.

CHAPTER EIGHT
ADOPTION WOES

While the council temporarily turned its attention to approving the next City budget, opposition to the City of Villages gained momentum. Political expediency increasingly trumped planning principles.

By no later than April 2002, the Friends of San Diego had begun considering legal action if the analysis in the EIR was not substantially improved. On June 14, the City released the final draft of the City of Villages EIR. It disappointed its critics. This meant the plan was in for a contentious finish.

At its June 25 meeting, the Community Planners Committee took up the Strategic Framework Element and its five-year action plan. Despite sharing the widespread concerns about how the infrastructure would be paid for, CPC members were still sufficiently enthusiastic to pass a motion, 21–3–2, approving the plan, albeit with nine conditions.

The conditions were far reaching. The first condition capped the additional housing at 17,000 units, consistent with Gail Goldberg's letter the preceding December which had reduced the total from 50,000 units. (The EIR analyzed a range of 17,000 to 37,000 units.) Additional conditions left it to each community to determine how much additional growth to take and required that the planning groups have a greater say in design of the additional housing.

Out in the communities, opposition to the City of Villages was growing. While planning groups often liked the ideas but were criti-cal of specific points, residents had a more visceral reaction: they didn't want additional density near them. This kind of opposition was not organized on a city-wide level. It was, however, intense when it erupted, most spectacularly in Allied Gardens, where hundreds more people showed up for two meetings than were able to fit into the room. (The planning department estimated a total of seven hundred people in attendance at the meetings.)

August 2002: At the Planning Commission

Several weeks after the last CPC meeting on the project, a judge ruled against the City's Proposition F, which had short-circuited the ballot initiative requiring general purpose taxes to pass by a two-thirds public vote.[1] The judge declared the City's measure inconsistent with the State constitution, which only required majority votes to change a charter. Barring a successful appeal, Proposition F was void, and general purpose taxes faced the all-but-impossible two-thirds threshold in elections, making the prospects of adequate facilities financing even more remote as the City of Villages headed for adoption.

On August 15, 2002, the planning commission held its adop-tion hearing. In anticipation of a large crowd, the meeting was moved from the council chambers across the plaza to a much more spacious room in the convention center. As the meeting started on that Thursday morning, approximately seventy people were in attendance, and more trickled in. Towards the back of the room, a handful of people held up placards along the lines of "No! City of Villages in Allied Gardens."

Staff began with a PowerPoint presentation. The current plan, they said, needed revision. It was outdated. It was inadequate for

1. Ray Huard, "City Loses Court Ruling on Tax Vote," *San Diego Union-Tribune*, August 9, 2002.

dealing with the housing crisis, the growing population and the increasing traffic problems. With quarterly public workshops and over two hundred meetings, public participation had been extensive. Indeed, it was "certainly a citizen-guided effort" because of the work of the Combined Citizens Committee, especially its June 2000 workshops that selected the City of Villages as the growth strategy. The EIR, staff claimed, was at the program level and did not need the detail to be done later in the project-level EIRs. The components to be adopted that day were the Strategic Framework Element (and its EIR certified), a five-year action plan and the interim transit-oriented development guidelines for the villages. Staff explained that any village designation had been removed from the Allied Gardens portion of the map, a decision rationalized in terms of good planning but clearly a concession to community pressure.

The commission asked clarifying questions, the most pointed from Carolyn Chase. She asked what would happen if the Transit First program wasn't implemented. This led to nervous tittering in the audience, which was unusual because disagreements at City meetings rarely rose above someone saying, "We should have a discussion about that." Staff replied that the Metropolitan Transit Development Board had adopted the plan, so implementation was a question of speed. Chase then asked what would happen if Transit First wasn't funded. Someone in the audience yelled, "Answer her question." Staff said that if there were no funding, then there would be no density increases, a promise Chase asked to see in writing.

After a few more questions, the meeting was opened to public testimony. Members of the Combined Citizens Committee and a number of establishment representatives (SANDAG, the Economic Development Corporation, the American Institute of Architects) praised the plan and urged its adoption. They did not think it was the best possible plan, and they spoke with anxiety about financing. Indeed, the rhetoric was similar to that of environmentalists and planning groups: the concepts were great, but money remained a huge question mark. The supporters, however, felt that the only choice was to move forward.

Often, when their three minutes at the podium was up, they turned to leave and Commissioner Chase called them back to ask them a question: would their organization actively support efforts to raise taxes to pay for the City of Villages? Few could wholeheartedly say that indeed was the case. The one critic that Chase called back to the podium was Tom Mullaney representing the Friends of San Diego. He was so critical of the EIR that she asked him whether he was prepared to litigate, a question to which she probably knew the answer because, as mentioned earlier, she was a founding officer of the Friends.

The Friends were prepared to sue. In fact, their attorney had sent the planning commission a letter the preceding week, arguing that the breezy claims in the EIR were unsupported by evidence and that analysis at key points was missing. Later, the chair of the commission noted that it was easy to threaten to sue and that the City attorneys said the EIR was defensible.

Community-based opponents of the plan were disproportionately from Allied Gardens, who were adamant that their area be maintained for single-family detached houses and not apartments. Many of them were clearly inexperienced in speaking in such a setting. Their bald NIMBYism grated on the nerves of some of the commissioners, who stressed the need to take a realistic approach to growth and to look at regional impacts.

At the end of an extremely long day, the commission voted 7–0 to support the City of Villages and 6–1 to certify its EIR, with Chase excepting.

Council's First Adoption Hearing

On September 23, 2002—five and a half years after the land use and housing committee gave the plan update the green light—city council held its City of Villages adoption hearing. It was immediately clear, however, that the plan was in for a rough time: the public was hostile. And the public was present in numbers. Council policy required that two of its meetings each year be outside its regular chambers. It was decided to make the City of Villages adoption hearing one of them and to put it in a huge room in Balboa Park. Even though it was far larger than the council chambers, the room was packed. After the initial presentations by staff and planning commissioners, Mayor Murphy announced that he had a hundred speaker slips, sixty in favor of the plan update and forty in opposition.[2] There was no way to get through all the speakers and still have time for council to deliberate. A second hearing had to be held in October.

Council in fact had already received many communications from the public. Some of these letters, faxes and emails were in support; they tended to be from organizations and people connected with the City or the plan update itself. More were opposed. Some communications were detailed critiques of the Strategic Framework or a portion of it. A handful of businesspeople wrote a form letter, with minor variations. (Their most interesting point: wanting recognition that not all businesses worked well in mixed use developments.)

A slightly greater number of people sent in email supporting the "Responsible Growth Resolution" put forward by the larger local environmental organizations (Audubon Society, BayKeeper, Sierra Club, Surfrider, and the small but growing Friends of San Diego). The resolution made four main points, which would become a refrain in public comments on the plan. The first two points: they supported the concepts and the pilot village program. Third, they

---

2. Ultimately seventy-one speaker slips in favor and fifty-nine opposed were submitted. During meetings, people kept submitting slips while others spoke. On the slips of paper requesting to speak, a person could indicate that they didn't need to speak but were simply registering support or opposition to an agenda item. The idea was to strengthen the sense of sentiment in favor of a position without slowing down the meeting. Also, people could turn in speaker slips but not speak because, for example, they might have been using their vacation time from work and left in disgust if it looked like it would be hours before they had their turn. This situation strengthened the hand of development interests at meetings because frequently, they were paid to be there while their critics were volunteers. (The evening City of Villages meeting reversed this.) Speaker slips worked the same way at the County.

wanted the Strategic Framework Element and accompanying documents revised. They listed over a dozen changes, mainly calling for more analysis. In their list was also a call for an active program to deal with affordable housing and for a policy that required "existing deficiencies... be cured before or current with new development." The fourth major point of the resolution was a call for a consultant to oversee the revision of the general plan. Although this was framed as a positive recommendation, adopting it would have been a no-confidence vote on the planning department.

The meeting materials noted that the CPC supported the plans but with conditions and listed the degree of support of fifteen community planning groups. Eight were listed as being in favor. Five more were listed as in favor with conditions (with two more coming to the same conclusion after the agenda material had been printed). Two groups were opposed, though the Mission Valley group's opposition was based on not receiving enough information to decide.

The initial staff presentation was virtually identical to the one given to the planning commission a month earlier. The chair of the planning commission summarized its meeting and recommendations. "The public wants assurances," he told council.

By that point, however, many just didn't want the City of Villages at all. Again, the public had not been organized on a city-wide level, but residents got the information about the meeting from word of mouth, email, websites and newspaper articles. For some, political participation was undoubtedly a novel experience.

That the public testimony portion would not go well despite the number of speaker slips in support of the Strategic Framework Element was foreshadowed by a fax to council earlier in the day from the Rancho Bernardo community planning group. The first two sentences gave a sense of its tone:

> The Rancho Bernardo Community Planning Board learned Thursday that the City Council Agenda for today's hearing indicates this Board's position on the Strategic Framework Plan as one of support. Such a

misleading statement is extremely troubling to this Board, particularly in light of the serious concerns we have raised regarding the overall implementation plan for the Strategic Framework Plan and City of Villages concept.

At the beginning of the public testimony, Mayor Murphy insisted upon a corny rule that gave the hearing a surreal bent. To save time, if a person in the audience supported a speaker, they should clap—once. Murphy also decided that the chair of the CPC, Dave Potter, should speak first and be given fifteen minutes.

Potter eviscerated the planning department for bungling the plan update and alienating the community planning groups, which was especially disconcerting because "it provides us with an indication of how we, and the public, will be dealt with in the future." He stressed that he was not opposed to growth or to the concepts of the City of Villages.

He thought it a bad idea for the plan to go forward without the support of the CPC, which it did not have: CPC members were belatedly informed that the planning department rejected all nine conditions attached to their June resolution of support—and yet still claimed that the CPC supported the City of Villages without indicating that they even had conditions for support.[3] Furthermore, the department had misrepresented the planning groups' stance on the Transit Overlay Zones at the land use and housing committee three weeks earlier.

Potter blasted locating potential villages strictly on the basis of transit and commercial centers. Then he gave examples of arrogant statements made by planners. He also described an email survey he conducted. Of the twenty-one planning groups that responded, twenty said that staff did not ask them to participate in how many

3. The materials for city council's next meeting on the City of Villages noted that "[s]ome conditions associated with community groups were inadvertently omitted" and mentioned that CPC had nine conditions. The city manager's report for the September meeting noted the CPC conditions but that they were best dealt with at the community level.

additional units should be put in their area. Potter pointed out that the community planning groups had been called NIMBYs but added, "They can call us whatever they like, but they need to add to that lexicon 'angry, frustrated, disillusioned, disenfranchised, and distrustful of the planning process as it currently exists.'" Potter got many a one-clap for his observation that "[a]s a consultant, I am currently preparing an EIR for a general plan update for another jurisdiction. If I were to submit a document of this quality, I would be fired."

He described how an assistant director of Development Services and a City attorney appeared before the CPC to assure them that the EIR covered everything required. When asked whether they had read the EIR, the director said no and the lawyer invoked attorney-client privilege, which the audience at the council hearing found even more laughable than the CPC did. Potter called for the council to adopt the community groups' nine conditions and ended with an outline of a program to revise the plan update similar to the responsible growth resolution put forward by environmentalists.

Potter was followed by a lengthy presentation by the Friends of San Diego. Assisted by PowerPoint, they stressed the importance of maintaining the quality of life—they had a picture of kids playing tennis in the middle of a street because there wasn't enough park space—and ridiculed the EIR for making outlandish claims, such as saying that adding 12,000 more housing units into Mission Valley would not require even one more school. By the end of the presentations by Potter and the Friends of San Diego, the planning department had lost the initiative.

The remainder of the evening was devoted to public speakers. Proponents recognized flaws but argued that the best next step was adoption. They were afraid that problems that could be solved were jeopardizing the plan's good ideas.

Some of the opponents were planning group members with highly technical criticisms. Others, who sometimes suffered from stage fright or rambled, had classic anti-density knee-jerk reactions. One speaker slip summarized this view: "Don't want high density housing in the neighborhood. It will lower property values, increase congestion & lower quality of life for those now living there." In the margins was added, "Parking is already a problem!"

By the end of the meeting, the question, then, was what form of damage control would work. Passing nothing would look bad: it would solve none of the city's problems and squander the time and effort devoted to the plan. The City of Villages, however, was controversial at best and unpopular at worst. As one speaker ominously put it, "you can't force density on us and expect us to roll over and play dead."

The mayor ultimately found a face-saving maneuver, one that would make the plan advocates' early decisions blow up in their faces.

CHAPTER NINE

THE DARK UNDERBELLY OF

ENVIRONMENTALISM

"Developer"—A fancy name for environment-raping, tax-evading, cowardly, corrupt, dictatorial creeps!

—Graffiti on a restroom stall,
in a San Diego County building
since torn down

They absolutely hate the developers when they're proposing something, but I tell you what, when you buy a house or need a house, you love him to death. As soon as you buy your house, you kick him in the buns and say, "We don't need you anymore." If you look around... without the development community, there wouldn't be a damn thing in this county.

—A developer, 2002

Environmentalism in the United States is a funny creature.[1] On one hand, most people heartily endorse it. Nature with a capital *N* is a good thing. No doubt about that. On the other

---

1. American environmentalism comes in a variety of flavors. The focus here is on a form that engages in and follows the rules of local land use politics. Most advocates self-identify as environmentalists but, in their actions described in this book, they're actually a distinctive brand of conservationists. To be neutral, they'll be called *land use environmentalists*. They are relatively conservative compared to more radical

hand, few countries in human history have been as profligate in their use of resources as the United States. Central to this paradox is the idea of Nature itself. It's taken as something real, as something no way contaminated by human hands.[2]

Nature, in this view, is a wondrous thing. To be sure, sometimes it can be brutal or terrifying. As anyone who watches their PBS documentaries knows, the cute baby deer gets eaten; the mother deer falls through the ice; and the buck, as he dies of a cruel wasting disease that causes his hair to fall out, spends his final days staring pitifully back at the camera crew. But this is all morally invigorating, at least until Man (again, capitalized) comes through with a bulldozer.

As William Cronon's brilliant essay "The Trouble with Wilderness" demonstrates, however, this is an illusion. *Nature* is a human creation. There might be parts of the world (increasingly few) that are beyond our reach, but we project our ideas onto them.

The concept of Nature is predicated on a metaphor and a story. The metaphor: a wall or barrier. On one side of the wall is "the wilderness" and, on the other side, civilization. When humans cross the wall from their side to the wilderness, one of two things can happen. If the crossing is so modest that it leaves no impact, then it is spiritually uplifting. More typically, the crossing is a violation of the purity of Nature and represents a poisoning, such as with air pollution, or an invasion, such as the construction of a highway. In this kind of contact, humans have a Midas touch that turns everything to lead.

---

environmentalists that resist co-optation by political processes like the City of Villages. While some criticisms of land use environmentalism that figure here apply to other types of environmentalism, not all do. And some criticisms of radical types of environmentalism do not apply to land use environmentalism. For instance, one of the country's worst cases of eco-terrorism, the firebombing of a large condo construction site, took place in San Diego during the City of Villages adoption process. Such violence can (and should be) harshly criticized on a number of levels, but those criticisms don't apply to the policy-oriented land use environmentalism of this book.

2. In land use planning, Nature is reduced to the term "open space"—a concept so broad that it sometimes includes farmland and golf courses. A more pro-developer term for the same land is *vacant*, implying that it's just waiting to be filled by human uses.

This damage is often a story of theft: as a source of moral values and of life itself, the natural world must be shared by all. It is the original commons that belongs to no one person but is available to and must be husbanded by humanity as a whole.[3] Appropriation of the commons, the privatization of the commons, is both an outrage against Nature and a social injustice. For instance, air pollution, in this view, is taking something that belongs to everyone—fresh air—in the name of personal gain. A factory that is profitable but pollutes is not really profitable. Rather, the manufacturer makes money by stealing resources from the public. It's merely a transfer of wealth from the community as a whole to the industrialist.[4]

This understanding of environmentalism encourages a specific approach to land use politics, namely the desire to limit additional growth, both in terms of fewer houses constructed and less land consumed per house, which is a key reason why Smart Growth rhetoric appeals to environmentalists. The results, however, have been unsatisfactory. Environmentalists fight perpetual rearguard actions. Even in their large-scale efforts like the Multi-Species Conservation Program (MSCP), which tries to create a system to avoid development-by-development fighting by clearly demarcating which areas have to be preserved, environmentalists are still taking a last-stand approach.

William Cronon sees the mistake of this approach in how environmentalists understand "the wilderness," which:

> is not a pristine sanctuary where the last remnant of an untouched, endangered, but still transcendent nature can for at least a little while longer be encountered without the contaminating taint of civilization. Instead, it is a product of that civilization, and could hardly be contaminated by the very stuff of which it is made.

3. David Bollier, *Silent Theft: The Private Plunder of Our Common Wealth* (New York: Routledge, 2003).

4. This damage is called by economists *negative externalities* and green economics emphasizes strategies to get polluters to pay what are seen as the true costs of their actions.

That is, wilderness is a concept that comes with baggage. Lots of it. Like the American Dream, it is not the unmitigated good that it is often taken to be. While the American Dream of homeownership is often considered unique but isn't, the American conception of Nature is taken to be universal but in fact is distinct.

Its beginnings were steeped in violence. When the British arrived on the American shores and saw uninhabited land for the taking, they were engaged in a spectacular act of doublethink because they were very much interacting with the natives, who lived off the land but somehow did not inhabit it. This doublethink was made possible by denying the humanity of indigenous peoples and dismissing the legitimacy of how they exerted control over the land. They were seen as devoid of civilization. Akin to the animals, they were part and parcel of the wilderness, which was there to be exploited.

In the nineteenth century, two shifts occurred in the thinking of European Americans. First, wilderness came to be valued. With the advent of industrialization, the threat that the wilderness posed to white Americans was decreasing, and it was becoming clear that humans were in fact a threat to it. The wilderness, now less of a danger, stood in positive contrast to the overcrowded satanic mills and was celebrated by the likes of Henry David Thoreau and John Muir. Second, as Nature was being romanticized, so were indigenous Americans (at least by whites not near the frontier themselves). The upshot, however, was that if Native Americans were people and not megafauna, then they were polluting the wilderness with their presence. European Americans took this to its logical conclusion: after designating Yosemite and Yellowstone as national parks, the National Park Service slowly drove out the Indians: they were deemed incompatible with the natural state of those areas.[5]

The logic underlying this expulsion has continued to shape the modern American environmental movement. As some environmentalists admit, the movement has looked down upon rural

5. Mark David Spence, *Dispossessing the Wilderness: Indian Removal and the Making of the National Parks* (New York, Oxford: Oxford University Press, 1999).

Americans, especially those reliant on resource extraction industries like mining and lumber.[6] This view, which defines Nature as that which has not been contaminated by humans, likewise has affected how American environmentalists have approached conservation in the developing world. They sometimes have perceived environmental problems as being caused by peasants trampling on high-value habitat. The sin of these indigenous groups, in this view, is that they are the wrong side of the barrier dividing civilization from Nature. They are humans, but they are traipsing through the natural world.[7]

The flip side of criticizing natives for meandering around the wilderness has been to pay less attention to what happens on the human side of the wall as long as it doesn't push the wall outward by visibly destroying more habitat. This has led environmentalists in the developing world to complain that consumption patterns in the developed world receive insufficient attention as environmental preservation focuses not so much on reducing consumption on a per-capita level but instead working to prevent the expansion of environmentally wasteful lifestyles by slowing growth, freezing inequalities in place.[8]

The moral dimension that is missing from this perspective is the recognition that existing residents were growth too at one point. In a kind of reversal of Faulkner's comment on the past, past growth, according to environmentalists, was never growth.

6. See John Echeverria and Raymond Booth Eby, eds., *Let the People Judge: Wise Use and the Private Property Rights Movement* (Washington, DC: Island Press, 1995); Frank Popper, "Rural Land Use Policies and Rural Poverty," *Journal of the American Planning Association* 50 (Summer, 1984): 326–334. Richard Louv has argued that we're also expelling our children from wild spaces, in effect domesticating them with video games and soccer. Louv, *Last Child in the Woods: Saving Our Children from Nature-Deficit Disorder* (Chapel Hill, NC: Algonquin Books, 2005).

7. This paragraph is very much the product of conversations with Seiko Matsuzawa whose research has focused on China.

8. Ramachandra Guha and Juan Martinez-Alier, *Varieties of Environmentalism: Essays North and South* (London: Earthscan Publications, Ltd., 1997).

As such, land use environmentalism is stuck in an eternal present in which proposed developments are fundamentally and morally different from what happened before but without a clear explanation of why, creating a trap:[9]

> If this is so—if by definition wilderness leaves no place for human beings, save perhaps as contemplative sojourners enjoying their leisurely reverie in God's natural cathedral—then also by definition it can offer no solution to the environmental and other problems that confront us.[10]

The full parking lots at Earth Day events epitomizes the difficulty for environmentalists: it's very difficult to reflect upon your own consumption patterns.

Some environmentalists, however, don't try. Instead, they see themselves as defending Nature and believe the way to do that is to oppose new development, as if people will disappear if no homes are built for them. These environmentalists do not necessarily explicitly reject growth but find reasons to oppose any specific project. A "no growth" position for San Diego could be done honestly—in truth, it makes little sense for population growth in the United States to continue to be funneled into water-dry southern California—but it would require supporting a national urban policy that would

9. William Cronon, "The Trouble with Wilderness," in *The Best American Essays of 1996*, ed. Geoffrey C. Ward and Robert Atwan, 83–109 (New York: Houghton Mifflin Company, 1996): 97. The only way I've seen this moral distinction of different kinds of growth justified is with the lifeboat analogy—that is, the claim that past growth was acceptable but any more would overload the ship and cause it to flounder. The people who make this argument invariably and conveniently believe the cut-off occurred after their arrival on the scene.

10. See also Stephanie Pincetl, "The Preservation of Nature at the Urban Fringe," in *Up Against Sprawl: Public Policy and the Making of Southern California*, ed. Jennifer Wolch, Manuel Pastor, Jr. and Peter Dreier, 225–251 (Minneapolis: University of Minnesota Press, 2004): 247–48.

direct resources disproportionately to more environmentally robust regions, which are much more logical places for growth to occur. This is not done.

Defensive environmentalism, then, risks paralysis and mystification: by emphasizing that all of humanity is dependent upon Nature for water, clean air, food and the like, it makes it look like people are equally affected by ecological damage and allows middle-class environmentalists to discount questions about who pays costs, a slippage encouraged by general plans that focus solely on the costs of future growth and not the ongoing costs of existing development. Environmentalists involved with the City of Villages or the County's parallel general plan update didn't try to use the plans to rethink their own impacts on the environment. The plan updates could have been an opportunity to advocate for green architecture, to find ways of living that stressed harmony and balance—but they weren't. Instead, environmentalists approached—or at least accepted—the general plan updates as a numbers game, an exercise in conservation to be won by holding the line against growth.

Some environmentalists at least recognized that current residents contributed to ecological problems and hoped that Smart Growth, by steering growth away from the urban fringe, would lead to more sustainable cities. The most sophisticated environmentalists saw that slow- and anti-growth positions had moral dangers but likewise recognized that Smart Growth, by continuing to accept growth unquestioningly, had problems as well. These environmentalists tended to be eclectic in their thinking: they had to think through a whole host of issues singlehandedly, leading them to come up with idiosyncratic positions. (But, as the County case study will demonstrate shortly, the eclecticism of environmentalists had troubling political consequences.)

In short, land use environmentalists tended to understand environmental problems as the problems of other people. Seen this way, this brand of environmentalism was not about the natural world but rather a novel approach to the most basic political science question of them all: "who gets what?" As such, it offered limited ability to truly guide our interactions with the natural world: it was actually a theory of human relations.

Seen this way, its logic is surprisingly similar to that of the American Dream of homeownership. Each community can be divided into good residents who truly belong and outsiders who are a threat. While both groups consider developers to be an enemy, environmentalism focuses on population growth as the alien threat the way homeowners focus on renters.

CHAPTER TEN
OH WELL, WHATEVER,
NEVER MIND

After the September 23, 2002 adoption hearing for the City of Villages, not much happened for several weeks. Mayor Murphy's office let it be known that he wanted the planning department to reach a compromise with both the community planning groups and the environmentalists. He had, however, already found his own resolution to the standoff.

An unexpected weakness in the plan was its dependence on SANDAG's population forecasts. As discussed previously, early on, planners jumped at SANDAG reports calling for additional housing for the year 2020, which morphed into the official reason for the plan. For its 2030 estimates, however, SANDAG changed their demographic modeling: instead of treating the gap between the housing capacity in the current general plan and the estimated population as a housing shortage, the model assumed that if people could not find housing in San Diego, they would live outside the county—either in Tijuana or Riverside County—and commute to their jobs. If people who worked in San Diego but couldn't find housing were assumed to have a lengthy commute instead of creating a need for

The title of this chapter is with all apologies to Kurt Cobain.

more housing, then, by definition, San Diego's "excess" future population disappeared. In short, the model stopped fighting sprawl but embraced it. Staff dutifully gave the estimates to SANDAG's board in August. And went back to what they had been doing.

But the intense opposition to the City of Villages before the council made Murphy more interested in those numbers. As he described it, "Actually, I sorta had to extract those [new lower population estimates] from SANDAG at the SANDAG meeting three days after the last meeting [in September]."[1] If the mayor knew about or cared about the changes in modeling and thus understood that they reflected no demographic changes but merely meant shifting growth to outside the borders of the county, he gave no indication of it in public. Instead, he saw in the numbers his out: "the 2030 regional growth forecast does suggest that fewer people coming to San Diego in 2020 than we originally contemplated which means that there were fewer residential units that will be required and they can all be accommodated under existing community plans." In short, the new approach for dealing with San Diego's growth was, "Never mind."

On October 16, Mayor Murphy and Councilmembers Atkins and Peters issued a joint memo.[2] It said that they did not support the density increases proposed for the general plan update. They gave three reasons: community opposition, recognition that the City couldn't afford the infrastructure and the SANDAG revised 2030 figures showing that the existing capacity of 108,000 housing units was more than adequate to meet the demand for 89,000 units by 2020. But this was pure political expediency: the same figures also showed that the City would be almost 25,000 units short by 2030. As a *San Diego Union-Tribune* headline described it in the next day's

---

1. I was not in attendance at that meeting but the audiotapes convey no sense of resistance by staff to Murphy's routine information request. As already mentioned, they had given his office the information previously.

2. Shortly after becoming mayor, Murphy created a Smart Growth Implementation Committee, but it supposedly did not discuss the plan update. Since it met in private, there is no way of confirming that. The three members of council on it, however, just happened to be the ones responsible for the changes to the City of Villages at the end.

paper, "S.D. Villages plan deflated."

The mayor's office hosted two sets of meetings between city planners and CPC members and then with the environmentalists. The meetings were focused on changes that the planning department could make in light of the revised SANDAG forecasts. Apparently the meetings bore little fruit, however, as the planners went back and forth between trying to compromise and defending their actions.

On October 22, 2002, the San Diego City Council held its second adoption hearing on the City of Villages back in its usual chambers. The meeting started at nine in the morning, and the City of Villages was the only major item on the agenda. Nonetheless, with all the public speakers on non-agenda items, the plan update was not discussed for more than two hours. Attendance was much lower, especially among the plan advocates and those with a professional interest in growth. It was as if they had done their duty by speaking at the first adoption hearing and then washed their hands of the matter. For the final month, the City of Villages was about environmentalists and community planning groups, who were still dissatisfied and distrustful.

The hearing began, of course, with a presentation by the planners. They said that a full staff report had been given at the September meeting, so it was unnecessary to repeat it. They did, however, list extensive changes for the council to consider. Gail Goldberg assessed them by saying, "the planning department is not recommending all of these changes. We're telling you that we would not object to any of them, but these are for your consideration today."

The changes were extensive: the proposed density increases were dropped; the table showing the additional growth for each community plan area was deleted; the map of potential villages was removed from the Strategic Framework Element and put in the action plan where it had less legal weight. The transit-oriented development guidelines would no longer be used as a stopgap measure to ensure appropriate design in the potential villages. The language suggesting that more development be allowed under ministerial review instead of discretionary review (speeding up project approval) was deleted.

New language was added saying that whenever a community plan was updated, the zoning for the area would be analyzed to make sure that it aligned with the new plan. Also, per a request by environmentalists, the package to council included stronger language on finding a regional-level funding source for infrastructure. Finally, there were minor modifications to the language of the EIR but not to its analysis.

The proposed changes were clearly new to the planning department. Indeed, one of the PowerPoint slides still included the TOD guidelines as part of the plan update and staff had to correct it during Goldberg's presentation.

To give recognition to the members of the Combined Citizens Committees for all the effort and hours that they had put in, Mayor Murphy listed their names and asked them to stand. While the committee had fifty members over its lifetime, only a handful were present. Murphy seemed surprised and amused when he called out Councilmember Ralph Inzunza's name. The new representative for district eight stood up but appeared a little embarrassed. (He was the only councilmember not to speak during the discussion before the vote.)

The chair of the planning commission talked about a letter they had written a week and a half earlier. He urged attention to the quality of the plan and not any particular set of numbers. He made one of the few comments of the day about what the new SANDAG numbers meant: more sprawl and more traffic on the already congested I-15 into Riverside County.

Then, after some discussion by council, Toni Atkins read verbatim the October 16 joint memo scaling back the City of Villages. It became the motion for the council vote. Then the meeting was opened to public speakers. The first two were accessible housing advocates, who blasted the plan for not being explicit in its support of the Americans with Disabilities Act. Then council broke for lunch.

After lunch, there were more public speakers. (Ultimately, 17 "in favor" and 22 "opposed" slips were turned in.) No one was happy. The supporters, who considered the plan gutted, urged support for

Atkins's version of the City of Villages but also expressed dissatisfaction. As Michael Stepner, who hadn't personally been actively involved in the plan update since early on, noted:

> We got too hung up on the numbers and tended to lose sight of the overall vision that gets incorporated in the City of Villages strategy. The numbers... as chairman of the planning commission, Mr. Anderson, said this morning, are sprawl oriented and will create problems for us later down the line and we'll have to deal with those.
>
> We have woefully underestimated the cost of doing the City of Villages and the need for doing it.... Let's work together to pay for the things that we need in this community that we've neglected for so many years.

The public speakers in opposition were still hostile. (One dubbed the plan "the City that Pillages.") They liked the elimination of the density increases, but they weren't sure what the other changes meant. They generally reiterated support of the concepts but wanted council to fix the problems before they adopted the plan.

The council discussion was typically disjointed, as each councilmember gave a semi-prepared speech instead of talking to each other and negotiating. Those in favor of the plan used "progress as forward motion" metaphors and called the Strategic Framework Element the first step. They said that Atkins's motion helped alleviate their concerns. The main theme, insofar as there was one, was financing, though it was much more on what to do with money if they had it instead of how to get it. Maienschein said that he opposed the plan because it would mean more taxes.

Paralleling the disproportionate attention paid to urban renewal in the 1965 plan, council's discussion was heavily weighted towards one obscure section that was probably unknown to most people working on the plan: one public speaker warned that the Framework encouraged companion units (smaller houses on the lot of an existing single-family house, also called *granny flats*). This got council's attention because of a new state law that prohibited discretionary review of companion units. This meant residents would have no chance to complain if their neighbors wanted to build one. Councilmembers, especially Stevens, ranted against companion units and the loss of land use control the state law entailed. He argued that it was a betrayal of people who bought homes with the expectation the surrounding neighborhood would remain single-family.

Scott Peters gave the most impassioned defense of the project. His speech, which he modified on his laptop to incorporate other people's comments as they spoke, began by saying that the planning department did not cause growth. Rather, he argued:

> Growth comes from births and it comes from jobs. And I can tell you that the city does not tell you how many children that you should have—and I don't think we should—and we really don't spend a lot of time looking for new businesses to come here. In fact, one of the criticisms of the mayor's first state of the city address, as you recall, was that he didn't make economic development one of his top ten goals and, as any councilmember will tell you, if you want to get the mayor's help on something, it has to be one of his goals. And this is not one.

Peters, who, within a year, would face an unsuccessful recall effort based on his allegedly being in the pockets of developers, discussed infrastructure and argued for the plan's vision. Without it, the city risked being "suburbs on steroids." He asked Atkins to accept a friendly amendment to reinstate the TOD guidelines with the word "encourage" instead of "require." He ended by saying that the city was overdue for a vision and that he'd "rather be an eagle than an ostrich."

He was followed by Donna Frye, who made the strongest case

in opposition. She argued against the plan on a mixture of technical matters and issues of trust. She had grave doubts about the unclear implications of adopting the Strategic Framework Element. She was concerned that while the planning department was saying individual communities could do what they wanted, the requirement in state law that the plan be internally consistent meant that when community plans were updated, they had to be made consistent with the City of Villages. She was concerned that the plan would perpetuate the infrastructure financing approach of the Popeye comic strip character Wimpy, who said he'd "gladly pay you Tuesday for a hamburger I eat today." (She also expressed concern that she dated herself with that reference.)

The Louisiana-born George Stevens asked:

> Why do we have to prepare for someone to come here from another region or another area or another state or another city for that matter? It's like we have been forced to do something because someone is coming here and that way we can't do anything about who we are. I believe that we can do something about those numbers. For example, I'm not knocking planning, I'm just saying, "Why do I have to prepare for someone who decides… to come here from St. Louis? Why do I have to have a place for them when they get here? Why do I have to prepare for that?" It's like being forced… But I don't feel an obligation to have to prepare for them and that's what I'm bothered by.

He rattled off the problems caused by other people: local colleges weren't educating students properly, requiring the in-migration of high-skilled workers; Congress did not exercise proper control over international immigration; state law allowed residential care facilities—even for drug abusers and the mentally ill—to be in single-family neighborhoods without even informing local government; that such facilities were using homes that could house local residents was "very sick." He then listed the planning groups in his area which voted no (one), hadn't even taken a position on the City of Villages (the rest), and announced, "I don't get any enthusiasm from my district on moving forward with this item." On the famous claim that sixty percent of the population growth would be births and forty percent in-migration, he added, "I want to focus on the sixty percent, not the forty percent."

For its critics, the City of Villages was a referendum on San Diego's past growth, and, as such, it was a clear "no" vote. For its proponents, past growth and all its problems could be separated off from the plan by simply not adding any more residential density. This allowed them to vote for it. In the end, the plan was adopted 6–3, with Frye, Stevens, and Maienschein opposing. Both support and opposition cut across party lines and the inner-city/suburban divide.

Afterward

What the council decision meant wasn't immediately clear. Planners were dismayed at this de facto rejection of Smart Growth. Some people claimed that the council wimped out, abandoning the substance of the plan in the face of opposition. As a realtor in *San Diego Metropolitan* described it:

> This housing deficit problem only will be exacerbated as the housing gap widens with shortsighted perspectives like the City Council's… The sticky problem of infrastructure funding is not positively impacted by the City Council backing down on housing; it is only delayed and complicated.[3]

Other people argued that the council action was a PR trick, a way

3. Gary H. London, "Planning for Sprawl: Political Convenience Removes the Muscle from the City of Villages Plan," *San Diego Metropolitan*, November 2002.

to appease the plan's critics without doing anything differently. They pointed to the way the planning department and planning commission had supported City of Villages projects even before its adoption. The Friends of San Diego still sued the city on the EIR, arguing that its language was about adding density even if the density target had been removed. (The lawsuit was eventually settled.) Community planning groups were still suspicious of the City of Villages map and concerned that the planning department would try to sneak it into the land use element when the rest of the general plan was brought in line with the Strategic Framework Element.

It is hard, however, to imagine what city council could have done differently at the end. A mess had landed in their laps: people were wound up and deep-seated problems had been pressed to the fore, but, ultimately, the scope of the issues was beyond council's powers. Any kind of grand solution would have not fit within the confines of one element of a general plan.

The Strategic Framework Element went forward as it was originally conceived: a vision statement. It went through a long detour of trying to accommodate additional housing growth, but that was defeated. The Strategic Framework Element was never structured to handle the detour: the massive amounts of data about "on the ground" conditions necessary to add population was never collected, as would normally be done at the beginning of a plan update. The detour added perhaps two or three years to the process: the latter phases of public outreach and so many hundreds of meetings would not have been necessary if the point was merely to endorse the popular City of Villages ideas. And the EIR would not have become a lightning rod for opposition to growth.

In 2003, the planning department began work on revising the rest of the general plan, making it consistent with the vision put forth in the Strategic Framework Element. It decided to do all the other elements at once. In a March meeting, staff claimed that city council had told them to put the map of villages into the land use element, exactly as planning groups feared. Staff also said that they were doing the detailed analysis of communities—that is, belatedly doing what planning theory considered the first step. It was as if the city was right where it was five years earlier. By spring of 2006, the full plan was moving towards adoption, and the situation was essentially the same: the rhetoric was still the simultaneous (a) support for growth only with proper infrastructure and (b) a refusal to consider tax increases to support infrastructure. It was adopted in March 2008 with much less controversy than the Strategic Framework Element because the map the planning groups feared was not in the plan and, perhaps more importantly, the housing market was in a free fall, making concern about growth a luxury that people would have loved to have. There was, however, one lawsuit over the EIR by an historic preservation organization.

Despite the institutional support for Smart Growth at the City, the Strategic Framework Element was, in many ways, business as usual: a controversial general plan watered down and lacking infrastructure funding. Eight pilot village applications were submitted, largely from the same areas that were targeted for the Liveable Neighborhoods program in the early 1990s. It quickly became apparent, however, that even funding the pilot villages would be a challenge: the national economic sluggishness, which had been relatively gentle to San Diego, finally was catching up with the City budget—as was the deliberate underfunding of the city pension program, which was well over a billion dollars in the red. Planners worked to develop ways to go forward with the pilot villages while relying as little on City moneys as possible.

The center of attention at the city, however, was shifting to more immediate crises: in October 2003, San Diego County was hit by three simultaneous wildfires, one of which destroyed hundreds of homes in the city as it became the largest recorded fire in California history to date. (The fires of October 2007 were on the same massive scale but did not lead to as much soul-searching.) Three of the new Democrats on city council were indicted for accepting bribes from a strip club owner. One died unexpectedly of liver disease; the other two were convicted, though the legal case against one was thrown out.

On the March 2004 primary ballot appeared an initiative to

raise the city's hotel tax. The initiative was supported by the tourism industry, which had long opposed such tax increases. Their enthusiasm came from the ballot language that specified that much of the increased revenue would benefit them, so much so that many people who normally would support such a tax increase got cold feet: they felt that the City had more pressing ways to spend the money than making hotel magnates richer. The ballot measure failed.

Over the summer of 2004, the Fourth District Court ruled against both Propositions E and F. This allowed the City to raise taxes with a majority vote of the public. City council acted swiftly to put a measure on the fall ballot to raise the hotel tax from 10.5 percent to 13.0 percent, almost in line with the Strategic Framework Element's Combined Citizens Committee recommendations. The money did not have the kind of strings attached that the March initiative had. Without being guaranteed a significant cut for themselves, the tourism industry opposed it, resurrecting arguments it attacked earlier in the year. The initiative was also defeated, continuing San Diego's long tradition of fiscal anorexia.

The long-simmering but well-hidden pension underfunding scandal was so bad by the summer of 2004 that Donna Frye jumped into the mayoral race between Dick Murphy and Ron Roberts. Frye's write-in candidacy garnered the most votes but enough were thrown out on a technicality for Murphy to be reelected. But he had so little credibility that he resigned within six months.[4] Jerry Sanders, a developer-backed conservative, beat Frye in the special election to replace him. He moved planning under the aegis of the Development Services Department without kicking up much opposition. Much of his time in office was spent trying to undo the paralysis caused by the City being shut out of bond markets for releasing highly misleading financial data. His successor, the intense and controversial liberal Bob Filner, not only restored planning but lured Bill Fulton, one of

4. Murphy's 2011 autobiography devotes one paragraph to the City of Villages, noting that they passed the plan and it won awards but provides no sense of its adoption process. Murphy, *San Diego's Judge Mayor: How Murphy's Law Blindsided Leadership with 2020 Vision* (San Diego: Sunbelt Publications, 2011).

the biggest names in California planning, to lead the new efforts. Filner, however, had to quickly resign amidst multiple scandals. In a special election, he was replaced by the business-backed Republican Kevin Faulconer (and Fulton soon left afterward). The wheel turns.

Indeed, hindsight humbles the drama around the Strategic Framework Element. As I was documenting it in real time, I was very much caught up in the uncertainty and intense emotions the final stages elicited. But, compared to the tremendous damage that was about to be caused by the subprime mortgage scandal or the myriad of municipal horror stories unfolding (like the pension debacle), the fights over the Strategic Framework Element, no matter how significant to the participants at the time, now look more like a distraction for idealists than a defining moment in City history.[5] This is no mean lesson for those who wish American city planning to be visionary.

And a final kicker: since the City's charter status allowed it to ignore the requirement to make its zoning and general plan consistent, it's not clear whether anything would have happened even if the village maps were approved.

This legal consistency requirement, however, was at the heart of the County's general plan update, the rural twin of the City of Villages. The County's general plan ran parallel to the City's in many ways, but the reader should be warned about a key difference. The City planners prided themselves on their professionalism, and they and their allies were conscious of national shifts in planning and were aware of what other cities were doing in terms of tax policy and strategies for raising revenue. It was only in the final months of the plan that it entered a death spiral in which broader principles and context were abandoned to expediency.

On the other hand, the San Diego County supervisors ranged

---

5. As previously mentioned, the pension scandal, the infrastructure shortfalls and other problems are well documented in Steven P. Erie, Vladimir Kogan and Scott Mackenzie, *Paradise Plundered: Fiscal Crisis and the Governance Failures in San Diego* (Palo Alto: Stanford University Press, 2011).

from mildly critical to outright hostile to planning, so the planners never had a chance to develop dreams of professional grandeur. Instead, they were buffeted by the jockeying of intensely focused interest groups. The broader context was not a concern, and the results were maddeningly self-absorbed: Smart Growth made a delayed entrance; sustainability, hardly at all.

Yet the events at the County contain many lessons for planners—to the point that one participant suggested I entitle my book *How Not to Write a General Plan*. Indeed, the plan went on so long that it went through so many phases that it became a *tour de force* of what can go wrong with planning.

PART III

MEANWHILE, BACK AT THE SUBDIVIDED RANCH

THE COUNTY'S NEVER-ENDING EFFORT TO REIN IN BACKCOUNTRY SPRAWL

The lover of the countryside who wants above all that its traditional appearance should be preserved and that the blots already made by industry on its fair face should be removed, no less than the health enthusiast who wants all the picturesque but insanitary old cottages cleared away, or the motorist who wishes the country cut up by big motor roads, the efficiency fanatic who desires the maximum specialization and mechanization no less than the idealist who for the development of personality wants to preserve as many independent craftsman as possible, all know that their aim can be fully achieved only by planning—and they all want planning for that reason. But, of course, the adoption of the social planning for which they clamor can only bring out the concealed conflict between their aims.

—F. A. Hayek, *The Road to Serfdom*

CHAPTER ELEVEN
THE FLAP OF THE
BUTTERFLY'S WINGS

If the City of San Diego's general plan update is a lesson in what can go wrong with top-down planning, then the County of San Diego's general plan update—covering all the unincorporated land not controlled by the Indian tribes, the cities or state or federal governments—is a lesson in what can go wrong in a bottom-up, grassroots approach.

It started innocently enough.

In 1965, to protect agricultural lands from rapid suburbanization, the State of California passed the Williamson Act. Sprawl was being fueled by farmers on the urban fringe selling their land to developers. The tax structure encouraged this: as sprawl crept closer to a farm, the value of its land increased, raising its property tax, which made it tougher to make a living from agriculture. Selling to developers was a profitable escape hatch. To discourage this, the Williamson Act allowed farmers to enter ten-year contracts agreeing to keep their land in agricultural production in return for a break from their real estate taxes.[1] (The loss of revenue for the local

---

1. The Williamson Act was repeatedly revised, usually in the direction of requiring less commitment from the State, counties and farmers. See Robert C. Fellmeth for a history of how the act failed to achieve its goals and benefitted wealthy landowning corporations. Fellmeth, project director, *Politics of Land* (New York: Grossman Publishers, 1973): 36–42.

jurisdiction was partially reimbursed by Sacramento.)

To further protect agriculture, San Diego County placed the land under contract—and the surrounding land—in an agricultural preserve. All the land within a preserve, even if the owner had not signed a contract, had to be used in ways compatible with agriculture. The bureaucratic way of doing this was to change the zoning on the farmer's and their neighbors' land so the land could not be split into lots too small for farming.

In the early 1990s, a woman, who had not signed a Williamson contract but whose land was within a Valley Center agricultural preserve, wanted to subdivide her forty-seven acre parcel into four lots, with two of the lots on the small side: about four and six acres. The zoning ordinance said that this was acceptable since lots as small as four acres were permitted.

The problem arose, however, with a chart in the County's general plan called the compatibility matrix that said what uses were permissible on a parcel of land based on its regional category, its land use designator and its zoning—a chart that was as confusing as it sounds. (As one retired planner put it, the person who designed it obviously never had to worry about being the one to use it.) Although the matrix *did* say that the woman's Ag 70 zoning, which allowed four-acre lots, was consistent with the designator for agricultural preserves, the matrix also said that every lot in a preserve had to be at least eight acres. So in one place the plan said that land in agriculture preserves could not be split into lots smaller than eight acres but elsewhere said four-acre lots were acceptable. In other words, the County plan contradicted itself, and such inconsistencies were, according to California law, illegal.

County planners, the planning director and the Valley Center community planning group—they all opposed the subdivision. They went with the interpretation they believed technically correct and supported by good planning principles. The property owner went with the interpretation that maximized the economic value of her land. A common tension. The planning commission sided with staff, but the board that handled planning and zoning appeals sided with the applicant, and the matter was kicked up to the board of supervisors.

The five supervisors took a middle-of-the-road approach: they let the woman have her subdivision, but they directed staff to fix this inconsistency in how land in agricultural preserves appeared in the planning documents. Fixing this minor glitch, however, led to a controversy of epic proportions. At stake would be billions of dollars and the future of San Diego's backcountry. Supervisor Horn would later observe, "I can't think of another issue in the nine years that I have been here that has generated more public interest than this."

County planners had several options for eliminating the inconsistency in the planning documents. The approach the planners picked was to make eight-acre lots the minimum for all the land in the agricultural preserves. Since this merely regularized existing practice, they claimed, it was too minor to need environmental review. This change was part of a general plan amendment that the supervisors approved in March 1994.

If actions are judged by their consequences and not by their intentions, then this was a disaster.

Stage Left: Enter the Environmentalists

While the landowner in the Valley Center agricultural preserve was fighting for her four-acre lots, a much bigger fight was brewing in an area twenty miles to the southeast in the beautiful and sparsely populated area that went in land use circles by the decidedly unromantic name of the *Central Mountain Subregional Planning Area*. It was relatively remote, but Interstate 8 ran through it before heading west into the heart of San Diego. That opened it up to development pressure. As open land with easy access to a major city, it was ripe for exactly the kind of growth that environmentalists feared the most: low-density estates that consumed tremendous amounts of land but housed few people. Any major development in the area was sure to garner their wrath.

Rising to the bait was the developer who owned Roberts Ranch. The *San Diego Union*, at the same time it was following the sex-and-hush-money scandal that was undermining the City of San Diego's planning department, covered the story.[2] The developer wished to build a subdivision on the seven-hundred-plus acre tract. The zoning code, which had been in place since the 1970s, allowed this, as it allowed such subdivisions most everywhere else in the unincorporated parts of the county. Roberts Ranch would have by no means been the largest subdivision in San Diego history, but a number of environmentalists treated it as Armageddon: the ranch was an inholding of the Cleveland National Forest, a massive but fragmented federal property that covered much of the middle of the county. While the forest surrounded a number of smaller communities, no suburban subdivisions had been built on the inholdings. If Roberts Ranch were developed, environmentalists believed it would be increasingly difficult to block other developments within the forest, leading to an ecological break up of San Diego's mountain region.

The environmentalists organized in opposition, forming an anti-sprawl group called Save Our Forests and Ranchlands (SOFAR). It quickly became a legalistic *infante terrible*, deftly leveraging the potential for judicial activism inherent in the American legal system into a form of power not dependent on wide membership. Its founder, Duncan McFetridge, rapidly became one of the most admired and most hated environmentalists in San Diego.

All concerned with the Roberts Ranch, including the developer, hoped that the US Forest Service would buy the land. The project, despite donating a considerable portion of the land for permanent

2. For Roberts Ranch and backcountry development battles, see (noting that the *Union* and the *Tribune* had not yet merged): David Harpster, "Lawsuit Filed to Block Forest Subdivision," *San Diego Union*, B3, January 17, 1992; Irene Jackson, " Preservation of Cleveland Forest Urged," *San Diego Union*, B2, October 16, 1991 and "Minimum Lot Size of 20 Acres Is Set for Mountain Land," *San Diego Union*, B1, 6, October 17, 1991; Bob Rowland, "Key Step Taken to Help Preserve Cleveland Forest Site," *San Diego Union*, B3, June 21, 1991; Katharine Webster, "Ranch Plan Hits Snag in Descanso," *San Diego Union*, March 7, 1991.

open space, was opposed by the planning committees of both nearby communities (Descanso and Pine Valley). The board of supervisors rejected the Roberts Ranch proposal in October 1991.[3] The following month, however, the board approved a project on the nearby ninety-one-acre Peterson property. SOFAR sued on grounds of an inadequate environmental review.

SOFAR, still a microscopic group, launched several other lawsuits. A plan for the entire Central Mountain region had been in the works for several years. The new plan for the 35,000-acre area downzoned much of the land, changing the zoning that permitted four- or eight-acre lots to zoning that required that each house have at least twenty acres. SOFAR, wanting even larger minimum lot sizes, sued, again on grounds of an inadequate environmental review.

Since victories concerning environmental impact reports (EIRs) were inherently temporary—a project could go forward once the EIR was revised enough to be legally valid—and since SOFAR did not trust the County, the group launched a ballot initiative to bypass the supervisors and more decisively protect the national forest. The initiative was dubbed the Forest Conservation Initiative (FCI)—the Forced Conservation Initiative to some—and it called for at least forty-acre parcels on private land within the Cleveland National Forest until 2010. SOFAR succeeded in qualifying the measure for the fall 1993 election.

Property rights activists and landowners argued that ballot-box planning was a clumsy tool, that the initiative was an unconstitutional taking of land, and that some people would be economically wiped out. The campaign opposing the initiative never gathered much steam, however. It won by an almost two-thirds majority of voters in the entire county.

---

3. The same week, the supervisors expressed extreme disappointment in SANDAG's draft Regional Growth Management Strategy, with Supervisor (and soon to be San Diego Mayor) Susan Golding calling it a waste of paper and staff time. See the SANDAG chapter and Emmet Pierce, "Supervisors Assail Growth Control Plan as Wasteful Rehash," *San Diego Union*, B3, October 16, 1991.

The County and SOFAR Collide

Less than half a year after SOFAR's ballot initiative passed, the board of supervisors approved the general plan amendment that included a fix to the glitch of small-lot zoning within the agricultural preserves. The decision to cover all the land within the preserves with eight-acre minimum lots looked much less innocent to SOFAR than it did to the County. While it eliminated the problem with lots smaller than eight-acres, SOFAR claimed that much of the land in question was in fact zoned at twenty-acre minimum lot size, meaning that converting them to eight-acre minimum lots was a substantial increase in residential density throughout the agricultural preserves. That, they feared, would fragment hundreds of thousands of acres of open space.

SOFAR's lawyers examined County planning documents and found several leverage points. In May 1994, they filed suit in state superior court against the County, claiming violations to the California Environmental Quality Act (CEQA)—the law that was the basis of the lawsuit against the City of San Diego in the last case study—as well as to the Williamson Act and the State's Planning Zoning Act. This became known as the "Ag 20 lawsuit" after the land use designator code for agricultural preserves. SOFAR demanded an injunction against the general plan amendment, and a hearing was set for March 1995.

SOFAR and its lawyers attacked how the County had written its general plan in the 1970s. Each of the seven elements mandated by Sacramento required analysis to legitimate their findings. The County, however, wrote into three of those elements that the analysis would be done in an optional agricultural element. The agricultural element was also supposed to establish a systematic approach to the creation of Williamson Act agricultural preserves, which planners had been doing in a stopgap fashion. County staff wrote an agricultural element, but in December 1979 the board rejected it and the matter was dropped. This meant that some of the analysis that was to be in the general plan—on soils, for example—was never included. SOFAR claimed that because the proper analysis had never been adopted by the County, it had to conduct an environmental analysis when it changed the twenty-acre lots in the agricultural preserves into eight-acre lots.

A war of motions ensued. The environmentalists' attorneys accused the County of extreme unhelpfulness in allowing access to documents, calling the production of discovery "analogous to Chinese water torture."[4] After postponements and a change of judges, in November 1996 a tentative ruling in favor of SOFAR was issued.

Judge McConnell issued her final ruling in January, agreeing with most of SOFAR's wide-ranging arguments. Sharply rebuking the County, McConnell ordered severe corrective action: until the environmental analysis was done properly, no building permits could be issued on the Ag 20 lands without SOFAR's approval. In effect, a local government had temporarily lost land use control over almost three-hundred square miles of land to a private organization—an unusual, if not unprecedented, situation. Adding to the County's humiliation, it was ordered to pay SOFAR's attorneys $427,434.04 in legal fees, with more pending.

Virtually everything the County did to respond to this spectacular setback sunk it lower into a quagmire. The County's Department of Planning and Land Use (DPLU) became the planning world's equivalent to Sisyphus, condemned to repeating itself over and over again.

The County's Strategies

The County took a three-pronged approach to SOFAR's legal victory. First, elected officials and planners tried to undo the decision. Then they tried to quickly comply. Their final strategy was to make sure they could never lose a lawsuit like that again.

4. Kilpatrick, Jerry, "Petitioner's Reply Memorandum in Support of Motion to Augment Record," California State Superior Court, case no. 676630. March 1. (San Diego, 1995): 4.

The County appealed Judge McConnell's decision. In February 1997, however, the appeals court largely upheld her opinion, only tempering it by allowing construction on legal lots and rebuilding if a structure was destroyed.

Unable to escape the verdict, the County worked to correct the legal deficiencies noted by Judge McConnell. This proved frustrating and grueling: ultimately, it took three tries over six years to get the environmental analysis to pass muster. During this time, many of the Ag 20 landowners, never knowing when the subdivision moratorium would be lifted, were deeply distressed by the legal paralysis of their property. Once the judge was satisfied, however, SOFAR ran out of legal tools and the matter ended in the first half of 2002.

The third and most extensive reaction the County took in response to the lawsuit was to overhaul the general plan and thus "bullet proof" the County against future legal actions.[5] It created widespread unhappiness and galvanized deeply hostile interests. Trying to reconcile them created a tremendous sinkhole of time and money.

5. A question sometimes asked while the lawsuit was still pending was why didn't the County simply fold the Ag 20 issues into the general plan update instead of running them in parallel and wasting staff time, to say nothing of putting itself in the awkward position of developing a plan for the Ag 20 lands, getting it approved by a court and then overwriting it with the general plan. Staff's answer was that the court required this approach. It would probably be more accurate to say that the County initially believed it could correct the Ag 20 problems quickly while the general plan update was a long-term project. It didn't make sense to accept SOFAR's control of agricultural lands while the general plan update meandered its way to completion.

CHAPTER TWELVE
"LEGALLY BULLET-PROOFING"
THE COUNTY

Both winners of the 1992 County board of supervisors district elections—Republicans Dianne Jacob (East County) and Pam Slater (North County coastal)—campaigned on platforms of fiscal conservancy. Jacob, the more aggressive of the two, had her sights on land use planning. She pushed for a seventeen-point program to streamline the DPLU. The DPLU, however, was imploding already.

Like many other planning departments, the DPLU received much of its funding from fees collected by those seeking development permits. The recession of the early 1990s, which led to a deep decline in construction and thus fees, hurt its budget. Between fiscal years 1991–92 and 1995–96, the revenue generated by the DPLU dropped from $5.7 million down to $3.7 million. The budget plunged, from slightly over $10 million a year to $5.7 million. Staff shrunk accordingly, from almost 170 staff-years to less than 90.

This was devastating to many long-term employees. To prevent losing their retirements, some essentially started over in other County departments at lower pay. The higher-level planners, not protected by civil service rules, were laid off, including all three deputy directors. Planners saw these cuts as politically motivated because the cuts continued even as the recession was coming to an end.

The blows to the department came from other directions as well. While the workload had fallen as development slowed, staff had been cut even deeper, increasing the work for those left, who also had to respond to SOFAR's legal challenges. Missed deadlines further damaged the reputation of the department (as did SOFAR's string of victories). In this environment of apparent incompetence, against a background of free-market euphoria at the end of the Cold War, Planning Commissioner Gary Piro suggested that the department be eliminated and its functions consolidated with parks and recreation department and public works.[1] The proposal—similar to what was actually happening at the City of San Diego—went nowhere, however.

Gary Pryor

In the fall of 1995, the County offered the position of planning director to someone who turned it down. The position was then offered to Gary Pryor.[2] He began in March 1996, less than two months after Judge McConnell ruled in favor of SOFAR and froze building on hundreds of square miles of the backcountry.

Gary Pryor had been the planning director of Omaha, Nebraska from 1990 to 1995. The recently elected mayor, wanting to establish a tradition of having department heads serve at his pleasure, had fired Pryor along with several others.[3] Previously, Pryor had been the planning director of Polk County, Iowa.

In San Diego, Pryor was a lightning rod for controversy. Few

1. Caitlin Rother, "County Selects Planning Director," *San Diego Union-Tribune*, February 25, 1996.

2. Unfortunately for the reader, this story of planning at the County really does contain a man named Gary Piro and another named Gary Pryor. (At least there is no need to mention by name the County CAO at this time: Larry Prior!) As a mnemonic device, remember that Pryor with a "y" worked for the County, which ends with a "y." Piro was a private consultant.

3. Jena Janovy, "Daub Wants His Cabinet Civil Service-free," *Omaha World-Herald*, April 13, 1995 and "Mayor Names Two to Fill Cabinet Posts: Three Directors Lose Their Jobs in Shake-up," *Omaha World-Herald*, April 13, 1995.

publicly praised him, and his critics saw the failings of the general plan update as his personal defects. If, for example, he said something would be done and it wasn't, even for circumstances outside of his control, it was seen as dishonesty.

He was, to many people, an enigma. It wasn't clear the extent to which he had independent authority over the plan and he was tight-lipped about what he wanted. He spoke about the plan's structure, not its contents. Some saw in this support for grassroots planning. Others thought it meant that he was little more than a bureaucratic survivalist, as he didn't appear to stand for anything other than expediency. On the rare occasion he showed his cards, it was to be emphatic that sprawl across the backcountry was not acceptable and that the County needed to change course.

Pryor wanted an orderly document, with all the parts appropriately interconnected in a clear hierarchy, with each serving a distinctive role. It would be a streamlined document that made sense of a hodgepodge of chaotic, improvised practices. In effect, he wanted to finally tame the western frontier.[4] The attempt to turn the current general plan—a mess, but a mess rich in history—into a smoothly running machine proved to be as much as the County could bear.

Planning to Plan

The desire of Pryor (and other planners) to reexamine the general plan added to the momentum to update it. Some community planning groups had also been pressing for an update, at least of their local plans: during the budget cuts of the early 1990s, the DPLU had stopped updating community plans, which were becoming dated. The ending of the recession meant more flexibility with the budget and thus a chance to address all of these concerns.

4. On the continuation of many characteristics of the western frontier into the present, see Patricia Nelson Limerick, *The Legacy of Conquest: The Unbroken Past of the American West* (New York: Norton, 1987).

In April 1996—two months after the City of San Diego decided to revise its general plan—the County planning commission requested that the board of supervisors fund a task force to examine the feasibility and costs and benefits of updating the general plan. As this was a new budget item and not recurring spending, it was not automatically funded in the chief administrative officers's proposed budget but put on a list of unfunded projects.

The plan update was formally added into the budget discussions by Bill Horn, the North County supervisor who became one of its staunchest critics. Horn, an avocado farmer and a firm believer in property rights, was well known for his hostility to planning and for receiving a disproportionately high percentage of his campaign money from developers. Nonetheless, perhaps out of a desire to undercut SOFAR, Horn's Letter of Change for the 1996–97 budget called for $130,000 to be devoted towards initiating a general plan update. The board unanimously approved the request in June.

The DPLU that embarked upon a general plan update, however, was a shadow of its former self. It was the victim of both political ideology and opportunism. It did not have the support of the supervisors. Its legitimacy was weak. It lost the experienced staff necessary to conduct a general plan update. In other words, it was in a similar situation to that of the City of San Diego's planners when they started their plan update, save that the City planners had enough allies recently come to power to have a measure of confidence in themselves.

Scope of Work

The County's approach to updating its plan was fundamentally different from the City's. City staff, supported by a cadre of professionals and elected officials, were motivated by a clear vision and did not emphasize the nature of the process itself. In effect, they winged the entire update: they never wrote down a time line except when requested to do so.

At the County, however, conflict over process was the norm. An observation that Francesca Polletta made about the civil rights movement could have been made about the County's plan update:

> People talked about and argued about decision-making rather than thrashing out goals because the latter was so difficult to do…. Activists, like politicians and policymakers, may champion participatory democracy precisely because it spares them the hard work of having to make choices among possible goals.[5]

When uncertainty engulfed the plan update, the process became an end in itself—as if some properly designed process could magically lead to a consensus. Or at least create a plan with enough legitimacy that people wouldn't fight it. Emphasis on the process helped create the appearance of rationality, and people fought as much over process as substantive goals. It wasn't meant to be this way. The County's first step in the general plan update, however, was already in this direction.

The DPLU began with what's called a *scope of work*, the plan for the plan, so to speak. It specified, in sequential order, each action to be completed. It laid out everyone's responsibilities and was sufficiently detailed that the consultants could calculate the cost of each service they provided.

The board of supervisors took up discussion of the scope of work in August 1996. Their initial meeting led to a motion by Supervisor Dianne Jacob that ordered that the word "comprehensive" be deleted from references to the plan. The plan update was only to fix what was broken and not be overly ambitious. The board also asked the DPLU to write letters to all the community planning and sponsor groups requesting input on what changes they would like to see in their local plans. (Sponsor groups were appointed bodies for areas

5. Francesca Polletta, *Freedom is an Endless Meeting: Democracy in American Social Movements* (Chicago: University of Chicago Press, 2002): 214.

too sparsely populated to have elected planning groups.) On the surface, the request was routine and perfectly logical, yet the initial deference to these groups during the plan update would ultimately tie the general plan into knots as it started down the road of each community doing a quasi-independent update.

When the board returned to the general plan update two months later in October, they requested changes to the scope of work that were intended to make sure that the revised general plan would be legally defensible. To ensure that the plan had no loose ends that a mischievous lawyer could unravel, the plan was to make no references to future actions (which might not be done, like the never completed agricultural element of the current plan) or to board policies or ordinances (which might change). In short, the plan was to be self-contained.

Still not having received feedback from all of the planning groups, the board gave them another month to say what they wished to see in a plan update. The feedback they had received, however, was wide ranging. The Hidden Meadows sponsor group wanted a complete overhaul. The planning group for Ramona, a large East County town impacted by rapid growth, wanted extensive changes. Others wanted more modest revisions. Lakeside, for example, wanted the demographic and statistical data in their plan updated, an already approved trail plan included, a section of Interstate 8 designated scenic, a right-of-way development standard implemented, the circulation element reviewed and, most curiously, a new zoning category created for "miniature animals."[6]

The Bonsall planning group's October 1, 1996 letter gives a sense of strain between the DPLU and some local communities. The group wanted the tone of its plan strengthened. "Many of us who were

---

6. The zoning ordinance considered any split-hoof animal a large animal, which meant adhering to a more extensive set of regulations than the Lakeside planning group thought warranted for the miniature versions of some animals. (The gap between the practicalities of everyday life and arcane ordinances, especially those promulgated by a "local" government that was twenty miles away, was an enduring source of frustration with County planning.)

involved with the composition of our present Community Plan," they noted, "have never been happy with the way it was formulated." As they explained:

> We feel that our input was severely limited by the County. The whole process was very similar to that of a kangaroo court. Language that we wanted included was excluded by the County with weak language established. The result is an insubstantial unfathomable document. Thus our main problem with the existing Bonsall Community Plan was purposefully weak language and some key omissions that were by design never covered.

The group had specific changes they wanted to see, like banning clustering and landfills.

Clustering would prove to be an enduring tension in the plan update. Usually, it is not particularly controversial, but in San Diego County planning, community groups felt the term had been misused in the past. To planners, clustering meant building the houses near each other instead of scattering them throughout an entire development. This preserved more open space and lowered the cost of providing services like roads. Residents, based on past experience, considered clustering a density-bonus program for developers: after the original houses of a subdivision were lumped together, the open space saved was then used for *more* houses. Clustering to residents was then not seen as a way of building efficiently but as a way of shoving more density down their throats.

Nine groups said that they did not wish any changes to their community plans. This didn't mean that they were completely happy with them. Rather, the problems they had with their local plans were more bearable than the risk of opening them to any and all revisions. In particular, the group from Valle de Oro, a cluster of upscale suburbs adjacent to the incorporated suburbs on the City of San Diego's eastern side, had an unpleasant experience with being bombarded with requests for upzones—that is, increases in allowable building densities—during their partial community plan update in the 1980s.

The Scope of Work, Revised

While the County was still receiving input from the community planning and sponsor groups, it went ahead and selected the local firm of Lettieri-McIntre & Associates to write the scope of work for General Plan 2020, or GP 2020 as it was most often called.[7] The scope of work, a four-hundred-plus page monster that detailed every step of the process, took months to prepare and was published in draft form and sent to the chairs of the planning and sponsor groups. Its proposed process was broadly similar to the City's approach with a citizens advisory committee and meetings in which the plan was presented to the public.

This was immediately controversial and ultimately rejected. The meetings with the public were cut without much protest to save money. Rather, the fuss about the scope of work revolved around the citizens advisory committee. It would have had up to twenty members, selected by the board of supervisors, and would "review proposed elements of General Plan 2020 and… help evaluate goals and policy options." This committee would be assisted by three study groups. The first would be an environmental group; the second, a planning and sponsor groups group; and third, a development and business group. The goal of this arrangement was to "maximize… the number of viewpoints brought into the process…"[8] This organization of committees, however, was deeply threatening to the community planning group members, who,

7. Lettieri-McIntre & Associates, *General Plan 2020: Scope of Work* (San Diego, September 5, 1996). Tony Lettieri was on the City's planning commission during the events covered in the last case study, and another commissioner worked for the consultant firm that won the County contract for GP 2020 itself.

8. Both quotes are from the September 5, 1997 draft, page 6.

being formally elected on the same ballot during a general election like all other public officials, saw themselves as *the* representatives of their communities.

A six-page letter from Jack Phillips—chair of the Valle de Oro group—to Gary Pryor outlined how the planning and sponsor groups' "worst fears for the County's are now realized in the GP 2020 proposal." The proposed process was, in his view, completely insensitive to the communities in the unincorporated area:

> Prepared for County Government by a firm that is closely involved with the development industry, the proposed process, timing, and actions are designed to force changes upon the County's unincorporated communities and severely limit their self-determination and ability to respond.

> Our issues with this proposal go to the very heart of its origins and intent. Although claimed otherwise by its supporters in DPLU, the words and charts spell out a scope and process that will open every community plan in the county to "plan busting" changes. It cannot be improved by changing a few words—the basic thinking that put this together is faulty.

The letter spelled out eleven problems with the proposal. The main point, though, was simple: the proposed process for updating the plan would overturn the County's tradition of cobbling the general plan together from the plans of the individual unincorporated communities. The representatives of environmental and building interests would be on par with the local communities. By starting with a regional, top-down approach, the plan could call for changes that were undesired by the planning and sponsor groups.

Two weeks later, the chair of the Crest/Dehesa/Harbison Canyon sponsor group wrote to the DPLU, saying that they had voted unanimously to recommend cancelling the plan update:

"The expenditure of public funds in excess of $3 million for the changes recommended is unnecessary and promotes much change for the sake of change."

———————————————

The planning commission held three workshops on GP 2020 in the fall of 1997. The commissioners had their own anxieties about the proposed citizens advisory committee. They worried that it wouldn't be representative of a wide range of interests or would become bogged down in self-interest. As the commissioners worked through the proposed scope of work, they came up with a number of changes. First, they scrapped the citizens advisory committee. Instead, the planning commission would hold a series of workshops earlier in the process. The advantage of this was twofold: it increased the involvement of the planning commission while freeing staff from dealing with an advisory committee. This would give them more time to concentrate on working with the planning and sponsor groups. The chairs of these groups—and not a citizens committee—would guide the process.

Staff was also able to convince the commission that an agriculture element, which Duncan McFetridge of SOFAR and ten planning and sponsor groups advocated, was unnecessary. The state-mandated elements, they argued, could fulfill the tasks that the agriculture element was to accomplish. Having fewer elements would also give SOFAR's lawyers less leverage in future lawsuits.

On December 10, 1997—a year after the planning and sponsor groups initially wrote letters saying what they wanted—GP 2020 returned to the board of supervisors. The changes the supervisors ordered that day would widely be seen as the fatal flaw of the whole update process, the reason the plan would go into a tailspin two and a half years later.

It was the last agenda item of day. As the meeting was called back into session from a break, Supervisor Horn, the chair that year, said into the microphone, "Shouldn't take too long, I hope." The staff report detailed the rationale, implementation process and cost of the general plan—the last of which was estimated at

$2.6 million for the consultant contract and $600,000 to update the community plans.

Staff explained the process of using "issue papers" to build consensus by having staff work with the planning and sponsor groups to write them. Then staff and the planning commission would hold intensive workshops. The process for writing the papers was convoluted, but the hope was that by hammering out problems through iterations of these papers, the plan update wouldn't come to the board "at the end as a big mess"—a rather ironic hope. The papers themselves were never written, though that would be least of the problems with GP 2020.

Four members of the public spoke. Three of the four speakers were chairs from East County planning groups: Valle de Oro, Alpine and Ramona. All three men admitted they had serious reservations with the proposed scope of work—George Vanek of Alpine called it having a tiger by the tail, given how unstoppable and dangerous it was—but they all expressed satisfaction with the changes that had been made during the workshops with the planning commission (that is, the advisory committee had been scrapped).

The men had, however, one more request, a modest one. They asked that they be consulted before anything was finalized. Between staff turn-over and the use of consultants, there might be someone making decisions about their communities who did not yet know their areas well. Jack Phillips said he would feel one hundred percent comfortable if the board said that "if you really see your community plan taken down the wrong road by County staff or these consultants, we will listen to you and correct that direction." Three years later, the board would show itself quite willing to change directions in response to concerns that GP 2020 was going down the wrong road. That road, of course, was the road these men helped put it on.

The preceding day, the board of supervisors had seen SANDAG's estimates for the county for the year 2020, which forecasted a forty-three percent increase in population. The supervisors were emphatic that they would guard their land-use authority and not have their hand forced by demographic estimates. The SANDAG figures were, in the words of Supervisor Pam Slater, "a tool—they are not a mandate."

Supervisor Jacob set the tone of the meeting. She stressed the uniqueness of each community:

> It's real important as we go through this that we do not forget that these are plans that belong to the community. It's not the SANDAG plan; it's not the Sacramento plan; it's not a County staff plan. And that's what I feel that we have before us [i.e., a plan belonging to the community].

Continuing in this vein, she went beyond the staff recommendations. She made the first step of the process, not establishing goals and policies as staff suggested, but to find out what each community wanted for a population in 2020. She asked staff to return in a 120 days with these community's population standards. The other supervisors present each discussed the motion. They supported the self-determination of each community, passing the motion 4–0, with Ron Roberts absent.

His absence allowed him to be self-righteous about this decision. Years later when GP 2020 was sinking in controversy, he complained that he was:

> skeptical of a process in which we add up what each city is doing in the county and we get to a precise number that's equal to what we're projected to need over the next twenty years. God only knows, if anybody ran a business like this you'd never get to the target. It wouldn't happen.

The board apparently saw a choice: go with SANDAG's numbers or let the communities decide. When put in those terms, the supervisors—never fans of SANDAG—were, of course, on the side of the people.[9] So began GP 2020.

The fourth public speaker was a rambling environmentalist. She began her comments thus:

> I hope you had a chance to read Richard Louv's column this morning, page A-3 in the *San Diego Union-Tribune*. The headline is "One needs vision to set the boundaries on growth." The first paragraph [reads], "Our region's leaders and citizens may finally be forced to become visionaries. Last week, a coalition of environmentalists, landowners and elected leaders proposed the Rural Heritage and Watershed Initiative, an ambitious plan that would limit urban sprawl in San Diego's back-country."

SOFAR was at it again.

The Rural Heritage and Watershed Initiative

While the County prepared to update its general plan in response to SOFAR's legal actions, the environmental group was making preparations of its own. Its success in invalidating the EIR for the agricultural preserve zoning was inherently temporary. Once the County was able to adopt an EIR that passed legal muster, it would regain its land use authority over the 190,000 acres in dispute. SOFAR, having once been resoundingly successful in using the ballot box, again crafted a ballot measure to make more permanent its vision of the San Diego backcountry.

9. County hostility to SANDAG can be traced back to the early 1970s when it was still called the Comprehensive Planning Organization (CPO). It had begun as a County department, but as local cities and the County began fighting over control of its spending authority, staff, with the help of mayors like Pete Wilson, essentially seceded from the County to establish an independent organization.

Although not all states use them yet, across the country ballot initiatives have become a common approach to dealing with growth. One survey of the 1998 general election counted 240 local and state initiatives nationwide supportive of conservation, quality of life or Smart Growth.[10]

There are several distinct reasons for putting a measure on a ballot. First, public votes are sometimes required by law. This is especially the case for conservation initiatives that want to borrow money to buy private land to protect it from development. Second, elected officials either want to pass the buck on a hot-potato issue or they want to increase the legitimacy of a measure.

Duncan McFetridge of SOFAR had a good name for a third category: *legislative failure*—that is, a situation where an initiative was believed to be required because elected officials had failed to take necessary action. The most famous case of this is California's Proposition 13, which was passed after the state legislature responded in a leisurely fashion to rapidly rising real estate taxes. The underlying assumption behind most of such initiatives is that government is unresponsive to the public's will because it has been captured by special interests, which, at the local level, usually means supporters of further growth.[11] This was certainly SOFAR's view of the County.

The campaign for their 1998 initiative, which included environmental and good government groups, elected officials and scientists, was underway by 1997. It qualified for the fall 1998 election. Most people found the title "the Rural Heritage and Watershed Initiative" a forgettable mouthful and called it Proposition B or simply "Prop B." Many of those who would go on to become major players in GP 2020 actively participated in the campaign for or against, including the Building Industries Association, the Sierra Club, the Audubon Society, the Farm Bureau and members of the planning and sponsor groups.

10. Phyllis Myers, *Livability at the Ballot Box: State and Local Referenda on Parks, Conservation, and Smarter Growth, Election Day 1998*, discussion paper for the Brookings Institution, (Washington, DC, 1999).

11. John Logan and Harvey Molotch, *Urban Fortunes: The Political Economy of Place* (Berkeley: University of California Press, 1987).

Prop B proposed an extensive urban limit line, covering the eastern two-thirds of the county, largely following the County Water Authority line, which limited where imported water would be provided. It amended the general plan to cover areas outside of designated Country Towns with forty-acre minimum lot sizes, or, in the case of environmentally constrained areas, eighty-acre lots. The overall effect would have been to preclude suburban subdivisions over much of the county until the initiative's expiration in the year 2028. It aimed to directly affect 578,000 acres, reducing the number of allowable residences by 54,133 units (though such calculations were misleadingly precise).

The radical reduction of building in this area was widely believed to lead to a serious deflation in land value if enacted, which did not endear SOFAR to property owners, and the initiative itself would have preempted the County's general plan update, which did not please either the board of supervisors or the DPLU. The initiative, then, found ready-made opponents, who, having felt the barbs of SOFAR before, were not going to be caught off-guard again. Indeed, SOFAR found the County's reaction so objectionable that it sued, claiming the government had illegally campaigned against the initiative. (This would not stop one of the more conspiracy-minded property rights activists from suggesting that the reason the DPLU opposed Prop B was that it had even more dire designs on the backcountry.)

Individual property owners engaged in spontaneous counter-campaigns, like writing letters to the editor. The actions of the more powerful private opponents of the initiative, however, were generally credited with its massive defeat. In early 1998, opponents polled the public to see what arguments against the initiative voters found compelling. Based on this information, they launched a last-minute campaign blitz, stressing how the initiative would hurt farm families, who would find it harder to split up their land to give to their children and to expand their operations.

The initiative lost. Slightly less than 60 percent of the 621,900 ballots cast were against the measure. This initiative, however, set the tone for the GP 2020 process. Property rights activists claimed their victory was a mandate against reducing construction in the backcountry. However accurate the claim of a mandate, what can't be debated is that the defenders of private property rights had laid the groundwork for further activism. When they felt threatened by GP 2020, they already had practice at organizing themselves and could do so again quickly. Thus not only did the initiative fail, it strengthened the opponents of the regulation of privately held land.

On the other hand, the defeat of the initiative gave the more politically astute—or at least those who considered themselves such—an incentive to compromise with environmentalists: if the environmentalists were not mollified by the new general plan, then they would claim that its shortcomings were evidence of the County's incompetence and use that as ammunition for another initiative.

CHAPTER THIRTEEN
THE CONSEQUENCES
OF A WHIM

E stimates of population growth are perhaps the most telling indicator of a jurisdiction's future and a key guide to antici-pating future infrastructure needs. Decisions, for example, about where to build or widen roads and where to build schools depend on such projections.[1] These projections and general plans are like the fit of clothes to a person's body: they are useful only insofar as they match. If a plan is written in anticipation of a signifi-cant population increase that never arrives, then it is a waste of paper. If the population grows in unexpected ways, then the plan rapidly becomes obsolete.

---

1. Local population estimates came in several guises. In addition to the population estimates for the general plan, the County also worked with another set of numbers. State law required that jurisdictions provide in their plan's housing element enough land for multifamily housing, which was taken as a proxy for affordable housing. The amount of land so zoned was based on the jurisdiction's *regional share number*, which SANDAG calculated for local jurisdictions. State law also allowed jurisdictions to demonstrate that another number was more accurate. Not wanting anymore multifamily housing within their borders than necessary, they invariably discovered that their regional fair share number was lower than what had been calculated for them. William Fulton, *The Reluctant Metropolis: The Politics of Urban Growth in Los Angeles* (Baltimore: John Hopkins University Press, 2001): 112–114.

188

As described earlier, SANDAG calculated the population growth for the region and then applied it to the general plans of all the San Diego jurisdictions. Once they had allocated future residents to all the potential housing construction in the cities, they distributed the excess persons according to Smart Growth principles and announced that each city needed to accommodate a certain number of additional people.

The County was different. The supervisors' decision to allow each planning and sponsor group area to determine its future population meant that SANDAG wouldn't allocate excess population growth to any unincorporated area. The planning and sponsor groups not only failed to accept additional population, they endorsed figures substantially lower than what the current general plan allowed. Much of the "excess" population that SANDAG said the jurisdictions would need to accommodate by 2020 was, then, population that in earlier calculations had been assumed the unincorporated part of the county would take. That is, the anticipated shortage of land for new homes that was so central to the City of Villages was created by the County government.

SANDAG did not object to this downward adjustment of the figures. When asked about this, SANDAG staff put it thus: "They asked and we did what they asked. It's as simple as that." This easy acquiescence may have been political. The shift in population was consistent with SANDAG's agenda: the organization's staff had embraced Smart Growth, which meant concentrating the population in already built-up areas. That the County would take a slower growth approach was what they wanted, though they may have wished that the growth in the backcountry be better concentrated according to Smart Growth. In other words, the aversion to additional growth by the County planning and sponsor groups gave the plan update an accidental Smart Growth tone by funneling growth back to the urbanized coast. Years later, the DPLU would explicitly embrace Smart Growth, but the planning and sponsor groups did not share the enthusiasm: they were wary of applying external principles to the actual design of their communities.

Pick a Number, Any Number

As SOFAR geared up for its ballot initiative to put most of rural San Diego County off limits to development, the planning and sponsor groups were determining the population of their communities in 2020. These numbers were uncontroversial at the time but ultimately would put GP 2020 in conflict with powerful interests.

The groups approached developing a 2020 population in different ways. Some sponsor groups were working with relatively small numbers of lots and could count the parcels and their potential housing densities. Other communities, like Valle de Oro and Sweetwater, didn't want to change their existing plans and asked that their build-out under their existing plan be their 2020 population target.

Some groups all but invented numbers. The only real tool they had was a set of low, medium and high projections by SANDAG. They had little time or resources, to say nothing of expertise, by which to make such determinations. Fallbrook, for instance, simply told the DPLU that they couldn't provide population figures. Since they disagreed with the SANDAG projection of almost 70,000 persons, they decided on 50,000, a rough average between that projection and the then current population. Years later, when trying to convince the supervisors to not take these numbers so seriously, a member of a sponsor group on the other side of the county admitted, "We were just pulling things out of our... you know, thin air."

The general theme of the community planning and sponsor groups' population standards was limiting growth. In no case was the group's recommendation higher than both the projection from SANDAG and the existing plan's capacity. Indeed, when the planning and sponsor group chairs met in February 1998 to establish target numbers, any absent group that had not submitted its population target was assumed to want the lower of either the SANDAG or the existing plan figures.

Under the existing general plan, the capacity for the entire unincorporated county had been calculated to provide housing for approximately 877,000 persons.[2] Initially, the total of the planning and sponsor groups estimates was about 670,000. Within several months, this was reduced to 660,000 and became the immutable bedrock of the plan. This committed the County to a population target of roughly 216,000 fewer people than the current general plan allowed. Although the exact meaning of the 660,000 number would be a perennial source of confusion and technical debate over the years, the direction was clear: cut back on the planned housing development in San Diego's backcountry.

Rural San Diego was not unique in being overzoned. Throughout the country, the initial zoning put on land was often high. As Yale Rubin notes, "Los Angeles zoned enough land for business to accommodate all the business activity existing in the United States at that time."[3] And a number of urban jurisdictions tried to revitalize run-down areas by increasing the zoning in hopes that it would encourage developers to replace existing buildings with new ones. A 1990s Maryland report estimated that the state had the zoning for 1.4 million homes when it needed closer to 600,000 by 2020.[4]

San Diego County could have limited the population in several ways. One approach, never considered, was an annual cap on the number of building permits issued each year. By the 1990s, planners were disenchanted with housing caps, and conservatives had largely discredited them as artificial interference in housing markets.

The County took a zoning-based approach. During the quiet revolution of planning in the early 1970s, Sacramento required that all properties be zoned, which limited uses and their intensity. The

2. Such calculations make assumptions about household size, which can vary over time (and potentially undermine the accuracy of the projections). Typically, a single-family detached house was assumed to house about three people and an apartment unit, closer to two.

3. Yale Rubin, "Expulsive Zoning: The Inequitable Legacy of *Euclid*," in *Zoning and the American Dream: Promises Still to Keep*, ed. Charles M. Haar and Jerold S. Kayden, 101–121 (Chicago, IL: Planners Press, 1989): 106.

4. John M. DeGrove, *Planning Policy and Politics: Smart Growth and the States* (Cambridge, MA: Lincoln Institute of Land Policy, 2005): 262.

total number of homes allowed in the zoning was the maximum that could be built. Since the zoning had to be consistent with the general plan, controlling the residential densities in the general plan gave the County broadbrush control over their location, giving them the power to minimize infrastructure costs and environmental damage.

The zoning-based approach had a serious problem, however, one that buried a bomb of landowner fury under the general plan, gave it a two-year fuse and lit it. If the current zoning allowed, say, five houses on a particular parcel and the new map only permitted one, the land would be said to have been *downzoned*. Downzoning could cause the economic value of the land to plummet. Cutting the projected population by 216,000 persons meant that the zoning would be lowered on perhaps tens of thousands of lots. Landowners often felt personally targeted when it happened to them.

In April, the board of supervisors received the population standards from the planning and sponsor groups. The chief administrative officer (CAO) sent a letter to SANDAG saying that the planning and sponsor groups numbers were to be used. It was followed by an additional letter from Supervisor Greg Cox (chair of the board for that year), and another by Planning Director Gary Pryor. The County was now aiming for 660,000 persons.

This approach to laying the foundations of the general plan update process would later be decried as arbitrary. In its defense, County representatives said that 660,000 persons was 17 percent of the region's 2020 estimated population, and that that was approximately the same percentage of growth the unincorporated county had taken for the last several decades. This elided several important points.

First, since the 660,000 population target for the entire unincorporated area was created by adding up the individual planning and sponsor groups' targets, it was only a coincidence that the sum was 17 percent of the region's total. Second, as both affordable housing advocates and building industry representatives noted, continuing to take the same percentage as in the past ignored that the cities themselves were running out of room. Thus an increasing percentage of the vacant land in the region was in the backcountry. Similarly, even if it made sense to funnel growth into cities, then some parts of the unincorporated area, which were cities in all but legal status, should have received additional growth.

After the April 1998 board of supervisors meeting in which the 660,000 number was approved, GP 2020 entered a deceptive calm. Many stakeholders negotiated quietly or simply were not yet involved. Campaigns to pass and defeat SOFAR's Proposition B absorbed people's time and attention, at least for the summer and fall.

———————————————————————————————

Over the summer of 1998, the consultant contract was signed. As originally envisioned, a consultant would do much of GP 2020, to the tune of $2.6 million. The winner of the bidding competition was Wallace, Todd and Roberts (WRT), an international consulting firm, well-known for its work on Baltimore's Inner Harbor, one of the most visible American downtown revitalization efforts of the 1990s. While consultants often took the lead—and thus the heat—in plan updates, WRT was eventually focused on the behind-the-scenes technical analysis to save money as GP 2020 became unimaginably drawn out and convoluted.

The contract was approved, on consent, by the board on August 12, 1998.[5] It envisioned a process that would last three years and assumed that SOFAR's ballot initiative would fail. (If it had not, the scope would have had to be revised to account for the increased

———

5. To say that a governing body approved an item "on consent" means that it was approved unanimously without discussion. At both the City and County of San Diego, every item requiring a vote begins on the *consent agenda* and is only pulled off it for discussion by elected officials or by members of the public, who do so by submitting a speaker's slip, either in favor (green slip) or against the item (pink slip). Most routine matters of business pass on consent.

When GP 2020 exploded into controversy and drew in many people unfamiliar with the rituals of local government, they would sometimes become upset when they heard the board talking about "pulling an item from the agenda," as it sounded like an item was being shelved, when in fact that meant that the item was to be discussed.

complexity of backcountry zoning.) The approval of the contract was taken as the official beginning of GP 2020. What had taken place had simply structured the process while everything afterward was geared towards creating the actual general plan. With hindsight, however, decisions already made would be just as responsible for the myriad of controversies as decisions to come.

The Conflict That Wasn't

Like the City of Villages, the County's general plan update began with two years of quiet, for much the same reason. Unless one was a land use addict or was paid to follow the DPLU's activities, its planning exercises were academic and less engrossing than PTA meetings, *Friends* reruns or the evening news. It was only when people's everyday patterns were threatened did planning attract widespread interest.

No one felt threatened by GP 2020 until the summer of 2000. In the meantime, the plan proceeded at an almost leisurely pace set by the community planning and sponsor group chairs. The planning process was to proceed along two major tracks.[6]

The first major track of the plan update process was the planning and sponsor group chairs' committee, known as the steering committee. The board direction of December 10, 1997 stressed a community-driven plan. That was interpreted to mean that this committee was to run the show. The committee had many tasks over its life. Initially, it crafted the *goals and policies*, as well as standards (quantitative benchmarks, like "*x* number of acres of parks per thousand persons").

Goals and policies were seemingly innocuous statements that said what each element should achieve. On the surface, most appeared to be bland statements of good planning, like protecting ridge lines

6. There were two other minor tracks: engaging the cities in a dialogue about the plan and gathering baseline data for the plan (something the City had failed to do).

and enhancing community character. Nonetheless, their wording was fought over repeatedly. What made them so contentious was that every development proposed in the unincorporated county had to be found consistent with them and slight changes in wording could have profound effects.

The classic example was the difference between *shall* and *should*. As commonly understood, the former absolutely mandated something. The latter was practically meaningless, as it expressed a good idea but new developments were not compelled to conform to it. Consequently, to say "ridge lines *shall* be protected" meant that no ridge lines were to be built on, while to say "ridge lines *should* be protected" meant very little.[7]

Planners considered the goals and policies a perfunctory first step that might last three months. To their chagrin and frustration, the committee, conscious of the importance of the exact wording and suspicious of the DPLU and developers, took eight months, starting in October 1998, to get a draft to the planning commission. But committee members were pleased with their progress. According to the planning commission minutes of May 14, 1999:

> The vast majority of Planning/Sponsor representatives present at today's Workshop express great appreciation for the work done by Staff thus far, and for being allowed to provide input and direction to Staff. The Commission is also quite impressed and encouraged with what has been presented to them today.

The commissioners recommended that the board support the goals and policies as written.

The goals and policies then ping-ponged between the commission,

7. The state guidelines said that *should* meant that a policy was to be followed "in the absence of compelling or contravening considerations" but recognized that jurisdictions used *should* to "give the impression of more commitment than actually intended," which the guidelines condemned as "common, but unacceptable." Office of Planning and Research, *General Plan Guidelines* (State of California, 1998): 14–15.

the board of supervisors and the steering committee for over half a year. The board endorsed—but did not formally adopt—the goals and policies on September 15, 1999. The steering committee made its last significant changes in February 2000.

While the steering committee was hammering out the goals and policies, it developed its routines. Although twenty-six groups could send representatives, fewer than twenty groups attended on average, though some groups had more than one person sit at the table. The committee met in the lunch room of the DPLU at the County Annex in Kearny Mesa. The meetings lasted from nine to twelve on Saturday mornings, usually with a break. The committee chair and DPLU staff met the day before to prepare for the meeting, discussing the agenda and possible points of controversy.

Bryan Woods, a Ramona pharmacist and planning commissioner appointed by Supervisor Dianne Jacob, was the chair. He constantly stressed two points: sound planning principles and common sense, which, in his rhetoric, were the same thing. He was not treated by the committee members as one of "the County," with all its connotations of distrust. He dealt with conflict by emphasizing the importance of being reasonable and assuring the committee that others in the process were reasonable as well.

The committee members were thoroughly parochial—to the point that in interviews for this research conducted when the group was still actively meeting several people got other members' names wrong despite serving together for years. They were mainly interested in how anything applied to their communities. Likewise, they were sensitive to not impose their views on other areas, stressing the importance of flexibility to deal with the diversity of the unincorporated county. By embracing the uniqueness of each community, their ability to provide coherence to the general plan update process was limited, with little convergence beyond issues that they agreed on—that is, those issues that defined them in sociological terms: Anglo homeowners and property owners suspicious of a distant "local" government. The committee, then, engaged in little to no bargaining or politicking beyond crafting motions that allowed them to all do what they wanted.

Jack Phillips of Valle de Oro and Gordon Shackelford of Lakeside, who had each been on their respective planning groups for approximately twenty years, were viewed as the leaders of the process. They gave voice to a deep suspicion of the planning process, the DPLU and the board of supervisors. They viewed any change with skepticism, trying to see whether it could become a crack in the dam holding back developers.

The other major thread of the plan was a special interest group committee. It represented a wide range of organized interests, from farmers to environmentalists to developers to sporting dog enthusiasts. The inclusion of all stakeholders was standard in American planning. Indeed, the original scope of work gave such interests a significant role. But when the citizens advisory committee was deleted and the planning and sponsor groups were put in charge—not the idea of the DPLU—special interests fell into a shadow. They still had their own committee, but it was a modest affair. Unlike the steering committee, which was limited to planning and sponsor group members, the interest group committee had a very fluid membership. If someone showed up claiming to represent a group, they could take a seat and talk. The interest group committee started in mid-November 1998, six weeks after the steering committee began meeting regularly.

At the interest group committee's first meeting, those present were encouraged to submit comments on the draft goals and policies. Several such letters indicated the directions in which these interest group representatives would try to push the plan. Bonnie Gendron, representing the Alpine Land Preservation Action Committee, wrote a dense three-page letter blasting the County on numerous points, arguing that "Alpine is an obvious example that county planning is more concerned with facilitating public and private investment than it is with community character and preservation of [the] natural environment." The coordinator for the Endangered Habitats League, Dan Silver, observed that the "General Goal [sic] portrays a happy but illusory world in which hard choices do not have to be made. Pleasant-sounding but ultimately ambiguous goals which mean different things to different people are inadequate for our task." Al Stehly, who argued against the Rural Heritage and Watershed Initiative in a televised debate with Duncan McFetridge, wrote that the "Farm Bureau of San Diego County is enthused about participating in the General Plan 2020 process." Since three of the goals discussed agriculture, he suggested that all references to agriculture be removed and placed into one goal, of which he provided draft language. It focused exclusively on farmers' rights and needs.

The new committee was a non-starter—to the point that several people who had served on it had to be reminded of its existence when they were interviewed for this book. As its open membership suggested, it was quite informal. The time and dates of the more or less monthly meetings were not standardized and were subject to last-minute changes, which members sometimes learned about belatedly. While its recommendations were presented to the planning commission, no one had any illusions that it was on par with the steering committee. The interest group made formal recommendations to the steering committee, which had little compunction about voting them down, though the minutes reveal more of a willingness to examine the recommendations than that committee was subsequently given credit for. Staff appreciated the different perspectives on the plan update, but the interest group representatives were unsatisfied, feeling that the meetings mainly were informational.

This placed a second incendiary device under the general plan update. Not only were landowners going to be upset when they found out that their land was to be downzoned, powerful interest groups, especially in the building and development industries, were growing dissatisfied with their venues for input. Since the general plan was legally considered the "constitution for land use" for San Diego County, these interests would not accept being sidelined.

CHAPTER FOURTEEN
CONFLICT REACHES
THE SURFACE

What became known as "the Alternative III controversy" caught people off-guard. People either hadn't heard of the plan or it had seemed of so little gravity at first.

In mid- to late winter 2000, planning and sponsor groups went down to the DPLU to develop land use distribution maps. Sometimes a subcommittee came; other times, the entire group. For months, they had been discussing with staff what they wanted their communities to look like. Such discussions were the *raison d'etre* for planning. Where was housing to go? How big were the lots to be? How much commercial development should an area have? What should be preserved for open space? Planning and sponsor group members sometimes answered questions like these simply by drawing with a marker. They literally sketched out the future of their areas on sheets of paper that the planners then used to create precise computerized maps.

From the standpoint of the planning profession, this was an unusual approach. From undergraduate policy classes onward, the emphasis was on a distinct process: gathering data, developing a range of alternatives and then analyzing their implications. The package of alternatives and their outcomes was then presented to decision-makers. Indeed, EIRs were required by law to examine alternatives, so sooner or later, GP 2020 had to have them. At the moment of crafting of the future of their communities, however, the planning and sponsor group members had little in the way of distinct options. They just came up with one vision for each community.

Ultimately, an analysis of the maps created by the planning and sponsor groups would have spelled out the implications of their input. The groups were to be given a chance to modify undesirable impacts. In a delayed way, then, what was to be done was to have partially followed the planning profession's norm of alternatives and analysis. The political consequences, however, of handing the group members, with varying amounts of planning experience, a marker and a blank map proved to be too severe.

With hindsight, it's not clear how seriously the planning and sponsor group chairs had taken their own input. While the chair of the Fallbrook group was noted for insisting on involving the entire planning group in the process, some chairs created a subcommittee that did not necessarily keep the rest of the group abreast of developments. One of the group members later confessed to staff that they hadn't realized a map was going to be created from their input. The maps, however, were concrete proposals that would seriously impact a complex of regulations that controlled how land could be used, regulations that did much to determine the price of the land. The maps, then, could upend the land market.

Once the staff gathered the input from the planning and sponsor groups, the consultants used the information to create maps for individual groups as well as a map for the entire unincorporated area. The new overarching map was called *Alternative III* or the *Community Preference Map*. Alternative I, in this system of naming, was the existing general plan. It was a baseline by which the new plan would be compared (in terms of traffic congestion, open space preservation, etc.). Alternative II was a rough sketch made by the consultants to see if in fact the new plan, with its target population and constraints, was even possible. It proved that it was.

The Community Preference Map was and was not a map. While it showed the input from each planning and sponsor group across the entire unincorporated area, the only real connection between the chunks of the map was that the total population had to be 660,000 persons. Otherwise, the individual segments created by the groups were effectively independent of each other. If, for example, one group's vision led to traffic congestion in another community, this was to be dealt with later.

The requirement of the 660,000 figure, however, meant that the different chunks of the map were not truly independent. If the adjustments were changed in, say, Sweetwater, and they reduced the 2020 population capacity by several hundred people, adjustments had to be made elsewhere, perhaps on the other side of the county, to increase the total population capacity by several hundred. This led to tinkering that pushed the community maps away from what the planning and sponsor groups had wanted.

The mandate from the board of supervisors to stick to a particular population projection for the entire unincorporated county, as well as for individual communities, coupled with giving the planning and sponsor groups the green light to plan as they pleased, created a goofy situation: the groups were to provide two forms of input—a total population for their area and a land use map—that were independent from each other yet logically were inseparable: the map implied a population because it designated land for homes. Unless someone had the intuition or luck to draw a map that matched their population target, they were guaranteed to be unhappy: one thing they said they wanted would be inconsistent with something else they said they wanted. If a compromise was constructed between the map they drew and the populations they wanted, they likely wouldn't recognize it as their input. The existence of this quirk in the process was all but ignored in the controversy that followed.

When staff received the maps back from the consultants, they gave copies to the members of the steering committee. They expected the steering committee members to take the maps back to their communities, discuss them with their group, perhaps post them some place public and generally take the lead in generating discussion about the general plan update. This was in June 2000.

Staff gave out the maps.

And then nothing happened.

Or rather, it appeared as if nothing was happening but a political crisis was at hand. In the East County town of Ramona (2000 population: 33,000),[1] the community map was like drops of water on boiling oil. After the maps were released in late June, Brenda Foreman, the chair of the planning group, scheduled a series of ten two-hour workshops for people to view the map. She also kept her only copy of the map in the community library. While word got out that a new map defining the future of Ramona was under discussion, frustrations quickly mounted as people had difficulty seeing it, and those who did get a chance were startled by the dramatic changes that were proposed.

On July 20, 200, the *Ramona Sentinel* devoted a lengthy cover article by Eric Leins to how the County was handling the plan update.[2] Its headline was to the point: "Scarcity of county density maps here irritates residents." It described how there were only two maps available for the entire community, which many residents felt was ridiculously insufficient. (Ramona was unique in that it even had a second map, as Bryan Woods, the planning commissioner and chair of the steering committee, put up his copy in his pharmacy.) The GP 2020 project manager was quoted as justifying only having one map available on the grounds that it was important that "people work through their planning group" and that they view the map in the context of the constraint maps (maps of environmental resources, steep slopes, etc.). When Supervisor Jacob read the

1. Ramona was arguably the most contentious site of growth in the unincorporated county. Books could be written about it alone and the discussion here makes no pretense of being a comprehensive examination of the factional fighting that surrounded that community planning group.
2. See also Leins, "Got Maps? We Soon Will Have," *Ramona Sentinel*, July 27, 2000.

article, she ordered that more copies be made available.

From there, the local politics rapidly grew byzantine as one community planning group member sued nine others for violating the Brown Act (California's sunshine law) because they privately discussed revisiting the town's proposed 2020 population of 60,000. On August 3, the planning group passed a no-confidence resolution for the town center portion of the map and claimed that "[t]he alternative 3 plan does not represent input from the Community Planning Group or reflect the stated community character." The planning group, however, continued the process of making it available and working with the DPLU on it.

The map inflamed virtually everyone. It called for increased densities in the partially Wild West town center, which was unpopular because the traffic was already bad during rush hour when people in the surrounding subdivisions drove through it. On the outskirts of the community, some areas were downzoned dramatically, going to as low as one house per 160 acres, all but wiping out the monetary value of the land. Furthermore, some of the Specific Plan Area (SPA) designations were stripped off, essentially killing any development that might have been in the works. (Such a designation didn't mean that a plan was actively being developed; sometimes, a project stalled out after the SPA was formed but the designation had yet to expire. In this case, however, active SPAs were being challenged.)

While in Ramona the Alternative III map—no one called it the Community Preference Map because clearly few in the community preferred it—was causing a storm, other communities were fairly quiet through the summer of 2000. The community and planning group chairs, however, must have realized that a crisis was brewing because, in August, thirteen of them met in a Ramona hotel to discuss the grievances they had with the DPLU. They talked about forming some kind of organized assembly of planning group representatives. They voted the idea down 3–10 for fear of antagonizing the board of supervisors.

While the public involvement of Ramona was not common,

people were beginning to get wind of the plan update elsewhere. Some planning and sponsor group chairs, however, seemed to get cold feet and all but kept the maps under wraps, as staff discovered when they conducted a series of GP 2020 community workshops in September and October.

The steering committee continued to meet in the summer and early fall 2000. A major topic of discussion was whether building moratoria should be put in place while the Alternative III map was discussed. The committee members feared a flood of development applications as builders tried to move their project far enough through the permit process that the changes in regulations couldn't affect them. In the face of a rapid onslaught of criticism of Alternative III and the steering committee, however, discussion about halting building quickly became moot.

Stage Right: Enter SOLV

Back in June, another stream entered the river of events. On the fifth of the month, representatives of Stonegate Development Company, which was working on a several-thousand-acre project in North County, went into the DPLU to discuss their proposal. They were told that a general plan update was underway and that their project would not be looked upon favorably if it were inconsistent with what was being proposed for the area. They were shown a map of the relevant area. In a June 14, 2000 letter to owners of the land, they described their reaction:

> We were aghast! The map designates the entire Merriam Mountains as one dwelling unit for forty acres! The one unit per forty acres does not distinguish between flat or steep land, [sic] it is all one unit per forty acres! These designations eliminate any development potential and effectively reduce land value to the value of one raw lot per forty acres. The cost of getting a road to each

forty acres would wipe out the land value. I am still reeling from what we saw. This plan amounts to the most massive confiscation of land and redistribution of wealth since the Russian revolution!

Under the then current plan, this hilly area allowed houses on four- to twenty-acre lots, depending on the slope. Alternative III reduced the area to 40-acre lots, lowering the yield from 434 units (plus one hundred affordable senior units) to 50 units. This struck the developers as irrational, as the site was on a major transportation corridor, the I-15, and not out in the boondocks.

In the eyes of the developers, the rest of the map didn't look much better. It called for massive downzoning throughout the unincorporated county, and the possible logic behind it seemed strained.

Furthermore, it was quite apparent that the plan was being created without the input or knowledge of landowners. The planning process was conducted through the planning and sponsor groups, which large landowners typically avoided because they were viewed as the enemy when they proposed developments. If they did not live in the community in which they held property (or in some cases even the United States), they were unlikely to see the public notices for planning meetings anyway. Consequently, few landowners knew that their investments were at risk.

The developers had no faith that the DPLU would do a better job of involving landowners as the plan update progressed. They decided to organize. The leadership came from North County—many of the men were on good terms with Supervisor Horn's office—but the membership owned land throughout the county.

The developers called other people they had known in the business for years. With seed money from Stonegate, they formed a group called Save Our Land Values (SOLV) and hired Jack Orr, an abrasive North County political consultant, as their executive officer. SOLV set about to inform landowners about what was happening, using personal connections and a mailing list developed to fight the Rural Heritage and Watershed Initiative.

Some landowners were apathetic and didn't want to be bothered. They had no near-term plans to develop and didn't care about other potential uses of their land; others saw their properties as long-term investments that would take care of themselves, at least for the moment. But others were more responsive.

To convey a sense of urgency, SOLV described GP 2020 in dire language. A letter Jack Orr sent out to property owners in October began, in all capital letters and bold-face, "Your property rights are under siege again!" It didn't pull any punches:

> Two years ago, Duncan McFetridge succeeded in putting Proposition B on the ballot. Proposition B would have DOWNZONED 54,000 dwelling units out of existence in the county of San Diego. Your contribution to the campaign against Proposition B (Rural Heritage and Watershed Initiative) made it possible to defeat Proposition B by a 60%-40% margin. No sooner was Proposition B buried, than the County Planning staff began an "update" of the County's General Plan. As you may have read, The [sic] County's General Plan Update 2020 (GP 2020), as now proposed, will DOWNZONE over 180,000 properties (one or more of which is yours). Some of the properties are DOWNZONED from 1 unit per 4 acres to 1 unit per 160 acres! In other words, the county's UPDATE is actually a DOWNZONE, and it's more than three times as bad as Proposition B!

The letter proceeded to draw a further connection between the specter of Prop B and GP 2020: Gordon Shackelford and Gene Heisel "were sponsors of the petition to qualify Proposition B" and were also "two of the more influential people on the County Steering Committee who established what properties would be DOWNZONED and by how much." The letter claimed that the loss in property values could amount to three billion dollars (according to "some experts"). The letter closed by stating the first goal of SOLV was to delay hearings until all property owners have been notified and by requesting money for the organization, at the rate of $100 plus a dollar for each acre of property.

This letter was more emphatic than accurate—it contained numerous errors, the most glaring of which was confusing the number of housing units and the people who would live in them, thus exaggerating the impact of Alternative III by threefold—but it certainly helped raise the alarm: by January, SOLV would have six hundred members.

Between the growing news coverage, the clamoring of private property rights advocates and word of mouth, landowners learned about GP 2020 and its potential downzoning. Many were shocked and angry.

This fury should be seen in historical context: those who wanted to use the land to make money in the American West had a lengthy tradition of seeing regulation as a threat and of portraying themselves as victims, with government (especially the federal government) as the cause of their woes.[3] Since the Sagebrush Rebellion of the late 1970s, in which western states tried to gain control of federal lands, antigovernment sentiment has coalesced into two intertwined right-wing social movements, the *wise use movement*, which co-opted conservation rhetoric to justify environmental exploitation, and the *property rights movement*, which attacked government regulation, interpreting the Takings Clause of the Fifth Amendment to mean that the government must compensate property owners for any restrictions on their land. This ongoing resistance to environmentalism and government regulation, largely from rural whites (and corporations), gave San Diegan landowners a ready-made explanation for why Alternative III was immoral.

At the beginning of fall 2000, the DPLU made available a hundred-plus page consultant report contrasting the impacts of

---

3. Patricia Nelson Limerick, *The Legacy of Conquest: The Unbroken Past of the American West* (New York: Norton, 1987): 42–46.

Alternative III and the existing general plan that was intended to be one of the main ways that people involved in GP 2020 would learn about the new general plan.[4] Public speakers at meetings occasionally selected passages to strengthen their position, but otherwise the report had little impact. Tellingly entitled *Evaluation of Regional Land Use and Population Distribution*, it was very much a technical document. It praised Alternative III in comparison to the existing plan because the lower population meant fewer negative impacts from development. It was intended to be studied, and not merely glanced at by property owners who had been told the sky was falling. As such, it was inadequate to the ensuing political controversy in which the very legitimacy of GP 2020 was in doubt.

The report did not spell out the defects of the current plan or put them into context. It did not explain how San Diego was typical of many jurisdictions whose exuberant zoning decades earlier made it difficult to manage growth, and that sooner or later, the County had to face the choice of a backcountry fragmented by single-family detached homes—a sea of roofs—or an extensive adjustment to the general plan and zoning code which would restructure the market for land, to the potential detriment of many people who currently owned it. Instead it talked about "LOS" (Levels of Service, a measure of traffic congestion) and "mgd" (millions of gallons of water or sewage daily).

The community maps likewise did not reassure. They were created with GIS (Geographic Information Systems), which was, in the late 1990s, spreading rapidly through planning. In essence, GIS supported a software environment for analyzing data spatially, which allowed an experienced user to quickly create highly professional-looking maps. Although it is obvious now, at the time, the dangers of GIS maps were unappreciated. Before GIS, rough drafts looked rough. GIS maps, however inchoate they were conceptually, looked polished and thus set in stone. This heightened anxiety about GP 2020.

---

4. San Diego County Department of Planning and Land Use, *Evaluation of Regional Land Use and Population Distribution* (San Diego, 2000).

Long-standing arcane technical matters also added to the confusion about the potential impacts of GP 2020. The most significant was the DPLU's desire to change how residential densities were calculated. In the 1930s, San Diego, like many other places throughout the country, suffered when the housing market collapsed during the Great Depression. Part of the problem was that speculators in the 1920s had cut up the land willy-nilly into odd arrays of small lots and sold off what they could and then skipped town, leaving the land broken into lots that couldn't be built upon and whose ownership was ambiguous. To prevent that from happening, San Diego began establishing rural zoning based on having lots a certain minimum size. This pretty much guaranteed using land as inefficiently as possible. So the DPLU wanted to switch from this *minimum lot-size* zoning to *density-based* zoning, which allowed homes to be clustered together away from constraints like endangered species. Landowners, fearing any change, often resisted the density-based zoning. Ironically, the idea to switch from minimum lot sizes to zoning that allowed clustering was developed and campaigned for by the development industry on the national level in the early 1960s.[5] It saved them money, and, in places like San Diego, which had significant environmental constraints, would allow them to steer construction around areas that could not be built upon. The tension between minimum lot-size and density-based zoning would prove to be one of the most enduring issues of the plan update.

Those with limited knowledge of planning tended to overestimate how many houses could be built upon their land because they would take their total acreage and divide by the minimum lot sizes. So an owner of ten acres with one-acre minimum lot sizes might think they could build ten houses when in fact a variety of constraints (like steep slopes) could potentially limit that to five or six. And there was no guarantee that water was even available.[6]

5. Evan McKenzie, *Privatopia: Homeowner Associations and the Rise of Private Residential Government* (New Haven: Yale University Press, 1994): 86.
6. The desert community of Borrego Springs (year 2000 population: 2,582), for example, had a current plan capacity of almost 44,000 persons. Given that the aquifer was already

The Workshops That Weren't

The next step for GP 2020 was to have workshops at the planning commission. Having extended workshops instead of a citizens advisory committee had worked successfully for crafting the goals and policies and the standards. This time, however, the workshops were filibustered by landowners and their consultants, leaving planning staff and the planning commission frustrated.

The first workshop was September 29, 2000, as part of the regular commission Friday agenda. Four days earlier, a *North County Times* article gave the property owners' perspective on GP 2020 and mentioned the time and address for the workshop. It quoted Supervisor Horn, whose property would be downzoned, as saying, "As it stands now, I couldn't vote for it. My opinion is it's very harmful. Hopefully, we can get this back into reason."[7]

On the morning of the workshop, the hearing room was packed, with at least one member of SOLV out in the hallway, coaching property owners on what to say, stressing the lack of notification and downplaying the loss of money. The minutes show that all but one of the sixty-four people who submitted speaker slips were in opposition. Not all of them spoke, but enough did that they left the commission little time to workshop with staff.

The planning commission's second workshop was six weeks later. The meeting was held at the Al Bahr Shrine Center, down the road from the DPLU: the larger space had more room for the public and allowed tables to be set up more informally to facilitate interaction between staff and the commission. Staff, who were by no means satisfied with Alternative III and wanted guidance, hoped to finally get down to the business of workshopping with the commission.

Repeating the first workshop, the public testimony took almost the entire day. By the time the speakers were done, the commission

---

being overdrafted (mainly by agriculture), this plan capacity did not, as one observer quipped, "pass the giggle test."

7. Katherine Marks, "New Group Targets County's Rural Plan," *North County Times*, September 25, 2000.

was exhausted and ready to go home. The developers and landowners again spent disproportionate time at the podium. One developer, for example, instead of being granted—per a longstanding rule, three minutes to speak, was given eighteen minutes because he represented six clients and implied that he could have them all come down and speak individually.

A third and then a fourth workshop met the same fate as the first two. During the last afternoon, the planning commission and staff finally had several hours to discuss the plan. The commissioners only had time to stake out basic political stances and recognize what they felt were the serious shortcomings with Alternative III.

The workshops were excruciatingly repetitive. Each new day was another opportunity for more or less the same speakers to approach the podium and pontificate for three minutes. By the time of the third workshop, the commissioners began discouraging repeaters. Even some property rights activists grumbled about the delays at that point, though their impatience might have been partially fueled by the environmentalists belatedly organizing themselves for presentations.

Speakers across the political spectrum blasted Alternative III. Some political experts were smooth. Others, especially small landowners, weren't. A handful became quite agitated, including, most memorably, a Chinese immigrant, who saw Alternative III as the Cultural Revolution all over again. He practically shouted as he compared the downzoning to the government dictating in which room of their house people could have sex, an observation that brought bemused cheers from the landowners.

Developers spoke in great detail about how the Alternative III proposal completely ignored Smart Growth and thus unreasonably affected their clients' properties. Landowners complained that they had been shut out of the process, that they had been railroaded, that the government was taking their land. They challenged the legitimacy of the planning and sponsor groups, doubting their competency, intentions and ability to represent communities in their entirety.

Farmers had distinctive concerns. Since their land was their main wealth, it was their de facto 401(k)s. Undercutting their ability to sell their land at high prices would impoverish them in their old age. They argued that their land was collateral on their loans which they needed to tide themselves over lean years. If the property dramatically lost its value, then banks would call in the loans, putting them in an impossible economic bind. (As GP 2020 dragged on, farmers eventually stopped claiming this, as it probably was not true, and instead claimed it would be hard to get loans if their land was worth less, which probably was.)

Environmentalists thought that the future growth that Alternative III permitted, even if it was less than the current general plan, was too much. Further, by failing to follow Smart Growth principles, Alternative III spread out future development excessively and caused unnecessary damage.

The planning commission chair kept reassuring people that the map was a beginning, not an endpoint. To his visible frustration, this reassurance did nothing to calm landowners, as it sounded like he stressed the tentative nature of Alternative III simply to get them to acquiesce until it was too late. Property owners thought it was a formality that the County called the map a draft.

The commissioners represented a wide range of viewpoints. Patsy Fritz, a Horn appointee, was the staunchest supporter of property rights. (She was on the mailing list of SOLV that became public record in May 2003.) She fought for the notification of property owners as well as compensation for loss of economic value of land. At the other extreme, Michael Beck, the chair of the San Diego chapter of the Endangered Habitats League, challenged the property rights view. For example, he responded to the common landowner argument that their property was treated differently from adjacent land by pointing out somebody's property was always going to be on the border between zoning classifications.

In December, a week and a half after the last planning commission workshop, Supervisor Horn pulled Patsy Fritz from the commission and replaced her with Thure Stedt, claiming that they needed someone with his experience on the commission to guide GP 2020.

The *San Diego Union-Tribune*, which was frequently critical of Horn, depicted the move as politically inspired because Fritz might run against Horn for his seat again, as she had done in 1998.[8]

Other Fronts

The controversy embroiling Alternative III was not confined to the planning commission. It was played out in newspapers, at planning groups, in private meetings and at the board of supervisors.

During the fall, the community planning and sponsor groups held meetings to discuss Alternative III. Sometimes staff was present; sometimes not. Enthusiasm for the plan update was limited. The chair of the Valley Center group wrote an account of one meeting they held. He noted that "it would be inaccurate to suggest that the total audience of 100+ persons were hostile to alternate 3 of GP 2020 as covered. But it is equally clear that the great majority were in opposition."

Comparing the planning and sponsor groups' population targets with Alternative III can give a sense of how the groups came to reject what was ostensibly their own input. Their population targets added up to 660,731 persons in the unincorporated county by 2020. Alternative III had a total population of 661,304, a difference of less than a tenth of a percent. However, at least 86,900 persons (or about thirteen percent of the 2020 population) were not where the planning and sponsor groups wanted them.

But even this underestimates the differences between what the groups said they wanted for a population and what Alternative III gave them. In the sparsely populated sponsor groups, slight absolute changes led to huge percentage changes. Tecate had a target of 2,150 persons; Alternative III said in 2020 it would have 330 persons, one-seventh as many people. On the other hand, a small percentage

8. Bruce Lieberman and Luis Monteagudo, Jr., "Commissioner Calls Oust Political Ploy," *San Diego Union-Tribune*, December 13, 2000.

MEANWHILE, BACK AT THE SUBDIVIDED RANCH

difference in large planning areas indicated substantial development. Alternative III pegged Lakeside for 73,947. This was only five percent more than what the group requested, but it still meant almost 4,000 more residents.

Although lobbyists and a barrage of constituent mail kept the supervisors aware of GP 2020, it only came before the board twice in the fall of 2000. The first time was in October to extend the consultant's contract. Staff recommended renewal, and two speakers spoke in favor of it: Jack Phillips argued that stopping the plan update process would attract speculators from all over the Southwest and that the steering committee represented a balance of grassroots, not special, interests. Bonnie Gendron, representing the Sierra Club and the Backcountry Coalition, claimed that the plan update had been well publicized and the new map represented democratic input. She blasted developers for sitting on the sidelines for two years and then trying to upset the process. Gary Piro, who wrote five newspaper columns against GP 2020, Dave Shibley and Thure Stedt—most of SOLV's intelligentsia—and four other developer and real estate representatives attacked GP 2020 for a wide range of problems, from lack of public input to bad planning to lost real estate taxes.[9] They saw the matter as whether GP 2020 needed to be "revamped, revised or restarted."

Supervisor Horn claimed that the process was obviously not bottoms-up, that the community planning groups just represented those active in planning and not, for instance, the Chambers of Commerce. He criticized downzoning along the corridor of a new

---

9. Developers are often portrayed as grasping mindless villains in popular culture, with perhaps the iconic image being John Huston's portrayal of Noah Cross in the 1974 film *Chinatown*, who has his way with the law, the environment and his daughter. This is image was not helped locally by developers' close ties with Supervisor Horn and political consultant Jack Orr. While there are troubling aspects to their views on property rights (to be discussed in the next chapter), developers work in a field that demands tremendous initiative and political savvy, as well as creativity, and consequently they tend to be independent thinkers who range across the political spectrum.

rail line that he had heavily lobbied for. He held up a picture of the Hewlett Packard site. Three million dollars had been put into new infrastructure and it was being downzoned.[10] He said he would vote against renewing the contract.

Since Roberts was absent and the contract needed four votes, Jacob's motion to accept the staff recommendation, with the addition that all property owners be immediately notified about GP 2020, could not pass. To prevent a stalemate, Jacob reworded the motion, ordering the notification of property owners by mail and continuing the contract discussion until the following week. This passed unanimously, and the contract was renewed the following week.

Alternative III was the source of many letters and emails to the DPLU, supervisors, planning groups and newspapers. At a minimum, several hundred letters were submitted on paper—plus many more by email—to the supervisors and the DPLU. Their tone ranged from folksy to mildly threatening. Attorneys and developers wrote detailed letters explaining why the downzoning on their clients' property was poor planning and a betrayal of the good faith in which their clients had worked. A small number of letters were concerned about the environmental impacts.

November meant elections for the community planning groups. Half the seats were contested (with the other half in another two years). The composition of the planning groups and the steering committee did not change spectacularly.[11] While many members of the steering committee attended sporadically or cycled through, the steering committee had a core of regular attendees. The election added to the regulars Dutch Van Dierendonck of Ramona, who

10. In an interview for this research, a DPLU planner gave the Hewlett Packard site as an example of an obvious flaw, from the staff viewpoint, in Alternative III.

11. My attempts to demonstrate statistically that increased interest in GP 2020 led to more votes being cast for community planning group seats failed to show any countywide pattern once the Presidential election, which always brought out more voters, was taken into account.

was an outspoken advocate of compromise and an aggressive realist when it came to the power of special interests.

It is hard to convey the sense of tremendous tension, uncertainty and confusion that surrounded Alternative III. Many people felt that their future was on the line, either that their investments were disappearing before their eyes or that their communities were going to be overrun by sprawl. As a cover note on a letter faxed to the planning commission from a man in Ramona put it, "Myself & my family's concern about the downzoning has been very stressful on my family."

During the fall of 2000, it was not at all clear what direction the plan update would take. Alternative III increasingly looked dead, but there were no clear other options. Going back to the current general plan appealed to many property owners and SOLV, but the population growth that that implied appalled many others. The steering committee, which received much of the blame, was seen as dysfunctional, but they were their communities' elected representatives, so disempowering them would look antidemocratic. It was a crisis, by the Murphy's Law definition: that is, it was a situation in which it was impossible to say, "Let's just forget the whole thing."

For all the drama and backcountry news coverage of Alternative III, it had to compete with many other issues for people's attention. For instance, the confusing debacle of the Florida Presidential election took place in the middle of this. More immediately pressing was the California energy scandal. Over the summer of 2000, the energy problems were widely, but not universally, understood as a problem of production, which meant the price spikes and blackouts should have lessened with the approach of winter. (San Diego's balmy weather required little energy to heat buildings.) Instead, the situation grew worse, casting a shadow over the long-term viability of California's economy, leading one steering committee member to ask how they could possibly be planning for more people when they didn't even have the electricity for the present. Virtually everyone in the region was touched by the energy problems in an immediate sense, as extremely high electricity and natural gas bills invited people to reconsider their relationships with every appliance in their homes. Those upset with GP 2020 were but a handful in comparison, though that handful included many of the most powerful in the county.

The supervisors' webpages highlighted what they were doing about the energy crisis, even though their power was limited. The websites barely contained any mention of GP 2020.

CHAPTER FIFTEEN

JOHN LOCKE AND RESISTANCE TO LAND USE PLANNING

In no other country in the world is the love of property keener or more alert than in the United States, and nowhere else does the majority display less inclination toward doctrines which in any way threaten the way property is owned.

—Alexis de Tocqueville, *Democracy in America*

S an Diego's general plan updates have been profoundly shaped by the American Dream of homeownership and by environmentalism. Both are descendants of another philosophy of land, one that has a strong strain of hostility toward government planning: the celebration of private property rights. Even environmentalists, who fear that Nature is being sacrificed on the altar of landowner profits, have been heavily—and detrimentally—influenced by the philosophy of property rights they attack. This is hard to see because of the taken-for-granted quality of property rights. As William Scott observes, "[p]roperty, like water, has for the most part been one of those facts of life which seldom needed explanation or justification."[1]

Private property seems so natural because it is so central to the

---

1. William Scott, *In Pursuit of Happiness: American Conceptions of Property from the Seventeenth to the Twentieth Century* (Bloomington: Indiana University Press, 1977): ix.

foundation of the nation. The best way to demonstrate this connection is to concentrate on the man most responsible for placing strong property rights at the center of American political ideology, a man who never stepped foot on the continent and died before the country was born: John Locke (1632–1704). While the British were establishing colonies on the Atlantic seaboard, this philosopher wrote an idealized account of the origins of government, an account that stressed private property. His views—some he invented, many of which were part of the zeitgeist—were hardly shared by all of the Founding Fathers, let alone all of the colonists, but their influence has deeply shaped how European Americans think about land and profoundly shapes conflict over land use planning.[2] In his *Second Treatise on Government*, a foundational text of liberalism, Locke presents a *labor* theory of property. He begins at the beginning: Earth was given by God to mankind. Men are to privatize this

2. For an example of how Locke's ideas were part of the zeitgeist, see Andro Linklater's claim that John Winthrop invented the labor theory of property half a century before Locke wrote on the subject. Linklater, *Owning the Earth: A Transforming History of Land Ownership* (New York: Bloomsbury, 2013): 27.

For a review of the literature of Locke's influence (if any) on the Framers of the Constitution, see Barbara Arneil, *John Locke and America: The Defense of English Colonialism* (New York: Oxford University Press, 1996): 11–14 and ch. 7; William Michael Treanor, "The Original Understanding of the Takings Clause," (n.d. but accessed November 14, 2004): http://www.law.georgetown.edu/gelpi/. Popcock argues that Locke's influence has been exaggerated, but he tries to make his case by ignoring Locke as much as possible in his history of British and early American political thinkers and then claiming that his ability to make a coherent story without Locke proves his point. Such logic is questionable. J. G. A. Popcock, *The Machiavellian Moment: Florentine Political Thought and the Atlantic Tradition* (Princeton: Princeton University Press, 1976, 2003).

An excellent book on how New England colonists and Indians understood their own actions and misunderstood each other is William Cronon, *Changes in the Land: Indian, Colonists, and the Ecology of New England* (New York: Hill and Wang, 1983). Although Cronon barely talks about Locke, reading his ecological history of colonial times makes it clear how commonplace many of the philosopher's ideas were. (Concentrating on Locke, however, allows pointing out the flaws in the ideas without being accused of making a straw man.) Cronon also has an excellent discussion on how New England colonists left behind a legacy of profligate use of resources (ch. 6).

vast commons. In this state of nature, a man has to mix his labor with the land to take possession of it. If he merely picks fruit from an unowned tree, just the fruit is his. If he pulls a bucket of water from a river, that water is his and, theoretically, can be passed on to the next generation. The man has no claims on the river. But if the same man plants an orchard and encloses it with a fence, the land itself is his.

To make the leap from private property to government, Locke, as do other social contract theorists like Thomas Hobbes, makes an analogy to trade between merchants. Just like a contract in which each merchant agrees to establish a relationship in which they give something in exchange for something they want, men came together to establish government:

> [each] divests himself of his natural liberty and puts on the bonds of civil society... by agreeing with other men to join and unite into a community for their comfortable, safe, and peaceable living one amongst another in a secure enjoyment of their properties, and a greater security against any that are not of it.[3]

This "just so" story of the origins of government contains several powerful ideas: government is by consent and government is for the protection of property.[4]

In the face of an authoritarian king, Locke's theory was

---

3. Ch. 8, para. 95 of *The Second Treatise.*

4. Locke defines property as "lives, liberties, and estates" but slips between that definition and property as land (e.g., ch. 5, para. 32). Barbara Arneil argues that "the two definitions seem to be mutually exclusive and are used by Locke in very specific places in his argument." Arneil, *John Locke and America: The Defense of English Colonialism* (New York: Oxford University Press, 1996): 133. See William Scott for speculation on Thomas Jefferson's change of Locke's phrase to "life, liberty, and pursuit of happiness" in the Declaration of Independence. Scott, *In Pursuit of Happiness: American Conceptions of Property from the Seventeenth to the Twentieth Century* (Bloomington: Indiana University Press, 1977): 41.

utopian. Everyone, except slaves captured during a just war, is free. Government does not coerce and only exists to promote peace and the public good. Labor cannot be appropriated by others. Women and children are not, as was argued at the time, at the complete mercy of husbands and fathers. Together, these ideas represent a radical extension of freedom, making Locke's vision "one of the most powerful ideologies ever invented, if not the most powerful."[5] Even today, many passages are quite stirring, and the equality implicit in Locke remains potentially subversive. *The Second Treatise*, however, is not so much a blueprint for all governments as an essay fulfilling immediate and complex political aims.[6] At once radical and conservative, insightful and arbitrary, it celebrates both the concentration and decentralization of power and property. This push-pull quality makes Locke's rhetoric appealing to a wide range of peoples and too slippery to easily reject. The contradictory complexity of Locke's thinking means, though, that any modern interpretation is partial and selective because people cherrypick ideas they like and ignore those they don't.[7] Further, many modern interpretations tend to ignore that Locke understood that once created through a social contract, government had the authority to regulate property and to protect people from extreme depravation by taxing resources from those with surplus. As a result, modern interpretations apply the logic of the state of nature to the present to justify limits on government in a way that contradict Locke.

The messiness of his ideas that allow cherrypicking and inconsistent readings can most easily be seen in Locke's understanding

---

5. Robert N. Bellah, Richard Madsen, Ann Swidler, William M. Sullivan and Steven M. Tipton, *The Good Society* (New York: Alfred A. Knopf, 1991): 67. See also Carol Pateman, *The Sexual Contract* (Stanford: Stanford University Press, 1988): 39.

6. John Dunn, *The Political Thought of John Locke: An Historical Account of the Argument of the 'Two Treatises of Government'* (Cambridge: Cambridge University Press, 1969).

7. And this is just within *The Second Treatise*. David Wootton sees such disparities between Locke's different writings he asks whether it makes sense to think of them as being written by the same person. Wootton, Editor's introd. to *The Political Writings of John Locke* (New York: Mentor, 1993): 110–119.

of women. The main target of *The Second Treatise* was Sir Robert Filmer's *Patriarchia*, which justifies absolute monarchy by an analogy to a man's position as the head of his family. In response, Locke both denies the validity of the analogy and attacks men's lording over their families. Locke's insistence on the equality of women and criticism of what we would now call child abuse makes him sound like a proto-feminist. But he also addresses the question of what to do if husband and wife disagree: "it therefore being necessary, that the last determination, i.e. the rule, should be placed somewhere, it naturally falls to the man's share, as the abler and stronger."[8] No sooner does Locke put forth potentially radical ideas, he retracts.

The Second Treatise attempts to thread a difficult needle: defend the enclosure of public lands and the current distribution of private property in England; justify revolution against a tyrannical king without questioning the underlying political order; and legitimate British colonization while also undercutting Spanish claims in the New World. In the process of making an elegantly simple explanation for why all of these property relations are right and proper, Locke introduces profound problems that haunt any attempt to apply his ideas to the modern world.

A central problem is the way that the Lockean view, by basing property on the work a man performs, conflates possession (a physical fact) and property (a legal status granted by a state). Andro Linklater argues that this is what makes Locke "revolutionary" as it is grounded property in fairness and justice: a person's rewards depend on their own effort.[9] In the abstract, this may well be true. When put into practice in present times, however, it has several negative effects. By denying that property is a right granted by a state and instead seeing property as the result of a person's own determination, Locke's view blurs the line between property and

8. *The Second Treatise* , ch. 7, para. 82.

9. Andro Linklater, *Owning the Earth: A Transforming History of Land Ownership* (New York: Bloomsbury, 2013): 84–85.

theft. This encourages the tragedy of the commons and puts land-owners in the position of simultaneously wanting to define for themselves their property rights while expecting everyone else to defend those rights through the power of the state.[10]

Another concern is Locke's racism towards Native Americans. It's not an incidental feature that can be brushed aside with an observation about how he was a man of his times. His approach towards Native Americans was closer to cunning than naive. Locke's racism is at the heart of his understanding of property. *The Second Treatise* is "simultaneously a philosophical treatise expounding the natural right to property and a defense of England's right to American soil."[11]

10. Resources can become overtaxed in a number of ways, of which the tragedy of the commons is only one. In that scenario, social regulation breaks down or never existed, like when cowboys pushed their herds into the Great Plains past any legal controls and treated all the lands as a commons. William G. Robbins, "Introduction: In Search of Western Lands," in *Land in the American West: Private Claims and the Common Good*, ed. William G. Robbins and James C. Foster, 23–35 (Seattle: University of Washington Press, 2000): 8–9. Although defenders of property rights say that privatized property can prevent this overuse of resources, the Lockean view of property encourages its initial stages. This is why David Bollier argues that the tragedy of the commons is really a tragedy of open access, which is the antithesis of a commons, as a commons implies collective regulation. Bollier, *Silent Theft: The Private Plunder of Our Common Wealth* (New York: Routledge, 2003). On research in the most literal commons—animal grazing areas—see Emery Roe, *Narrative Policy Analysis: Theory and Practice* (Durham and London: Duke University Press, 1994): 37–41; on the frontier mentality of resource extraction, see Thomas Princen, *The Logic of Sufficiency* (Cambridge, MA: MIT Press, 2005): 28.

A second way to induce a resource tragedy is for people to misjudge how fast renewable resources can be replenished. In the West, even those trying to develop a sensitive approach to the land have at times overestimated how much grazing they can safely do. Patricia Nelson Limerick, *The Legacy of Conquest: The Unbroken Past of the American West* (New York: Norton, 1987): 155–56.

11. Barbara Arneil, "The Wild Indian's Venison: Locke's Theory of Property and English Colonialism in America," *Political Studies* XLIV (1996): 61; see also Robert A. Williams, *The American Indian in Western Legal Thought: The Discourses of Conquest* (New York: Oxford University Press, 1990): 248.

To create a government based on property in land while justifying land theft from Native Americans on a genocidal scale, Locke appeals to several distinctions. First, he sees land as either privately owned or part of a commons. Communal regulation—including the varieties of Indian ownership—doesn't count; tribal land falls into the category of the not-yet-divided commons. In 1609 Robert Gray explained this so:

> Some affirme, and it is likely to be true, that these Sauages haue no particular propertie in any part of parcell of that Countrey, but only a generall residencie there, as wild beast haue in the forrest... so that if the whole lande should bee taken from them, there is not a man that can complaine of any particular wrong done vtno him.[12]

Furthermore, Locke uses as a marker of land having been removed from the commons a symbol believed not to be used by Indians: the fence.[13]

Locke also carefully calibrates his ethnocentric definitions of labor. He splits work into two categories: gathering—the fruit, the bucket of water—only entitles the person to what they collect while labor that mixes with the ground itself—farming—turns the land into private property.[14] Conveniently enough, according to these distinctions, Native Americans did not engage in labor that transferred land from the commons into private property because they

12. Quoted in Gesa Mackenthun, *Metaphors of Dispossession: American Beginnings and the Translation of Empire, 1492–1637* (Norman and London: University of Oklahoma Press, 1997): 195; see also Barbara Arneil, *John Locke and America: The Defense of English Colonialism* (New York: Oxford University Press, 1996): 152–53.

13. Barbara Arneil, "The Wild Indian's Venison: Locke's Theory of Property and English Colonialism in America," *Political Studies* XLIV (1996): 63–64.

14. Peter Hulme, "The Spontaneous Hand of Nature: Savagery, Colonialism, and the Enlightenment," in *The Enlightenment and Its Shadows*, ed. Peter Hulme and Ludmilla Jordanova, 16–34 (London and New York: Routledge, 1998): 30.

only gathered and did not properly farm.[15] Therefore they had no legitimate rights to the land. Similarly, Spanish claims to the New World were based on discovery and conquest and not settlement, so they too had no recognizable land claims.[16] The New World in the seventeenth century, then, was still a primordial commons, there for the British taking.

Keeping to the universal pretense of his thinking, however, Locke sees Indians as capable of possessing land, but he offers them a devil's bargain: they can retain property if they cease to be Indians. They have to lead their lives according to the colonizers' norms of bearing, including enclosing their lands and engaging in English-style agriculture.[17]

---

15. Colonists themselves went to great lengths to avoid recognizing Indian agriculture as such, like insisting that an activity was only truly farming if plows were made out of iron and if crops in the field were neatly segregated. Gesa Mackenthun, *Metaphors of Dispossession: American Beginnings and the Translation of Empire, 1492–1637* (Norman and London: University of Oklahoma Press, 1997): 40–44, 272. See also Barbara Arneil, *John Locke and America: The Defense of English Colonialism* (New York: Oxford University Press, 1996): 40–41. Back in England, maintaining the fiction that Indians didn't farm required ignoring how Indian crops, like tobacco and corn, were seeping into British food culture. Peter Hulme, "The Spontaneous Hand of Nature: Savagery, Colonialism, and the Enlightenment," in *The Enlightenment and Its Shadows*, ed. Peter Hulme and Ludmilla Jordanova, 16–34 (London and New York: Routledge, 1998): 30. This hostility towards how Indians fed themselves also resonated with Puritan anti-royalist sentiments, as the Indians' hunting smacked of aristocratic hunting for pleasure. William Cronon, *Changes in the Land: Indian, Colonists, and the Ecology of New England* (New York: Hill and Wang, 1983): 56.

16. The belief that Spanish colonial claims were invalidated by the lack of settlement was suggested as early as the 1580s, concurrent with the first British attempts at settlement and well before Locke's time. Barbara Arneil, *John Locke and America: The Defense of English Colonialism* (New York: Oxford University Press, 1996): 71.

17. Barbara Arneil, *John Locke and America: The Defense of English Colonialism* (New York: Oxford University Press, 1996): 74. The view that Indians didn't own land was not universally accepted by colonists. Roger Williams insisted that land be purchased from Indians, though his view narrowed their original rights to land considerably. William Scott, *In Pursuit of Happiness: American Conceptions of Property from the Seventeenth to the Twentieth Century* (Bloomington: Indiana University Press, 1977): 16–17.

Resistance to Land Use Planning

If Locke's views were museum pieces, they would interest only historians. Locke's ideas, however, are very much alive. Indeed, it is not much of a stretch to say that we are all Lockeans now. But what people draw from the complex stew of Locke's thought often is concocted into diametrically opposed visions of the good life. People on the political left tend to dislike Locke, sharply criticizing him while failing to appreciate the extent to which their own values are indebted to his (equality, government to serve the people, hostility to war and exploitation, property regulated and taxed to serve the aims of the community, etc.). Those on the right embrace Locke explicitly, using his words to celebrate the mechanisms—limited government and private property—that are supposed to reach his ends. But the right often treats those mechanisms as ends in themselves. In short, the American left has implicitly embraced Locke's ends while the American right has explicitly embraced his means.

The conservative, Lockean interpretation is pervasive in a way that is hard to see because it feels so natural, especially to property owners. The way it can be invisible to its advocates can be seen in one of the most popular American novels of all time, *Gone with the Wind*. The novel's description of how the O'Hara family acquires the Tara plantation is telling. In a poker game, Gerald O'Hara risked, without his brothers' knowledge, the company they owned together and won a rundown plantation that had, within the lifetime of its oak trees, belonged to Cherokees. Borrowing money from the said brothers and mortgaging the property, O'Hara bought his first slaves, who worked the cotton fields. Then again he borrowed money from his brothers to buy more slaves, who built the plantation's mansion. This story of O'Hara's rise ended with the words, "He had done it all, little, hard-headed, blustering Gerald."[18] Mitchell saw this as pulling one's self up by the bootstraps and as great risks justly

---

18. Margaret Mitchell, *Gone with the Wind* (New York: The Macmillan Company, 1936): 42–48.

rewarded, but it could only be understood as such by an insistent obliviousness to familial resources and the exploitation of others even when describing it.

Locke's denial of the possibility of communal ownership also survived the centuries. To quote a 1974 radio address by then Governor Ronald Reagan of California:

> Over a hundred years ago Abraham Lincoln signed the Homestead Act. There was a wide distribution of land and they didn't confiscate anyone's already privately owned land. They did not take from those who owned to give to others who did not own.[19]

In the most literal form, the law still embodies the logic of Lockean land theft. Although rarely used, the doctrine of *adverse possession*, the acquisition of land by private parties without title, is still on the books.[20] It contains more than an echo of the legalistic maneuvers behind the conquest of the continent. One of the conditions for adverse possession is to show that the land has been occupied. In California, the statute reads:

> land is deemed to have been possessed and occupied in the following cases only:
> First – Where it has been protected by a substantial inclosure.
> Second – Where it has been usually cultivated or improved.[21]

This is Locke, undiluted.

What is widely seen as *the* American land ethos has a deep

19. Ronald Reagan, radio address. Quoted in Jeff Gates, *The Ownership Solution: Toward a Shared Capitalism for the Twenty-first Century* (Reading, MA: Addison–Wesley, 1998): 167.
20. Donald A. Krueckeberg, "The Lessons of John Locke or Hernando de Soto: What if Your Dreams Come True?" *Housing Policy Debate* 15, no. 1 (2004): 10.
21. California Code of Civil Procedures, Section 325.

Lockean strain. Ann Strong delineates its six main points, which are reminiscent both of Locke and the homeowner offshoot of his ideas, the American Dream:

1. Private ownership of land is a sacred right;
2. Interference in an owner's use of his land is contrary to the intent of the Constitution;
3. Eminent domain is wrong;
4. All profits from land development should inure to the landowner;[22]
5. Government, except for local government, ignores the wishes of the people and is untrustworthy; and
6. Big business is in league with government in derogation of the people's interests.[23]

Only the last point is not in the spirit of Locke. (It's curious to wonder how Locke would have responded to the rise of big business in the nineteenth century.)

22. Private property rights activists rarely explicitly stated in public during GP 2020 that many of them were not merely trying to protect their property; they want to protect their property's ability to increase in value (and would consider it a disaster if their land was worth the same in the year 2020 as it was when the plan update started). In general property rights advocates are hostile to the public sharing in increases in land value even when they result from public efforts, like the construction of a nearby highway interchange.
23. Ann L. Strong, *Private Property and the Public Interest: The Brandywine Experience* (Baltimore: Johns Hopkins University Press, 1975): 145. There are, of course, other ways to interpret Locke. For example, Locke argues, with complex caveats, that if a person wastes their property, then they can lose control of it. If this were stressed, then those in poverty could seize for affordable housing land held speculatively, as is done in Mexico. Some Marxists have even embraced Locke because they believe taking his ideas to their logical conclusion makes his views similar to their own. Lawrence Becker, *Property Rights: Philosophic Foundations* (London, Henley and Boston: Routledge & Kegan Paul, 1977): 94–95. For an example of an effort to defend the regulation of land, not on the basis of the "historical Locke" but on a modern interpretation of his words, see Kristin Shrader-Frechette, "Locke and Limits on Land Ownership," in *Policy for Land: Law and Ethics*, ed. Keith Lynton Caldwell and Kristin Shrader-Frechette, 65–84 (Lanham, Maryland: Rowman & Littlefield, Publishers, Inc., 1993).

It is not hyperbolic to suggest that the vast majority of US citizens believe in the Lockean philosophy of land at least part of the time.[24] Indeed, the American Dream is basically a twentieth-century variant of the Lockean perspective, one that has refocused the sanctity of land onto the home itself after the bulk of the American population moved off the farm and into the cities and suburbs, creating a class, if you will, of yeoman homeowners.[25] It's not as if Americans read *The Second Treatise* and were instantly converted. Rather, Locke's ideas just felt and continue to feel right. Private property has had the deep support of numerous institutions.

Indeed, despite the antigovernment rhetoric of this ethos, the federal government has been a strong supporter. The end of the Fifth Amendment states that private property cannot be "taken for public use without just compensation." The federal government has not merely recognized and protected private property. It has actively privatized swaths of the continent and made property the focus of many policies.

In the 1960s, however, this approach to land began to face tremendous skepticism from the rapidly growing environmental movement. Government had regulated property since colonial times, but the early 1970s witnessed a new wave of regulations at all levels of government, including laws that gave land use planning teeth. This in turn led to a right-wing backlash of the property rights movement, which emerged to resist eminent domain abuses and to defend property owners' discretion to exploit their land as they saw fit. Giving the concept of maximum economic return on their land an almost sacred quality, some property rights activists have made little distinction between land use planning and communism and

24. On the appeal of different, it not contradictory, belief systems, see Claudia Strauss, "Who Gets Ahead?: Cognitive Responses to Heteroglossia in American Political Culture," *American Ethnologist* 17 (1990): 312–328.
25. Neala Schleuning, *To Have and To Hold: The Meaning of Ownership in the United States* (Westport, CT: Praeger, 1997).

thus see planning as Satan incarnate.[26]

The main legal weapon of landowners in their battle against government interference is the concept of *regulatory taking*—the claim that government regulation can be so strict as to effectively seize property (discussed in chapter one). At the most extreme, such as Oregon's successful Measure 37 (2004) or California's failed Proposition 90 (2006), this approach interprets the phrase "just compensation" in the Constitution to mean that property owners should be paid money for almost *any* financial loss attributed to government regulation. This view so equates land and money that it ignores the possibility that it might be just for a land speculator to receive little compensation. This broad interpretation of regulatory takings goes well beyond the Supreme Court, which, while recognizing that regulations can go too far, has given jurisdictions wide discretion in regulating and seizing property.[27]

Yet property rights are embedded more deeply into American jurisprudence than the American Dream or environmentalism. This is not to say that property owners, especially smaller ones, always get their way—that is hardly the case—but their needs are a central concern of the system of land use regulation. There is nothing equivalent to the Takings Clause in the Constitution that protects the viability of ecosystems or the right to shelter. This privileging of property has tremendously contributed to the weakness of planning in the United States. It institutionalizes the veto power of wealth over land use planning, a veto that is difficult to override.[28] And the folk belief that "you can do whatever you want with your land" is backed by the political clout of large landowners and the moral authority of smaller ones, encouraging the attitude that land use

26. On why conservatives equate regulation and social programs with communism, see George Lakoff, *Moral Politics: How Liberals and Conservatives Think*, 2nd ed. (Chicago: University of Chicago Press, 2001): 170–71, 181–82.

27. J. Sax, "Property Rights and the Economy of Nature: Understanding *Lucas v. South Carolina Coastal Council*," *Stanford Law Review* 45 (1993): 1433–1455.

28. See Sidney Plotkin, *Keep Out: The Struggle for Land Use Control* (Berkeley: University of California Press, 1987).

planning is guilty until proven innocent.

Before turning to explore the fundamental weakness of this perspective, it is important to understand that it is not necessarily meant to be an elite perspective, that its vision is of widely distributed wealth. Indeed, its promise is quite similar to the quip of a Texas professor accused of communism, who, when grilled about whether he believed in private property, reportedly replied, "I believe in private property so much that I think everyone in the state of Texas ought to have some."[29]

The Flaw in the Modern Application of Locke's Views on Property

Since the property rights movement is so Lockean, looking at Locke can explain its conceptual weaknesses. To understand the flaws of Locke (and thus the limits of the property rights movement) requires looking at how Locke deals with inequality. In the state of Nature, each man can create as much property as he wants (by farming). There are only a few limitations. Specifically, privatizing land or materials does "not affect anyone else because enough and as good remain for others to appropriate." That is, someone can't take ownership of so much land that it inhibits others from getting a fair share.[30] With a small population, this is not a problem. One

---

29. The Texas anecdote is relayed in Nancy Folbre, *The Invisible Heart: Economics and Family Values* (New York: The New Press, 2001): 182. For a history of how middle-class advocates have explicitly promoted the interests of the wealthy, see Isaac W. Martin, *Rich People's Movements: Grassroots Campaigns to Untax the One Percent* (New York: Oxford University Press, 2013).

30. James O. Grunebaum, *Private Ownership* (London and New York: Routledge and Kegan Paul, 1987): 56. Locke feared that Carolina colonists were seizing more land than they could work. His concern may have been, à la Smart Growth, about the resulting diffuse settlement pattern. Donald A. Krueckeberg, "The Lessons of John Locke or Hernando de Soto: What if Your Dreams Come True?" *Housing Policy Debate* 15, no. 1 (2004): 13–14. Arneil's understanding of Locke provides implicit support for this view, including a quote from Locke's main supporter, the Earl of Shaftesbury: "A towne in a

family can only work so much land and there's essentially the same left over for everyone else. If, however, the population continues to grow, this effectively requires an infinite supply of land. Presumably, the conflict that then arises over land is what makes men willing to accept a social contract and leave the state of nature for a governed civilization. And consenting to government means consenting to taxes and regulation, meaning that government can control property conflicts.[31]

This, however, is where Locke stops. He says little about what happens next, which Thomas Jefferson recognized:

> Thus he [Jefferson] says in a letter to Thomas Mann Randolph Jr., dated 30 May 1790, that Locke's essay on government is 'perfect as far as it goes.' In other words, there is nothing flawed about the analysis as it stands; the problem is that Locke simply did not follow through far enough on his thought.[32]

Indeed, to apply the logic of the state of nature to modern times turns property into an oxymoron: the theory is about divvying up essentially infinite material resources and it is only conditions of scarcity that create a need for property.[33] (This is why homeowners and landowners can so frequently be hostile despite their similar

---

healthy Place will give more Reputation, Security and Advantage to us then ten times that number scattered about the countrey." Barbara Arneil, *John Locke and America: The Defense of English Colonialism* (New York: Oxford University Press, 1996): 123.

31. *The Second Treatise*, ch. 8, para. 120.

32. Barbara Arneil, *John Locke and America: The Defense of English Colonialism* (New York: Oxford University Press, 1996): 188. For another perspective on how the conflation of property and community made sense when most people farmed but has become a non sequitur in areas where farming is no longer prevalent, see John G. Francis and Leslie Pickering Francis, *Land Wars: The Politics of Property and Community* (Boulder: Lynne Rienner Publishers, Inc., 2003).

33. James O. Grunebaum, *Private Ownership* (London and New York: Routledge and Kegan Paul, 1987): 56, 59. Likewise, my preschooler suddenly develops a great willingness to share at an all-you-can-eat buffet.

attitudes: each feels their property rights should trump the other's.)

Thus, just as land use environmentalism offers little of help in understanding how humans should relate to the natural world because it's really a theory of how resources should be distributed among people, modern Lockean views of property offer little guidance to questions of who should get what because they ignore the ways that one person's property can impinge upon the liberty of another.

Locke didn't seem to have worried about this because he had an emphatic way of avoiding the land supply problem: the Americas. The New World, which dwarfed Europe in size, was to him a massive commons as the Native Americans (north of Mexico) did not properly claim it by engaging in English-style agriculture. It was, to Locke, vacant.[34] This, however, obviously only works as long as the ratio of land to people is tilted towards land.

When the supply of land is constant and demand is increasing rapidly, owners are able to extort money based on their monopolistic position. They are able to increase their own property, not by work, but by being able to charge what in effect is a private tax on other people's work. This turns property into a zero-sum game: for owners, they see the role of government as protecting their property and any limit on their property is a threat. On the other hand, nonowners hardly feel like they are part of a social contract. Their need for housing allows them to be bilked for the product of their

---

34. His solution forces him to view another group uncharitably: England's propertyless. If property is the result of work, then those without property must be lazy or suffer from "relaxation of discipline, and corruption of manners" in John Locke, *The Political Writings of John Locke*, ed. David Wootton (New York: Mentor, 1993): 447. Locke's position ignores the aggression of enclosing of the commons by the English elites, which had deprived many people of their livelihoods. The extent of Locke's hostility towards the poor was unusual for his time. David Wootton, Editor's introd. to *The Political Writings of John Locke* (New York: Mentor, 1993): 109–110. But in his time the impoverished were in fact treated and described in ways similar to Native Americans—the unemployed landless as savages, Indians as lazy. Gesa Mackenthun, *Metaphors of Dispossession: American Beginnings and the Translation of Empire, 1492–1637* (Norman and London: University of Oklahoma Press, 1997): 270.

labor. For them, a Lockean government devoted to existing property rights is far from liberating.

This fear that some day that land would no longer be readily available has in fact been a recurrent anxiety in American history. The Founding Fathers saw it as a possible coming loss of innocence. Their reading of European republics was that they declined through the same process.[35] A republic would start with some measure of political equality. Once land became concentrated and an aristocracy would emerge, however, the nobles would lose their virtue and become decadent. A landless laboring class would appear and the subsequent class conflict would weaken the republic, making it vulnerable to internal strife and invasion. The Founding Fathers thought that the United States had an opportunity to cheat death: as long as the country could expand through space, it could stay young. At the end of the nineteenth century, Frederick Jackson Turner, claiming it indicated that the frontier had closed, turned the 1890 census into a myth of anxiety for the country as it rapidly urbanized.[36]

Indeed, what happens when the frontier closes is an irresolvable problem for property rights advocates. It puts them in the metaphorical position of having to abandon the freedom of the state of nature for submission to the rule of government. It becomes the point at which their values and their preferred means for achieving them part ways. It's the moment the Founding Fathers feared. The results will not be pretty. It'll happen eventually. Indeed, the argument could be made that it's been long happening.

It's the moment in which the logic of Locke is reversed. Locke argued that property furthered the common good; many times people opposed to government regulation of land are effectively arguing

35. Drew R. McCoy, *The Elusive Republic: Political Economy in Jeffersonian America* (Williamsburg, VA: The University of Virginia Press, 1980); Gregory S. Alexander, *Commodity & Propriety: Competing Visions of Property in American Legal Thought, 1776-1970* (Chicago & London: University of Chicago Press, 1997): 36.
36. Lee Benson, "The Historian as Mythmaker: Turner and the Closed Frontier," in *The Frontier in American Development: Essays in Honor of Paul Wallace Gates*, ed. David M. Ellis, 3–19 (Ithaca: Cornell University Press, 1969).

that their property rights should be respected *despite* the common good.[37] Stressing the sanctity of property rights when land supplies are limited and demand is growing exacerbates the conflict already inherent in the situation. It becomes a way for those who already possess property to use the legal system and American values to press their advantages against others. It is not a way of working towards just solutions to common problems but a tool for landowners to maintain privilege and inequality:

> Liberty is too important a concept to rest on something that not everyone has or is able to acquire. Those opposed to or leery of government intervention imagine that their freedom, their liberty, is assured by their possessions, including land. But the history of the world's revolutions would suggest otherwise. Revolutions have arisen precisely because of the skewed distribution of the property interests in land and other assets.[38]

After this point, when newcomers, the poor huddled masses, enter the scene without property, they are in a position of vulnerability.

---

37. See Andro Linklater, *Owning the Earth: A Transforming History of Land Ownership* (New York: Bloomsbury, 2013).

38. Daniel Bromley, "Private Property and the Public Interest," in *Land in the American West: Private Claims and the Common Good,* ed. William G. Robbins and James C. Foster, 23–35 (Seattle: University of Washington Press, 2000): 27. In limited contexts, there is truth to the guarantor arguments. For people with a lot to lose, it has often not been worth the damage to the legitimacy of property to directly appropriate from others, and private property has limited the ability of government to wantonly take from citizens. Furthermore, property relations have created bubbles outside of elite control. The property southern blacks had in their churches limited the ability of whites to apply economic pressure to the ministers who were leaders of the civil rights movement. Douglas McAdam, *Political Process and the Development of Black Insurgency, 1930–1970* (Chicago: University of Chicago Press, 1982): 135. In looking at women involved in the early development of the Bay Area, Simpson claims that, "[p]roperty ownership was the great equalizer between men and women." Lee Michelle August Simpson, *Selling the City: Women and the California Growth Games.* PhD diss., (UC Riverside, 1996): 193.

They lack liberty yet are supposed to somehow be equal. Some intellectuals suggest decidedly unLockean ways out of this tension, like compensating the landless through money payments.[39] But that is unlikely to happen. Smart Growth tries to square the circle by putting forth an ideal of urban life and making the case that a slightly smaller yard around the house will do. Private property rights advocates, however, generally dodge the issue or argue that markets distribute resources justly. At some point, however, they have to face the issue and something must give.

Although they haven't framed it as such, San Diego property rights advocates have explored different ways of responding to the potential unraveling of a property-based republic. The first and main approach has been to double-down on the property rights of existing owners. Despite their relative affluence compared to many San Diegans, private property rights activists, like homeowners, are motivated to participate in politics by a sense of victimhood (which suggests the observation that everyone in politics thinks of themselves as victims). This feeling of victimization has proven to be a powerful mobilizing force among landowners involved in GP 2020. This easily makes sense when put into the context of Locke's views. Per Locke, they've earned what they have. The government's job is to protect the fruit of their labors. They would never submit to a social contract that robbed them of their property. This was perhaps the main rhetorical strategy used in public: GP 2020 violated the property rights of landowners.

Furthermore, in their view, property comes in two flavors: private property and common land not yet privatized. There is no room for wilderness as valuable in itself, so environmentalism—the motivation for much of the proposed regulation in the San Diego County general plan—is based on an illegitimate concept. Taken to its extreme, this collapses the value of land into its economic value.

---

39. See Donald A. Krueckeberg, "The Lessons of John Locke or Hernando de Soto: What if Your Dreams Come True?" *Housing Policy Debate* 15, no. 1 (2004): 1–24.

(Or, as Jack Orr put it in an interview, "My land is my money.") This sees the value of land as captured in full by its potential to generate wealth (in contrast to homeowners who also value their homes for shelter and emotional attachment).

Some landowners and the more sophisticated developers don't adhere to this strictly. They recognize ecological values. They object, however, to what they consider to be the unfair distribution of the costs of environmental protection. "Yes," they say, "protecting the environment is important. But why does one segment of society have to pay all the costs? Environmentalists say they want to preserve Nature, but they're not willing to put their money where their mouth is. They simply want to take our land."[40]

Another approach—perhaps best seen as an elaboration of the previous one—is to legitimate their interest in land and avoid the charge of speculation by defining whatever they themselves do as work. (Locke again.) One developer involved in GP 2020 denied that speculation was speculation if one researched the investments. And some property owners in effect claimed that paying real estate taxes was work that legitimated their property rights.

A third approach has been to blame land use planning for accelerating the problems in the Lockean model because it is restricting access to land and thus hastening the demise of a property-based republic. (Landowners have a quick solution to the housing affordability crisis: eliminate restrictions on housing construction.) This

40. This is where property rights advocates most differ from homeowners and environmentalists. Up to this point, there have been affinities between the property rights position and the American Dream of homeownership and environmentalism. Environmentalism, as it is applied to land use, is nothing less than Locke standing on his head. The story is the same. Whereas advocates of property rights define their making use of the commons as part of the common good and see the regulation of private property as theft, environmentalists instead see private parties taking from the commons as theft and the protection and restoration of the commons as the public good. Environmentalists, however, have adopted Locke's commons wholesale: it is the uninhabited wilderness of North America. As discussed in the chapter on environmentalism, it is this notion of the wilderness, a purity untouched by people (never mind the Indians), that puts environmentalists at odds with housing needed by others.

third approach was implicit in criticisms of land use regulation—made by the Building Industry Association—that tightening the housing supply through land use regulations was an intergenerational transfer of wealth from young to old. It was only during the Great Recession that it was more widely elaborated upon. The most sophisticated version of this critique of land use planning has strong parallels to world cities theory, a leftist critique of globalization that argues that inequalities in major cities is increasing because of the growing power of the super-wealthy, especially in the financial sector.[41] Property rights perspective sees the same result—deepening inequality—but places the blame on artificially constricted access to land instead of on the globalization of capital per se: limiting the supply of land for housing is driving away the single-family home-owning middle class. The region's appealing features (especially its weather and hi-tech industries) appeal not just to Americans but to global elites who can outbid middle-class Americans for housing. The result will be a region split between a small wealthy elite and a large working class providing services to them. As a possible future for San Diego, this is quite plausible. The property rights advocates' solution—allowing the construction of more housing, preferably single-family, on more land—could be seen, however, as merely delaying the inevitable without resolving the fundamental tension inherent in building a growing middle-class republic on a finite supply of land. Or it could be seen as buying time to straighten out the tangled logic of our country's Lockean roots.

An Aside: The Final Piece of the Puzzle

With this analysis of the logic of the defense of private property, we have the last puzzle piece to address a key question of San Diego politics, one that has only been alluded to so far. Why did the

---

41. Saskia Sassen, *The Global City: New York, London, Tokyo,* 2nd ed. (Princeton: University of Princeton Press): 2001.

participants in the general plan update processes think of them as democratic when the people who involved were not representative of the people of San Diego? The participants almost all felt that their own views weren't being given enough weight, but rare was the occasion in which someone pointed out how much of the San Diego population was excluded from the planning process. Except for community planning groups in the most diverse neighborhoods, the degree of segregation at planning meetings was extraordinary. Participants were homeowners (perhaps representing their business interests or their investments in land). Typically, they were Anglos—during the period in which Anglos lost their majority status in the County—and they were over forty. If someone was under thirty, they were mostly likely an intern with the planning department or an ambitious young architect. And, as argued earlier and will be touched upon again in the conclusion, this unevenness subtly but profoundly influenced the concerns that were addressed and the visions that were promulgated.

So why did the segregation by status, why did the exclusion of younger persons, of renters, of non-Anglos, not call into question the legitimacy of a political process that is supposed to be democratic? There are two major reasons. First, Americans have a very voluntaristic notion of political participation. It is seen as a passive right to be enjoyed and not as a duty or expectation. In the United States, major strains of political thought, especially libertarianism, idealize conditions under which people have the fewest possible obligations to each other. In other countries, citizenship is seen as an active duty, as more than a call to jury service that has to be dodged every couple of years. Not voting, for instance, can lead to a fine or loss of financial aid. In the United States, with the possible exception of debates about whether efforts to eliminate voter fraud are in fact deliberate voter suppression, there's little discussion about what conditions are necessary for people to actively participate in the affairs of government. So if people don't show up, then it's a shrug of the shoulders and more for those who do.

Distinctive to land use, however, is another reason that exclusion does not call into question the democratic character of participation in government affairs. Each of the three approaches to land use—the American Dream of homeownership, environmentalism and private property rights—splits the world into two types of participants: good citizens (to use a phrase of Michael Schudson) and those who can legitimately be excluded because they're not really members of the community. Homeowners question the value of renters, who "do not have a stake in the community." Environmentalists are opposed to additional growth. Landowners are deeply suspicious of those who do not own property: they're trying to take from others. If someone were to make a Venn diagram of these three groups considered illegitimate, it would immediately become apparent the extent to which they overlap. They are referring to a cluster of people that are poorer (renters) and younger than the people actively involved in land use. In San Diego, they are also disproportionately minority (largely Latino). In other words, as much as homeowners, environmentalists and landowners fight among themselves, they tacitly share a consensus about who should not be participating.

CHAPTER SIXTEEN
HITTING THE RESET BUTTON

T he office of County supervisor meant different things to different occupants. Candidates were often the product of one city's local politics: Greg Cox had been the mayor of Chula Vista; Pam Slater, of Encinitas. Ron Roberts had been on the City of San Diego's planning commission and then city council. As the board of supervisors was one of the few local elected bodies to not (yet) have term limits, it could be a final resting place for politicians pushed up out of city politics. The board was also a springboard for higher office. All three mayors of San Diego from 1983 to 2000 had taken this path. As discussed in the last case study, in 2000, Roberts unsuccessfully tried to follow in their footsteps. (The same year, Horn made a quixotic run at the US Senate.)

The supervisors then could have looked at GP 2020 from a position of comfort or with an eye on higher office. That is, they may or may not have had to live with the County general plan. And the plan, if the supervisors stayed, would affect them differently. The bulk of the unincorporated area—and thus the voters most directly affected by GP 2020—were in Dianne Jacob's and Bill Horn's districts. For the other three supervisors, the most direct impacts would be on the possible prestige of endorsements by environmental groups or access to developer campaign funds.

A common understanding of how the board would react to the general plan update was as follows: Supervisors Horn and Roberts would be unwilling to accept anything ambitious or detrimental to development interests, though it might be possible to convince Roberts that it was necessary. Slater—almost a throwback to the Republican Party before Reagan pushed it so far to the right—and Jacob were seen as willing to support preserving the backcountry, though Jacob had a more difficult balancing act. This left Cox, who said the least at each GP 2020 hearing.

Such figuring, of course, oversimplified. GP 2020 had no shortage of pitfalls that made it, in the words of one observer close to the board, a "political nightmare" because if handled improperly, it was supervisory suicide. How to avoid an untimely political demise was by no means clear given the gulf separating conflicting groups. Different interests knew what they wanted, but to keep all of them from becoming so unhappy that they might retaliate through a lawsuit or withdrawal of support was a challenge, one that the supervisors didn't ask for. (Recall that the board had deleted "comprehensive" from the general plan update in 1997 because they wanted the least revision possible.)

The Fate of Alternative III

The Alternative III controversy deepened for four months before the board of supervisors finally addressed it on January 10, 2001. That day, the board's hearing room, which seated approximately a hundred, was packed, and a sheriff deputy, concerned that crowded aisles were a fire safety hazard, directed people to the balcony and to an overflow room where the hearing could be watched on television. A Sierra Club activist commandeered one of the tables in the crowded hallway outside and distributed colored pieces of paper that said, "STOP SPRAWL" for people to tape to their shirts. Not many wore them, though a who's who of local environmentalists was present.

The meeting got off to an incongruous start. When, at the beginning, speakers had a chance to address items not on the agenda, a homeless man shared his views on "When art is not art," explaining that if art was conscious, then it was a craft. He claimed he "had mastered tennis from an eternal or universal perspective"—that is, as a mind-body exercise and not as competitive sport. He described going to city councils looking for assistance in spreading his ideas through a website.

Bill Horn was the chair. He said it was "an adjustment day" and that he particularly wanted to hear about Smart Growth ideas, especially focusing growth near transportation by, for example, tax incentives. There were seventy speaker slips, so each speaker had one minute at the podium; groups, five minutes. This did not please those anticipated the usual three minutes per person.

Then came opening remarks by staff and the planning commission. Planning Director Gary Pryor stressed that Alternative III was not a plan. It was a starting point. What staff wanted was direction on whether the board still supported the goals and policies as well as the population target of 660,000.

Three planning commissioners spoke. The chair, Herbert York, gave a synopsis of the plan update's evolution. He was frustrated with the workshops: "Regardless of how I presented it, property owners would nonetheless get up and consider Alternative III as *the* County plan, as if we had adopted a new plan and they wanted to show us how it squared with their existing property rights and so forth." Alternative III was, he thought, relatively uncontentious in the built-up areas, mainly in the south and east. The controversy was centered on the north suburban area, Fallbrook through Ramona and to some extent Alpine (to the east).

Commissioner Woods described the steering committee's work, emphasizing that development interests and the Farm Bureau attended as needed and that the vast majority of votes were unanimous. Michael Beck finished the commission's presentation, discussing mainly technical issues, like the need for good design standards. Presumably to short-circuit criticisms that the County wasn't allowing enough housing, he added:

We had a joint workshop with the City of San Diego Planning Commission and the message in that joint meeting was interesting because essentially the City, at least at the planning commission level, was saying, "Give us your density. We need density to make our system work." They were speaking to—and our planning commission as well—were speaking to this issue as a system's issue which acknowledges that the City of San Diego, the other jurisdictions, the County of San Diego are all players in this same so-called Smart Growth game.

Most of the first individual speakers were from the planning and sponsor groups. They had a wide range of concerns, from Pala/Pauma, in the north, worried about the Indian casinos to Potrero, down by the Mexican border, afraid that their group's right to determine the future for their area was threatened by the plan.

Two of the biggest concerns were that property rights were being eroded and that the steering committee might be contaminated by developers. Dutch Van Dierondonck's speech epitomized the second sentiment:

> Plainly and simply, the developers and their clients have been asleep for two years. Now they wake up and realize that they are behind the curve. So the obvious solution to them is to dilute and dissolve the planning groups that have been working their butts off getting things done, much to their dismay. Now, instead of working with the planning groups they want to do it all their way, destroy our county resources—ridge line development, forget the infrastructure, we don't have a water problem, just business as usual.
>
> This County and many people in it have labored mightily for two years. We've spent millions on a GP

2020. It may not be the best plan, but it is what we have to work with. We can modify it, we can learn to work together, we may compromise, but make no mistake: these planning groups are here because they have been put here by an electoral process guaranteed by the Constitution. They [the developers] do not have the right legally or otherwise to dissolve or otherwise destroy the planning group process. Essentially, these developers are looking for guarantees. However, there is nothing in the Constitution of the United States that guarantees them a profit or that they are protected by law from economic loss. They cannot dictate to the populace of this county.

Many environmentalists spoke, stressing that the board had an opportunity to stop sprawl. They wanted the County's plan to be based on resources and the carrying capacity of the land. During the lunch break, they held a news conference. One reporter attended.

The landowners, developers and realtors were out in force. They reiterated the arguments they used before the planning commission: they had been excluded from the process; the downzoning was a taking; the plan was arbitrary. Their *cause célèbre* of the day was Monte Vista Ranch, a proposed development in Ramona that went from one home per 5 acres to one per 160 acres, prompting Supervisor Roberts to ask Pryor, "So there could be other sites like this throughout this map that we might find a little shocking?"

After a lunch break and an hour of the board in closed session, Pryor gave the staff presentation. He portrayed the plan update process as very reasonable and as having followed board direction. The problem was that obstructionists had prevented staff from analyzing the kinds of deviations from good planning that they were accused of making.

The first supervisor to speak was Bill Horn. He again said he wanted to see density moved to areas along transportation corridors, especially the highways in his district and the proposed

Oceanside–Escondido railway. He also expressed support for property rights.

Dianne Jacob began by taking environmentalists to task for not concentrating their efforts on the growth that accompanied the new Indian casinos, a non sequitur that upset some of its targets. Jacob mentioned transfer of development rights as a way of preserving both the open space and equity. She expressed concern that the extent of parcellization—that is, the way the county had already been subdivided—would undermine the reduction in population: existing lots, which were allowed to build one house each regardless of the zoning, already made it possible to build extensively.

If the board of supervisors had been the San Diego City Council, they would have deleted the downzoning and approved the rest. The motion Jacob put forth was more like hitting the reset button on a computer. It reaffirmed support for the 660,000 population target and the steering committee's goals and policies. The motion, however, also eliminated the Alternative III map, on the grounds that only Boulevard and Lake Moreno/Campo sponsor groups liked it. In its place, staff was to develop three alternate concepts of growth. The most contentious point of the motion would:

> direct the CAO to establish an interest group that has the same influence as the steering committee, that would be compromised of a total of fifteen members, six from the environmental community, six from the development community, adding one from the American Institute of Architects, one from the American Planning Association and one from the American Society of Landscape Architects.

Just as Jacob typically made the motions for GP 2020, Slater typically seconded it.

The other supervisors tweaked the wording of the motion, brought additional items to attention and lashed out at the process. (Roberts: "I'm disappointed, to be honest, in the amount of money we've spent and where we are today. We spent an awful lot of money to be at the beginning of the beginning.") In a mark of the plan's unpopularity, only Slater thanked staff. The motion passed unanimously.[1]

According to County documents, two days later, the San Diego Association of Realtors paid for dinner for the County assessor, Supervisors Roberts and Cox, and Roberts's chief of staff ($59 each). The form submitted to the County was signed by a lobbyist who eventually became an alternate on the new interest group committee.[2]

Fallout

Alternative III was both routine and unique. It was routine in that the people involved were the usual suspects—environmentalists, developers and homeowners—and they used their usual means of trying to influence the DPLU and the board: private meetings, letters, newspaper articles, phone calls, email and appearances at meetings. They did nothing unorthodox by local planning dispute

1. The "when in doubt, form a committee" approach was not unique to the board of supervisors. Barbara Czarniawska once quoted an interviewee: "I don't think it's anything special to just the [Swedish] National Social Insurance Board. Appointing an investigative committee is a method employed by central government and Parliament to get out of difficult situations. In the private business culture you have to take decisions very quickly in order to get ahead." Czarniawska, *Narrating the Organization: Dramas of Institutional Identity* (Chicago: University of Chicago Press, 1997): 113. But Jonathan Dimbleby quotes a Hong Kong tycoon as saying, "In business, when you don't want something to happen, you put it through a committee." Dimbleby, *The Last Governor: Chris Patten and the Handover of Hong Kong* (New York: Little Brown, 1997): 87. Or, as the inestimable British television series *Yes, Minister* put it, "I regard the interdepartmental committee as the last refuge of a desperate bureaucrat. When you can't find any argument against something you don't want, you set up an interdepartmental committee to strangle it. Slowly." Jonathan Lynn and Anthony Jay, eds., *The Complete Yes, Minister: The Diaries of a Cabinet Member* (New York: Harper & Row, Publishers, 1984): 39.
2. See Form LO5 [lobbyist disclosure form], filled out by Tracy Morgan Hollingsworth (registrant no. 589), dated April 13, 2001.

standards. They launched no hunger strikes. They engaged in no acts of vandalism or sabotage. But Alternative III was also unique. Most land use issues that came before the board were specific to one community. GP 2020 affected the entire backcountry. This complicated the politics tremendously.

While the board resolution did not give SOLV exactly what it wanted—a return to the current plan's housing capacity and hence no downzoning—it was undoubtedly a victory for the property rights advocates. After spending two years letting planning groups play at redesigning their communities, the landowners, when they were displeased, sledgehammered GP 2020 and redirected it to a trajectory more to their liking. Few expected the new committee to be balanced: the development interests would be paid to be there and the environmentalists would be volunteers—a war of attrition with obvious results.

Environmentalists were put in an awkward position. While they had not yet played a significant role in the plan update and some were frustrated with particular planning groups, their new powerful role came at a high price. They provided legitimacy to developers and landowners, for without the environmentalists, the new commit-tee would have looked like a bald sell-out to property. Furthermore, by their being on the same committee as the development inter-ests, environmentalists reinforced their image as outsiders telling communities what to do. If any of them considered boycotting the committee, however, they didn't discuss it in public.

The board's actions had mixed impact on DPLU staff. On one hand, the Alternative III controversy hurt their reputation and demonstrated the board's lack of confidence in them. On the other hand, at least one planner was pleased with what the board had done. For two years, staff had labored without direction, slogging through an update basically in a facilitator's role to the planning and sponsor groups. The board's request for three different alter-natives of what growth could look like was a green light to go and actually do some planning.

The big losers in the controversy were the members of the steering committee. They had been blamed, not entirely accurately, for the problems with the Alternative III map, so their credibility was low. The creation of a new committee that was to be of equal influence substantially diminished their power and was seen as a rebuke. Before, they had been comfortable with the process, except for where they disagreed with the map, but, with the new interest group committee, anything could happen—a demoralizing turn of events.

CHAPTER SEVENTEEN
THE QUERULOUS TWO-
HEADED HYDRA

The January 10, 2001 board hearing did little to diminish the uncertainty about the general plan update. Scrapping Alternative III gave breathing room to landowners, but all the tensions between environmentalists, homeowners and developers remained. The mission of the new interest group committee was unclear, as was the point of the three new growth alternatives the board requested. Indeed, as Horn wanted the meeting over by four o'clock, the meeting ended in a rush and a few of the supervisors seemed a little unclear about what they were voting on.

In February, the steering committee met for the first time since September—that is, for the first time since the Alternative III controversy began in earnest. Attendance was high. The meeting revolved around the relationship between the steering committee and the new interest group committee. That the members of the new committee might not even live in the unincorporated parts of the county and might have serious conflicts of interest caused considerable consternation. The steering committee passed a unanimous motion requesting that their counterparts be required to fill out the standard Form 700 financial disclosure forms. There was much confusion about what was to happen next. If Alternative III represented their input and that was rejected, then what status did their input have?

The new interest group committee—whose name was often reduced to the "interest group" except by steering committee members who called it the "special interest group"—met for the first time less than a week later. Since some members knew little of GP 2020, the meeting laid out the plan update's framework. Staff described the three concepts as they had evolved since the January 10 board meeting. Concept A was compact village centers: growth would be concentrated in the cores of the existing country towns. Concept B was similar to the first but was more spread out—sprawl, pure and simple, in the eyes of environmentalists. Concept C was called *transportation corridors.* This was to keep Supervisor Horn happy.

Soon thereafter, Thure Stedt—SOLV member and Horn appointee—resigned from the planning commission when the County's committee on incompatible activities claimed he, as the owner of a development consultant company, had a high potential for conflict of interest. The *Union-Tribune* noted his resignation in a short piece and then blasted the supervisors for their role in the matter.[1] The paper conceded, however, that no one had suggested that Stedt had done anything improper.

In response, a small effort was made to get Michael Beck off the commission as well, on the grounds that the Endangered Habitats League, whose San Diego chapter he led, negotiated with the County on land purchases for open space preservation and thus he too had a persistent conflict of interest. The County did not pursue this aggressively, if at all.

With distrust between developers and environmentalists high, the interest group committee met again almost four weeks later. Like the steering committee, environmentalists wanted everyone to

1. Brian E. Clark, "Stedt Quits County Planning Board," *San Diego Union-Tribune,* March 14, 2001.

submit the Form 700 financial disclosure statements. The developers were opposed, arguing that everyone knew they had financial interests at stake—they were called the interest group committee for a reason—and that the form was irrelevant as their conflicts stemmed from their clients, not their personal finances. After forty-five minutes of haggling, the committee agreed on a compromise: everyone would go around the room describing their organization and its stake in GP 2020. The environmentalists admitted to few direct interests, save that downzoned land would be cheaper to buy for open space preservation. The committee decided to meet the following week.

During the intervening weekend, the steering committee met and again devoted much of its energy to venting about and struggling to define themselves against the new interest group committee. Many on the steering committee were opposed to cooperating with the new committee for fear of granting it legitimacy, especially as County counsel just declared that since the interest group was not a standing committee, its members need not submit Form 700. The steering committee members had to fill out this form annually to be on their planning and sponsor groups and found it galling that they had to disclose their financial stakes in the unincorporated county while an unrepresentative group of special interests did not. The steering committee voted almost unanimously to request that the board have the interest group committee disclose their financial interests, even though the law did not require it. Another motion, led by Dutch Van Dierondonck, who was vocal about being realistic, expressed support for a joint meeting with the new committee. It failed by one vote.

At the end of the meeting, steering committee members expressed one of their deepest fears: the plan would have loopholes which developers could exploit. They were worried about a repeat of the "plan-busting" 4S Ranch development, which they saw as the epitome of what was wrong with County planning.

Two days later, the interest group committee met again and discussed the new plan's goals and policies and the three new concepts (A, B, C) that the board had requested. The development interests argued that the committee was allowed to examine the goals and policies crafted by the steering committee because the board of supervisors's "endorsing'" them twice indicated only tentative support. The Building Industries Association representative, Matt Adams, had a list of ten policies he wished to reopen, all of which limited density. Others on his side had additional issues with the steering committee's work. Indeed, one complained that some proposed policies were counter to sound planning and precluded good developments... like the 4S Ranch.

Planning Director Gary Pryor admitted that staff did not completely agree with the goals and policies as written. He pointed out a contradiction between two policies and agreed to a reexamination of the steering committee's work. Tinkering was acceptable, he said, but a wholesale rewrite, however, was out of the question.

The discussion of the three growth concepts that the board wished to see was more confused because it was unclear what they should look like or what would be done with them. Everyone agreed, however, that no unincorporated community would fit any one perfectly.

Dan Silver of the Endangered Habitats League threw out some possible definitions for the concepts. This marked out the main environmental position for the early part of the life of the committee. Silver was especially interested in Concept A, which he envisioned as a kind of transit-oriented development. It began with a perhaps half-mile wide core. He wasn't sure the density necessary to make public transit viable there and grabbed at "two hundred dwelling units per acre." (If anyone else in the room had a better estimate, they didn't say.) Surrounding this core was the *core support area*, which was considerably less dense—four to ten dwelling units per acre—and stretched out for another half mile. Surrounding this would be "the semi-rural" with half acre to four-acre lots and no urban services. This would be surrounded by a greenbelt.

When members of the steering committee read the minutes of the meeting, they went ape: they couldn't believe that someone who could suggest two-hundred dwelling unit per acre housing was sitting on a committee that had a say in the future of the county. (In fact, the only buildings that dense in the region were a handful of skyscraper condominium projects in downtown San Diego.)

The Interest Group Committee, Habits and Behavior

Karen Scarborough, who had been a member of Mayor Susan Golding's staff and chair of the MSCP committee, became the chair of the interest group committee. She worked to build consensus in the heat of the debate, preferring to generate an atmosphere of give-and-take in which people had to compromise on the spot without the opportunity to go back and consult with their groups. She discouraged grandstanding and instead focused people on what motion language they would accept then and there. Since the essence of these meetings was compromise under pressure, the committee, unlike the steering committee, which had a more leisurely pace, did not take breaks except under special circumstances.

The afternoon meetings were typically held every other week in the tower of the County Administration Center and lasted for two and a half hours. They were focused on the wording of one motion that would represent their day's work. Often, agreement about the wording was not to be reached until the last ten minutes. Afterward, a few members of the public spoke, some every week.

Although the neat environmentalist vs. developer split would eventually be complicated by infighting and divide-and-conquer tactics, the sides were clear at first. The environmentalists held strategy sessions at the National Wildlife Federation office. Initially, they met at the same time on the weeks opposite of the biweekly meetings but then decided to meet less frequently. The developers, on the other hand, established a pattern of meeting for lunch at eleven in the County Administration Center cafeteria before the 12:15 meetings. They reviewed minutes and worked on strategies when their respective positions were in agreement. (They probably also dealt with how to deal with disagreements, as they rarely surfaced during the meetings.)

At first, the development side had an advantage. Not only did the huddles before the official meetings allow them to coordinate, for the most part they did not represent democratically organized groups but simply had to think economically about whether a given proposed motion penciled out. As long as they were opposing proposals that cost them money and not having to sign off on any replacement proposals, they were highly disciplined in public.

One case was particularly telling. The committee was discussing what kind of development was acceptable in the eastern portions of the county, beyond the area that the County Water Authority serviced. Since the lack of imported water meant that large-scale development was out of the question, the developers were initially willing to support requiring very large lots. Al Stehly of the Farm Bureau, however, objected strenuously, complaining that farmers, who were under-represented on the committee as it was, were being sold downriver. The developers withdrew their support, pending language that Stehly could accept. Nothing of the sort happened on the environmentalist side.

The developers had a laundry list of concrete grievances against GP 2020. Jim Whalen was especially interested in preventing what he called "double dipping"—that is, having additional land be prohibited from development for environmental reasons, which he saw as a penalty on landowners who had voluntarily set aside land in the MSCP program. Matt Adams focused on the steering committee's goals and policies. And, of course, they all wished to preserve the landowners' and developers' economic investments in land.

The developers fell into a good cop/bad cop routine. Jim Whalen, who was one of the founders of the Alliance for Habitat Conservation, a group of large landowners that wanted to rationalize the process of allocating land to development and sensitive habitat, was the good cop. Until he, like many others, grew frustrated with the whole process, he seemed to enjoy the game of diplomacy, trying to figure out what the environmentalists would accept and then creating "win-win" solutions. Most everyone else on the developer side played the bad cop.

In the early meetings, developer rhetoric stressed the importance of having a map that recognized "market realities," meaning that they be allowed to build the housing people wanted to buy. In other words, Smart Growth principles were not be used to force them to build multifamily housing or small-lot single-family houses when homes on one- to four-acre lots sold. Talk of "market realities" also had an undertone that suggested the amateurishness of the environmentalists, as it implied that their desires were pie in the sky.

The environmentalists began with serious disadvantages. As volunteers, they had worse attendance than the developers, and several were naive. Their agenda was also defuse. They spoke of staying within the carrying capacity of the land, an idea that was hard to define or quantify, and thus was of limited use in trying to hammer out concrete proposals. Indeed, it was slightly dangerous: there was the risk that in a compromise developers would get something concrete for their involvement while environmentalists would get planning platitudes. (Consequently, the environmentalists favored the more specific language of doing a "gap analysis" to understand exactly what ecologically was at risk.)

The environmentalists' testimony before the planning commission and board of supervisors suggested that at least some of them thought the 660,000-person population goal the planning and sponsor groups wanted was too high. But they became committed to it as the best they could hope for. The supervisors had twice approved the figure and reexamining it would likely have led to something worse. (After all, SOLV was pressuring the County to stick with the existing capacity of 855,000 persons.) Since the best case scenario for environmentalists was a general plan that allowed enough sprawl for 200,000 more people, environmentalists were not in a position to gain much from their presence on the committee. They had to search out the small compromises, like more density in the centers of town to preserve more open space.

The environmentalists, however, were unable to agree on the small compromises or maintain a united front, which became a great weakness. They epitomized a problem George Lakoff sees as endemic to the American left: after describing how the leadership of the American right meets weekly and hammers out compromises that ensure most everyone gets most of what they want most of the time, he observes, "Nothing like this happens in the progressive world, because there are so many people thinking that what each does is *the* right thing. It is not smart. It is self-defeating."[2] The environmentalists did meet regularly at first, but they were never able to stick to a message. They were divided between those willing to compromise quickly and those who had doubts about compromising at all. The most resistant to compromise was Eric Bowlby of the Sierra Club (which claimed to have 15,000 members throughout the county). Bowlby had deep reservations about the premises underlying the direction of GP 2020. While the developers insisted on some way to preserve the economic value of the land, Bowlby had serious misgivings about the practicality of the "equity mechanisms" they proposed. Since so many of the motions were predicated on the assumption that landowners' economic values were to be protected, he habitually abstained from motions. This was the ultimate sin in the eyes of the developers: he was not "someone you could work with." At one point, a developer asked him point blank whether he thought he had the votes on the board to get his agenda accepted, and his apparent unwillingness to even think in those terms frustrated the development side. When they spoke of him, it was with contempt (though, ironically, they came to share his views about whether equity mechanisms would work).

On the other hand, Dan Silver focused on making bargains with developers with little apparent concern for whether the other environmentalists were onboard. Typically, Silver proposed language; the developers attacked it; and then Whalen offered a modification acceptable to the developers, which they would support along with half of the environmentalists.

---

2. George Lakoff, *Don't Think of an Elephant: Know Your Values and Frame the Debate* (White River Junction, Vermont: Chelsea Green Publishing, 2004): 16.

The environmentalists, however, did have a few cards in their hands. First and foremost, the environmentalists believed they were right. No one could claim that they were merely hired guns. At times, they were dogged, and, once the committee began to fall apart, the advantages of the developers weakened. Arguably, even Bowlby's quiet stubbornness was effective—effective that is, at wearing down the developers: they were highly talented people who had to wonder whether there weren't more rewarding ways to spend the peak years of their lives than to interact, year after year, with someone who was impervious to their viewpoints. (At least one implied as much when talking to me.)

The reverse of developer "market realities" was the rhetoric of "preserving community character." This all-purpose club against growth—any major development, by definition, changes a community's character—was a favorite of community groups, and environmentalists sometimes took advantage of it as well since it implied that growth was an intrusion. Environmentalists were less enthusiastic when the steering committee and planning groups used it to fight the increased densities in town centers, which most, if not all, environmentalists believed a necessary trade-off to protecting open space.

Perceptions of the New Interest Group Committee

Insofar as people even knew of its existence, the interest group committee had little legitimacy in the unincorporated communities. It was seen as arrogant, developer dominated and ignorant of local conditions. Sometimes, representatives of backcountry groups attended its meetings to carry back news of its doings, and what they saw likely reinforced their preconceptions: some committee members talked as if they were hammering out the new general plan singlehandedly. Also, small property owners were not necessarily enthusiastic about either the Farm Bureau or developers, whom they saw as representing fat-cat interests—and not the average landowner with a handful of acres.

Many members of the steering committee, of course, hated the interest group and continued the antagonistic relationships they had with developers from before GP 2020. The developers on the new committee reciprocated the hostility. Then, to complete the picture, the property rights defenders on the steering committee saw the environmentalists on the interest group as a direct threat to their way of life.

The steering committee and the interest group were, per board direction, to have equal influence over GP 2020. This meant that the process had in effect two steering committees that were not on speaking terms—an awkward situation, though one that gave staff more room to maneuver.

This split-personality problem in GP 2020 was exacerbated by the lack of communication between the two committees. Formally, the committees learned about each other's activities through two sources. First, they were given each other's minutes. While at this time the quality of the minutes dramatically improved compared to earlier in GP 2020, nuances of meaning were invariably lost. This allowed members of the committees to assume the worst in each other statements—or rather it allowed the steering committee to assume the worst about the interest group, which all but ignored its counterpart. The second formal way the committees learned of each other's actions were briefings by staff or the committee chair. Staff, which was the source of information for the chairs, was aggressively optimistic, if not euphemistic, in its assessments.

The committees had several informal ways of learning about each other. Depending on who asked, staff on an individual basis probably gave committee members more candid assessments about what was happening. Some of the environmentalists had ongoing projects in unincorporated communities and thus worked with planning and sponsor groups. Also, the few people who attended the meetings of both were conduits of information. (In March 2003,

Bonnie Gendron, the Backcountry Coalition's representative on the interest group, was appointed to fill an empty seat on the Julian planning group, whose chair was also on the board of SOFAR.)

If information did not follow one of those routes, which all had their biases, it did not pass from one committee to the other. This led to some unusual situations. Early on, for example, one of the property rights advocates on the steering committee resented the environmentalists on the interest group for not having to fill out a financial disclosure form. He had no idea that the environmentalists had argued that the interest group members should submit the forms and had contemplated voluntarily filling out the form to pressure the developers to do so as well. If the two had joined forces, they might have succeeded at this modest mutual goal. But they didn't, so they didn't.

CHAPTER EIGHTEEN
LOOKING FOR COMPROMISES
AND MONEY

A round the time the supervisors nixed Alternative III, the project manager for GP 2020 transferred off the project. The position remained vacant until May because its pay did not tempt applicants. On May 4, 2001, the DPLU was reorganized. GP 2020 became its own division, whose titular head would be "chief," which would have a higher pay grade than project manager. An open search was held for that position. The thankless job fell to one of the DPLU's own, Ivan Holler. Holler, a resident of Fallbrook, had previously been on Supervisor Horn's staff. Despite—or perhaps because—he had no prior role in GP 2020, he quickly won the confidence of many people. In interviews for this research, in which people rarely offered any positive observations about anyone else, he was praised for the speed at which he came to understand the process, his political astuteness and his grasp of the details of the project.

The day after Ivan Holler joined the GP 2020 team, the steering committee met again. The chair of the interest group, Karen Scarborough, gave them an overview of what her committee was doing, which led into and-yet-another unhappy discussion of the relationship between the two committees.

The meeting was also a chance to discuss a new, extremely ambitious phase of the general plan update, the revision of all twenty-six community plan texts. Pryor's goal was to streamline and rationalize the general plan. He felt that there was material in the community plans that belonged in the regional elements of the plan or in the zoning code. While some information was merely redundant with the regional elements, other parts contradicted them. This allowed developers to argue for whichever interpretation best suited their interests but also allowed anyone disgruntled with a development to sue because of the plan's internal inconsistency.

The revision of the community plans began over the summer with three public meetings led by staff. Then community-created subcommittees crafted the actual language of the plans, which, true to GP 2020 form, sometimes became drawn-out affairs. The initial meetings took an enormous amount of staff time, required pulling in planners from other divisions. This meant that some of those who would be the public face of the DPLU had just gotten onboard GP 2020.

This revision of the community plans was controversial at the steering committee. At the beginning of GP 2020, many of the planning and sponsor groups had expressed an interest, to a greater or lesser extent, in updating their community plans. Indeed, several were in the midst of doing so. Wholesale rewriting of community plans, however, made uneasy those on the committee suspicious of change. They saw the redundancy between the general plan and community plans as a safeguard: if something a community wanted was only in either the general plan or the zoning code, a general plan amendment or change to the zoning code—something a community planning group had no control over—could significantly alter the community's future.

On May 19, environmentalists held a one-day Smart Growth conference on the University of California, San Diego campus. Supervisor Slater was a speaker. She claimed that a silent majority of Americans considered themselves environmentalists, including two-thirds of Hispanics. She said that Americans were not environmental activists because they felt everything was okay. They were increasingly realizing, however, that everything was *not* okay. It was impossible to build suburbs to infinity, and she offered an alternate vision of the future, based on vibrant cities, giving as an example Dupont Circle in Washington, D.C.

———————————

Four days later—Wednesday, May 23—the board of supervisors was presented with its first progress report since they had intervened in GP 2020 in January. Gone were the days when the reports were accepted on consent. Public comments fell into two categories.

First, members of the new interest group committee, as well as some observers, roundly endorsed the progress they had been making. The committee, after having gotten past the initial deep skepticism, was in euphoria, as the different sides agreed on a number of things in principle and hadn't yet analyzed their proposed solutions carefully enough to see whether they would actually work. They were optimistic about their Concept D, an addition to the three concepts the board requested, which would keep the eastern part of the county from developing. Furthermore, any concern about downzoning was mollified, at least temporarily, by the deputy CAO stressing that there was "no presumption of downzoning" in the process.

On the other hand, community planning group activists—the "usual suspects" in the eyes of developers (Phillips, Shackelford, etc.)—protested that the interest-group lovefest hid disturbing trends. They argued that the residents were being disenfranchised because the new direction of the update was inconsistent with Board Policy I-1, which described how community plans were to be written in coordination with the planning groups. They claimed that over 75 percent of the interest group committee did not live in the unincorporated county and that one (Dan Silver) lived in Los Angeles.

After all the controversy they had listened to in January, the supervisors were pleased with the accolades heaped on Scarborough and the interest group committee. They were not about to question its legitimacy by belatedly asking for financial disclosure from its members. Instead of following the CAO's boiler-plate motion to proceed with the creation of a new land use distribution and consider the financial disclosure issue, Horn instead proposed his own motion. After being tinkered with by the other supervisors, it in part read that the board "directed the Interest Group to evaluate the feasibility of using the existing General Plan and to incorporate Concepts A, B, C and D as drafted as soon as possible; return to the board within 90 days with a report on that decision and any suggestions that they have detailing out implementation plans."

At face value, this would be difficult to do, if not contradictory: applying the concept would require changing the land use distribution, which couldn't be done while using the existing general plan. The idea of "using the existing general plan" was what the developers wanted. It meant to them, in essence, not downzoning anyone but having a voluntary transfer of development rights to clear unbuilt housing units out of the eastern reaches of the county. In other words, all the housing units that could be built under the current plan would still be built, maybe just not in the same place.

The board also responded to a request from realtors to give them representation on the interest group, which also meant adding another environmentalist to maintain the numerical balance. One would not be found to join the committee until August. She would do much to deflate the high spirits of the committee.

Money Matters

According to County documents, the day before the board hearing, the interest group developer Jim Whalen donated $500 to Supervisor Horn's reelection campaign. His interest group alternate, Scott Molloy gave $250. The day before that, Bruce Tabb and Gary Piro—both developers on the interest group committee—gave $500 and $250 respectively. (The same day a past president of the Farm Bureau gave $500.) Six days before the meeting, Dave Shibley—future SOLV representative on the interest group—and his wife gave $500. And finally, the developer Greg Lambron gave $500 on the first day of the month. The only other development side member legally able to give money to Bill Horn's campaign, Al Stehly of the Farm Bureau, did not do so. He did, however, give $100 to Ron Roberts's campaign.

These donations were not unique, in two senses. First, they were simply part of a deluge of money falling into Horn's campaign chest from development and land interests. People with connections to SOLV, for example, donated at least $6,065 in May 2001 to Horn. Second, the donations to the board of supervisors by the men on the interest group were not their only times they opened their checkbooks.[1]

SOLV's Gary Piro donated $250 to Horn's failed senate bid (August 26, 1999). He also gave $100 to Roberts's 2000 mayoral campaign. For the day after the May 23 hearing, Supervisor Roberts's Form 700 listed receiving a gift of "Heritage Golf Classic" worth $85 from the developer Bruce Tabb.[2] Two years earlier, Tabb and his wife—occupation: homemaker—simultaneously gave $250 to Supervisor Greg Cox's 2000 campaign.[3] Eight months later, they did again: $1,000 each for Horns failed senatorial bid. On June 7, 2001, Tabb also gave $500 to Supervisor Slater's 2004 reelection campaign, as did a number

1. These donations can be found in Friends of Bill Horn/Bill Horn 2002 Form 490 for the first half of 2001. For Stehly, see Ron Roberts for Mayor, Form 460, same time period, p. 10. The federal contributions are from www.tray.com.

The estimate of SOLV contributions is conservative in that neither the SOLV membership list made publicly available nor the campaign contributions were alphabetized, and, in the case of SOLV, only one name appeared on each piece of paper. Thus a thorough cross-referencing would have taken days, meaning that the calculations were based on more prominent members whose names I recognized.

2. Roberts's campaign filled out the form incorrectly, putting the golf course's address and not the gift giver's address (see California Form 700, schedule E, signed off by Roberts on December 6, 2001). There does not appear to be any other Bruce Tabb living in the San Diego area at the time, however, and the developer Tabb gave to other elected officials so it is unlikely that it was someone else. Since the golf tournament was actually held on May 24 and supervisors have such busy schedules, the gift was probably given before the board meeting, as it seems unlikely that this gift would have been given after the hearing for a tournament held the next day.

3. Bruce and Cheri Tabb, 6/30/99, p. 55 of Form 490, Schedule A, Mr. Gregory R. Cox, Greg Cox 2000.

of people on the SOLV mailing list.[4] Five weeks later—that is, less than two months after giving Roberts the tickets to the golf tournament—Tabb donated $500 to his 2002 supervisor campaign.[5] (Also giving to the Roberts campaign was the president of a development company whose projects had been downzoned in Alternative III and who was employing Jim Whalen.[6])

The biggest contributor on the interest group, however, was the quiet Greg Lambron, who gave $1,000 for Horn's Senate campaign (March 31, 2000), and, on October 22, 2002, gave $500 to the Friends of Gregory Cox. The bulk of his contributions, however, were for persons and causes unrelated to GP 2020, including quite liberal ones.

The registered lobbyists on the interest group—Matt Adams, Dan Silver and Lynne Baker (Silver's alternate)—were prohibited from giving money to County candidates. A month after giving to the Horn campaign, Whalen registered as a lobbyist as well. Before GP 2020 was over, Al Stehly also registered.

Developers sometimes grumbled that these contributions were not in fact completely voluntary, but they were also themselves capable of cynicism about the influence of other people's money. At a meeting in September 2002, the interest group committee discussed a state bill that would have given Indian tribes a say in development within twenty miles of their sacred sites (including most of San Diego County). Those on the development side said that the tribes could buy good PR, just as they bought the state legislature. Another suggested that the governor's stance on the bill could be ascertained by looking at his list of donors.

The summer of 2001 was a busy time for the general plan update. DPLU staff worked on what they would call the *regional*

4. Friends of Pam Slater 2004, Form 460, first half of 2001.

5. Friends of Pam Slater 2004, Form 460, first half of 2001, p. 11. Ron Roberts for Supervisor 2002, Form 460, third quarter, p. 15.

6. Whalen's client was the Gildred Development Company. See Whalen's letter to Gary Pryor (October 20, 2000) objecting to the downzoning and Ron Roberts for Supervisor 2002, third quarter 2001 Form 460, p. 10.

structure map—the rough draft of a replacement to Alternative III. Communities kicked off the process of updating their local plans with introductory meetings that ranged from docile and poorly attended to hostile and overcrowded. In June, the board of supervisors, which earlier in the year had raised the maximum political contribution from $250 a person to $500, considered doubling it again but declined to do so. The Sierra Club worked with several backcountry communities to establish building moratoria to prevent a rush of development before the new general plan was finalized. The effort sputtered out after the proposed moratorium in Ramona was presented to the planning commission and no action was taken.

The interest group had two allegedly joint meetings with the steering committee during the steering committee's usual Saturday morning time slot. These weren't so much joint meetings as presentations that members of both committees were invited to attend. Steering committee members, leery of creating the impression that they accepted the existence of the interest group, literally kept their distance from its members. (When a developer tried to schmooze the steering committee member sitting beside me, he was met with cold monosyllabic responses.) Since these presentations took place in lieu of steering committee meetings, that committee did not meet for over two months, fueling the sense that the center of gravity of the plan update had shifted towards the interest group, which held six meetings during that time.

One of the joint meetings was a presentation by local transit guru Alan Hoffman, who discussed how the strategies he described to City's Community Planners Committee (last case study) could be applied to the unincorporated county. Since so much of the backcountry was rural, he did not have as much inspiration to offer. Steering committee members interpreted him through their suspicion of outside experts, even though it was the low densities they preferred that limited the options available.

Much more significant to GP 2020 than mass transit were the presentations on TDR (transfer of development rights). It was developers who advocated TDR, which then had also just caught the fancy of many environmental legal scholars across the country.[7] In theory, such a program would permit open space preservation while compensating landowners for their economic investments. It would have worked like this: if developers wished to build in a particular area (the receiving area) above the density allowed by the zoning code, they had to buy the right to build the additional units off the land elsewhere (the sending area). The land from which the units were bought would be preserved as open space. For instance, say a developer wanted to build ten houses on an acre of land in town but the parcel's zoning only permitted the construction of two houses. The developer then could buy permission to build the additional eight units from another parcel of land, perhaps belonging to a farmer whose land was zoned for urban uses but who wanted to keep farming. Once the permission to build the eight additional homes had been bought, the farmland would be covered with a conservation easement to prevent it from being developed.

This was an elegant compromise. For environmentalists, future growth could be directed to where they wanted it—in more built up areas—and the land they wished to be preserved would be, at low cost. For the property owners, they would retain the value of their land, even if it were downzoned. TDRs, then, were a potential win-win situation.

At the joint steering committee/interest group meetings, it became apparent that TDR programs were tricky to implement and maintain. No program had been done before on the scale of San Diego County and, to gain the acquiescence of property owners, the County would have to implement it quickly—simultaneous with any downzoning. The sheer magnitude of political and technical issues made such speed unlikely.

And it might well have been impossible. If the current plan's

7. Gregory S. Alexander, "Propriety through Commodity? Why Have Legal Environmentalists Embraced Market-based Solutions?" in *Private Property in the 21st Century: The Future of an American Ideal*, ed. Harvey M. Jacobs, 75–91 (Cheltenham, UK and Northampton, MA: Edward Elgar, 2004).

housing would generate enough development credits for a population of 855,000 persons and the new plan would only expend enough credits to reach 660,000, then there would be tens of thousands of excess credits. Each credit would be worth so little—supply would outstrip demand—that selling credits would not recoup the loss of economic value that downzoning entailed. This could have been mitigated by stipulating that developers had to buy more than one development credit to build each additional home, but this made a TDR program less appealing to them.

Also, there was a very basic political problem: as with many proposed TDR programs, no one was volunteering to be a receiving area. Residents there would have to pay more to live at higher densities so other people could live in a more pristine environment—a scenario that did not garner much enthusiasm, even though developers, seeing multifamily housing as too controversial, only wanted to increase the densities from approximately four houses to an acre to six or seven, claiming that it wouldn't make that much difference to the people who lived in modestly denser homes.

Simultaneous to the discussions of TDRs, the interest group implicitly at first and then explicitly established one of the major points of agreement, namely moving future housing out of the further reaches of the backcountry and focusing it west of the County Water Authority (CWA) line, a line that ran raggedly north-to-south through the middle of the county. It marked the limits of where imported water would be provided and thus the limit of major development. This line became the interest group's continental divide: Concept A (compact development), Concept B (more diffuse), and Concept C (transit corridors) were put in place to the west of the line and the low-density Concept D would apply to the east. (The place of farms in this schema was challenging. Everyone wanted to give farmers the flexibility to continue what they were doing, but it was hard to distinguish between small farms and large-lot residential sprawl.)

The developers understood the compromise as moving units from the east of the line to the west of it. The environmentalists had a more complicated vision because they were not willing to write off everything west of the CWA line. The controversy over what would be preserved west of the CWA line was largely played out in an ongoing debate about the "semi-rural lands" of Concept B. Based on their understanding of market demand, developers thought it logical that much of the future growth would occur in these areas surrounding existing towns. Environmentalists, however, considered "semi-rural" a nice word for sprawl and wanted to minimize it.

Attached to all of these concepts was a kicker: if a TDR program amounted to nought, then the densities in the concepts would be reconsidered. This became known as "the asterisk" because the committee once agreed to put it into a motion as a footnote. It became a principle of the negotiations: all of their agreements, all their work, was predicated on an understanding that landowners' investments would be preserved, though even that was understood differently by the different sides. The developers wanted their economic values preserved. Environmentalists thought that that was asking too much—local governments did not insure invest-ments—and interpreted their agreement to the asterisk to mean that some kind of mechanism would, within the context of the land market, provide support for land prices but with no guarantees if the entire land market went south.

A significant but little noticed event took place at the June 18 meeting. (It didn't make it into the minutes.) The developers pressed for action on part of the supervisors' May 23 motion, namely the language about considering using the current general plan's land use distribution as a basis for the new plan. This in effect called for an end of the discussion of downzoning. Staff creatively side-stepped this by saying the analysis of the current general plan done in preparation for Alternative III was the analysis the board motion wanted. In other words, they claimed to have already done what the board was asking. SOLV's Gary Piro, however, was unhappy with this. He said that he had talked to Horn's office about the motion and what staff was suggesting was not what was intended when the motion was written. But Scarborough didn't like the idea of getting into authorial intentions and wanted to go with motions as they would be commonly understood. So died the most direct effort by developers to undercut the direction of the general plan update.

On July 28, the steering committee met for the first time in almost three months. They tackled the interest group's four concepts. Simply put, they tore them apart. Staff and the interest group understood the four concepts as creating guidelines for developing a new map, something more coherent than just planning and sponsor groups drawing with markers. The steering committee members, however, were afraid that each community would be pigeonholed into one of the four concepts, even though staff and Karen Scarborough denied it. They were especially afraid that the concepts would be used to justify upzones in their downtowns because the village core and core support areas of Concepts A and B were defined by higher densities than existed in many of the communities.

The steering committee redefined the concepts merely as "tools in the toolbox" which individual communities could use insofar as they found them helpful. They wrote a preamble to the concepts to that effect. Then they revised the individual bullet points that described the concepts. They deleted all references to specific housing densities except Concept D's rural lands, which they changed from one dwelling unit per 80 or 160 acres to one per 40 acres. They deleted the references to clustering. They also nixed the prohibition of Concept A and B east of the CWA line, not because they wanted the densities those concepts implied in the eastern part of the county—many would probably be aghast at the notion if they thought it through—but because they didn't want limits on what they could do. They also strengthened the language about preserving community character.

As these changes were in the direction of making the concepts flexible to the point of uselessness, they likely had little effect on the map replacing Alternative III that was in the works.

From August to October, the interest group committee went on three tours of the backcountry. The committee members said the tours were helpful, but these trips also underscored their outsider status, as they wouldn't have been necessary if they had all been familiar with the backcountry. (The steering committee members were too focused on their own communities to tour.)

Meanwhile, the board of supervisors was embroiled in a controversy that further demoralized community participants in the GP 2020 update. The 2000 census showed that the county had grown unevenly over the 1990s, meaning that the supervisor districts needed to be reapportioned. A citizens committee developed two new maps, which were presented to the board at the end of June. Supervisor Horn proposed a third map, one that took wealthy areas from Supervisor Slater's district and put them into his, giving her in exchange the more working-class, Latino, Democratic Escondido. This left her district with an odd shape, like the cross-section of an I-beam with a fuzzy ball—Escondido—resting on the top of one section. Horn justified this map on numerous grounds: it reunited Carlsbad, it put the communities along the I–15 corridor into a unified district, and so on. A little more than two weeks later, the board approved this new map 4–1, with Supervisor Slater adamantly opposed.

Newspapers went ballistic. They portrayed the board as self-serving and Machiavellian, if not in violation of the Brown Act sunshine law because the new map was created behind closed doors but also the Voter Act because it was claimed to be an implicit quest to keep the board in the hands of white Republicans. In the conspiracy theory—rejected by a court two years later—Horn got developable land and wealthy areas that were a source of campaign contributions. He shed Escondido, which was the hometown of his last campaign opponent and which had not supported him electorally. Dianne Jacob got Spring Valley in one district.[8] Cox

8. Of all these changes, putting Spring Valley entirely into one supervisor district was arguably the one most motivated by the needs of the community, as it was a concrete

got some wealthier areas and Roberts had his district go from 59 percent minority down to 52 percent, increasing his chances of getting reelected. Slater was portrayed as the victim of her rapacious fellow board members.[9]

The redistricting did not bode well for GP 2020. The scenario was obvious: at the end, after people had poured incredible amounts of time and energy into a plan, the board would summarily toss aside their efforts and do whatever they wanted, namely please developers and landowners. At a steering committee meeting shortly after the new district map was approved, one community group chair expressed a common feeling: "I don't mind being out of order when I say that there's not a lot of confidence in the board of supervisors right now"—to which people clapped. The uncertainty of the plan update, then, went up a notch. No matter how well the plan appeared to be going, in the end, it could blow up in everybody's faces.

---

step towards overcoming the sense of political helpless that plagued residents. At one meeting I attended preceding the redistricting, a resident responded to the request of planner to brainstorm on community characteristics by suggesting, "Nobody loves us."

9. The newspaper coverage of this controversy was extensive. See: Christine Millay, "Fritz Announces Challenge to Horn for District 5 Seat," *San Diego Union-Tribune*, August 1, 2001; Caitlin Rother, "Horn Sets Off Tremors with Redistrict Plan," *San Diego Union-Tribune*, June 29, 2001; Dave Downey, "Horn Proposes County Redistricting Plan," *North County Times,* June 29, 2001; Downey, "Slater Offers to Negotiate with Horn over Redistricting," *North County Times,* July 4, 2001; Downey, "Escondido Officials Oppose Redistricting Plan," *North County Times,* July 10, 2001; Dave Downey and Marty Graham, "Supervisor Approve New District Map," *North County Times*, August 1, 2001; Luis Monteagudo Jr., "Board Faces Showdown Tomorrow on District Redrawing," *San Diego Union-Tribune*, July 9, 2001; Monteagudo, "Horn Remap Plan Wins," *San Diego Union-Tribune,* July 11, 2001; Monteagudo, "Supervisors Approve Redistricting Plan," *San Diego Union-Tribune,* July 18, 2001; Sherry Parmet and Jonathan Heller, "Redrawn Political Lines Viewed with Cynicism," *San Diego Union-Tribune* July 11, 2001; Lisa Ross, "Redistricting Games: The Rancho Santa Fe Chip," *Del Mar Times,* July 6, 2001. This section was also based on a September 4, 2001 document produced by the Office of Aguirre and Meyer entitled, "Re: Demand to Cure Brown Act Violation Regarding County Redistricting Made Under Gov Code §54960.1(b)(c)."

The New Map

At the end of August, DPLU staff presented to the steering committee and interest group the first draft of what would eventually replace Alternative III. To anyone expecting a full-blown replacement to the map that had generated so much controversy, the regional structure map disappointed.[10] To prevent a "this map is final and is the end of the world" reaction, the detail of the map was limited. While GIS software did not lend itself to fuzzy boundaries, the map key was vague. The map had four main colors, one for each of the main areas to be found in the interest group's Concepts A through D. To understand what the colors meant, the public had to consult other documents. Then, they would discover that each covered a broad range of densities and that the definitions of each color were fluid.

To further keep a lid on the map, staff did not make copies for distribution. In fact, there was only one copy of it seen by the committees, a 6' by 8' posterboard—tough to slip into a pocket while casually strolling out of the room. When the map was unveiled at the steering committee, however, at least one person took digital pictures of it during the break, allowing photos to be circulated.

In fact, with hindsight, this new map was the first expression of a philosophy that was developing at the DPLU. It would not become fully realized until later, but its general direction would quickly become apparent. This approach could be called the long seduction: go so slowly, make each decision so small, that no one would abandon the compromises being crafted. In short, boil a frog.

The steering committee was skeptical about the new map but were repeatedly assured that it was a draft not meant to hold up to small-scale scrutiny. But that was the only scrutiny the steering committee members wanted to provide. Typically uninterested in the kind of big picture discussion staff wanted, they couldn't do much with this map.

10. Ironically, despite the problems that beset Alternative III, staff found themselves digging it back out to figure out the implications of what they were doing, as it was the most detailed vision and analysis of possible change in the backcountry.

Two days after the steering committee saw the regional structure map, the initial spirit of cooperation on the interest group abruptly ended. As mentioned earlier, the supervisors had asked for a realtor to be added to the group. Liz Higgins agreed to do it, making her the only woman on the development side (out of seven members). Her positions were all but identical to the others, except she periodically reminded the group that they were ignoring housing affordability.

To maintain the numerical balance, Carolyn Chase joined the environmentalist side. She represented the Coalition for Transportation Choices but was recognized as a force in her own right. Adding her was like adding the final ingredient to nitroglycerine. Chase was, as one developer put it, mercurial: she worked towards compromises but also lashed out without warning, attacking developers in heavily moralistic terms. She had not participated in the months long process of building up rapport between members of the committee. She was not impressed by what the environmentalists had agreed to and wondered why they were sitting at the table if the plan wouldn't stop sprawl. She was blamed for poisoning the congenial relations on the committee. Actually, what she was doing was acting like the developers. That is, she was pushy, and having people on both sides push made it harder to maintain the illusion of common interests.

When Ivan Holler, the project manager, introduced the regional structure map, he assured the interest group it was a draft map, a "draft, draft, draft map." The discussion rapidly grew heated. Phil Pryde, who had been fairly quiet so far, thought his Concept D had been egregiously misapplied. He questioned whether whoever made the map even read the descriptions of the concepts the interest group agreed upon. How, he asked, could they be expected to have confidence if this is what happened to their input?

Bruce Tabb of Environmental Development was upset by the limitations to yellow (the map color for semi-rural). He wanted more land in the range of one- to four-acre lots. He was quite vocal about this, interrupting staff when they tried to explain that the concepts only included those size lots where they already existed. Stehly observed that maybe three percent of the land east of the CWA line was yellow and that if the yellow were wiped out there, they'd lose the support of the Farm Bureau. Not everyone was upset—some were guardedly optimistic—and by the end of the meeting the disagreements were patched up.

This meeting demonstrated the rhetorical upper hand of the developers. They issued ultimata, interrupted staff, did not even listen to others—they frequently got up during this meeting to consult in corners—and no one called them on it. When an environmentalist complained about how the developers were being unreasonable and when two other environmentalist pressed for implementing the concepts based on the compromises the committee had already reached, they were accused of being disingenuous.

As the steering committee meeting for September was cancelled in the wake of 9/11, the focus remained on the interest group. The compromise Scarborough was trying to craft began cracking up as the "grease of misperception" wore thin. It became obvious that the consensus was partially illusionary in that both sides agreed by defining the same thing in different ways.[11] Environmentalists thought they had been agreeing to minimize construction in semi-rural areas—"limit the yellow"—while the developers thought future growth should occur there, not in the village centers.

The second meeting of September revolved around a motion that spelled out what they had in fact agreed upon. The meeting repeatedly degenerated into multiple conversations, with Scarborough snapping, "Can we have one conversation please?" At one point, when developers noisily talked to each other while he was speaking, the usually soft-spoken Phil Pryde pounded the table and boomed, "The disrespect at this table must stop!"

The committee ended up with four variations of a motion to describe their progress at the board of supervisor's quarterly GP

11. Allison T. Graham, *Essence of Decision: Explaining the Cuban Missile Crisis* (Boston: Little, Brown & Company, 1971): 178. See also Patsy Healey, *Local Plans in British Land Use Planning* (Oxford: Pergamon Press, 1983): 6.

2020 update two days away. The committee went round and round on each point. The developers, for example, wanted to go ahead as if they had agreed to go forward with preserving the economic equity in the land. The environmentalists tactically embraced neoliberal rhetoric and claimed that developers wanted guarantees that went against the idea of markets (which might have been a better time to imply that they were being disingenuous).

Ultimately, they agreed to a statement that only a committee could devise. To wit: "Interest Group members agree to cooperate to zone areas to achieve the plan, with a concurrently activated mechanism program, to facilitate conservation values and the maintenance of landowner equity over time." This passed 13–5, with all five nays environmentalists.

CHAPTER NINETEEN
INFINITESIMAL PROGRESS

During the fall, the interest group worked on GP 2020's land use *categories*—Country Towns, Environmentally Constrained Areas, etc.—and the steering committee mainly focused on land use *designators*—office-professional, neighborhood commercial, etc. The *categories* dealt with the regional level, which was seen as the purview of the interest group, while the *designators* were below them in the general plan's hierarchy and too detailed (and too technical) for them. They were left to the steering committee, which of course took an interest in everything related to their immediate areas.

Steering committee members, especially Jack Phillips, had a number of specific concerns about the impact of the new system that staff proposed. Most of the uneasiness stemmed from the fear that changes could permit unintended reinterpretations of current rules, thus giving developers leverage to build bigger projects. If the terminology was changed, for example, what would happen to the mitigation required by an existing EIR since it was couched in a vocabulary that no longer related to anything in the general plan?

The committee approved several changes in the proposed schema, changes quite consistent with their (inconsistent) twin overarching objectives: change as little as possible and narrow the range of development as much as possible. For example, they voted to replace the "should" with "shall" in the sentence limiting infrastructure beyond urban limit lines and to delete the sentence encouraging infill. Both of these votes were aimed at limiting growth. But then they voted to allow estate development (one home per one to four acres) east of the CWA line if that was what was already in an area. This would allow growth where there was already similar growth.

This inconsistency had a method in its madness: it was a fusion of geographically specific rebellions against Smart Growth. The areas facing the more intensive suburbanization wanted to limit growth while remote areas that had little to fear from developers resisted restrictions from the distant County government. It was then a pact, embracing the whole of the unincorporated county, to not act regionally. It cut across the agenda of environmentalists and developers, meaning local community planning representatives could find allies and enemies in both groups.

At the interest group, staff and, to a lesser extent, environmentalists, pressed for change in the regional land use categories. The developers argued for retaining as much of the existing framework as possible. Explicitly, they said that they were skeptical of learning a whole new framework and that changing the categories would lead to a time-intensive rezoning of the entire county, but undoubtedly, they hoped that the less that changed, the more likely development projects then in the early stages would be unharmed by GP 2020.

Since there was so little communication between the two committees, the irony was lost on them: the community representatives and the developers, some of whom held each other in utter contempt, aggressively argued for nearly identical positions to thwart each other's aims. In both cases, what they resisted was staff's efforts to rationalize the general plan.

The interest group had a contentious fall. On every point—what kind of agriculture to allow east of the CWA line, whether existing specific plan areas should be grandfathered in, what residential densities were permissible in the semi-rural lands, how committed they were to TDRs—environmentalists and developers fought hard (and sometimes the environmentalists disagreed openly among themselves). They made progress on many compromises, but it wasn't clear whether they were making compromises faster than they were burning through goodwill.

Indeed, very little was clear. Not only was the interest group showing signs of falling apart, the compromises that they had reached were the product of intense negotiations that no one else felt bound by. Dutch Van Dierendonck, the chair of the Ramona planning group, said Planning Director Gary Pryor assured him that while the interest group would have equal *input*, it would not have equal *influence* with the steering committee. This was inconsistent with how the interest group committee members perceived their role.

Furthermore, the process of updating the community plan texts was proceeding apace, without a land use distribution map. If the community planning group wrote its text one way and the map of potential growth was inconsistent with its vision, then thorny questions would arise about how such conflicts would be resolved. Except for those who read into Supervisor Jacob's comments a guarantee for themselves—that changes wouldn't be forced upon communities; that everyone "would be made whole" (i.e., not lose money because of downzoning)—people seemed to be increasingly despairing of their views being respected in the end. As one participant put it, GP 2020 was like flushing a toilet: crap spinning round and round but ultimately going down the drain.

So the uncertainties continued, all cast against a backdrop of even greater uncertainty at a global scale after September 11, with daily headlines about elusive terrorists, bomb scares and missing radioactive material. In response, staff increasingly played a proactive role as it labored to craft the impossible compromise. With behind-the-scenes negotiation and baby steps, staff focused attention on the little concessions, trying to divert attention away the enormity of what had to be done.

Lurching towards an Alternative IV

In January 2002, the DPLU unveiled the next iteration of its replacement to Alternative III. Individual supervisors were briefed and then the map was shown to the interest group and the steering committee.

The basis of the map was the 6' by 8' uncorrected regional structure map. It was covered by a sheet of buff (tracing paper). Lines demarcating the densities were in pencil, so they could be (and were) adjusted with an eraser. The result, Holler warned the interest group before inviting them to take a closer look, was cluttered.

The committee's consensus was that the map was hard to interpret. To understand what was being proposed required looking at the buff and then lifting it up to see the underlying map, which was not easy to do in less than half an hour when other people were trying to do the same thing. Until the committee members could study the map more fully, they had no opinions.

When the steering committee saw it, they had the same reaction: they couldn't tell much just by glancing at it. A few sponsor groups—Boulevard, Twin Oaks and Pine Valley—complained that they saw no hint of their input in the map. The steering committee passed a motion to request that the map be digitized (put into GIS) so communities could take a look at it in a more readable format. The motion contained a caveat that the steering committee was not endorsing the map. During the break, again at least one person took pictures of it.

After this January meeting, the committee would not meet again until April. Before they met again, the interest group would meet seven times.

The January meeting was also the last time two longstanding members of the committee would sit at the table. Lakeside's community planning group rules kept Gordon Shackelford from continuing as its chair. The health of George Vanek of Alpine was diminishing, and he passed away five months later. Both were central to the steering committee's old guard, insisting that growth be on their own terms. Back in 1997, they had helped lobby the planning commission and board of supervisors to put the planning and sponsor groups in charge of the process.

The second time the interest group saw the new map, they voted to digitize it. The vote was unanimous except for Bowlby, who thought it had too much sprawl. The developers, however, spent much of the meeting resisting a list of corrections Dan Silver wanted taken into account before the map was put into GIS. The head of the Endangered Habitats League stressed that his corrections were deviations from the concepts that they had all agreed upon, deviations that didn't have any apparent justification. The developers didn't know what would be the implications of Silver's list, so, until SOLV's Piro said he had some changes he wanted incorporated as well, they were reluctant to entertain last-minute tweaks.

During the public comment period at the end of the meeting, Kevin Barnard, running against property-rights supporter Bill Horn in the district five supervisor primary, made a brief speech.

Supervisor Reelection Campaigns

Two district supervisors ran for reelection during the 2002 primary, Bill Horn and Ron Roberts. They were the most skeptical of GP 2020 and the least supportive of ambitious changes to the general plan.

In addition to Kevin Barnard, Supervisor Horn faced Patsy Fritz, who had long made it clear that she intended to run against him as she had in 1998 (coming in third in the primary). Since her views were so similar to Horn's, she ran a negative campaign to distinguish herself. Barnard, a retired police detective from the small unincorporated town of Harmony Grove, also ran a negative campaign but for the opposite reason: a Democrat in a heavily Republican district, he could only win by conveying the sense that something was terribly wrong with the incumbent. His support from the Sierra Club was so strong that the media portrayed him as its candidate.

Sierra Club members were quite hostile to Horn, for he seemed to think riparian habitat was a kind of golf hazard. Club members waded through the indigestible reams of financial and campaign disclosure statements Horn had submitted to the County, the results of which Carolyn Chase described in her February 1, 2002 column in the *San Diego Daily Transcript*. Most of Horn's donors, especially the most generous ones, were either developers or employees of a company with a stake in a project in or near his district. "Of Horn's donations," Chase wrote, "64 percent came from outside his district, with 20 percent of those coming from outside San Diego County, mainly from developers in Orange County."[1]

The environmentalists on the interest group (members and alternates) contributed $1,600 to Barnard's small campaign fund. These were unusual donations, as people connected with land development provided well over half of the contributions to supervisor races during GP 2020. Other unusual contributions came from Scott Peters (the San Diego city councilmember), Harry Frye (the husband of another councilmember), one of the County planning commissioners, Gordon Shackelford (leader of the Lakeside planning group vilified by SOLV) and Tom Mullaney of the Friends of San Diego (mentioned in the City of San Diego case study). These donations were probably all as much donations against Horn as they were for Barnard.[2]

Between a vastly larger war chest, a record of getting government money directed towards district five, and the release, shortly

1. The Sierra Club campaign against Horn had a subplot about trying to get him in trouble for allegedly illegal campaign contributions. Nothing came of it. See Carolyn Chase, "Horn: Contributions Legal and Proper; An Open Letter in Response to Marty Graham," February 7, 2002; Marty Graham, "Horn: Contributions Legal and Proper," *North County Times,* February 7, 2002; 10NEWS, "Supervisor's Campaign Contributions Questioned," online description of television segment, posted January 25, 2002: http://www.thesandiegochannel.com.
2. See the Forms 460, filed on behalf of Kevin Barnard for Supervisor.

before the election, of a national report claiming that San Diego was one of the best run counties in the country, Horn, with 53 percent of the vote, handily beat Barnard (29 percent) and Fritz (18 percent), avoiding a run-off in the general election.

Supervisor Roberts, whose district was largely in the City of San Diego, ran unopposed. Thus, the two supervisors friendliest to the development industry were securely in place for four more years, which could reasonably be assumed to see GP 2020 to the end. They were in no way beholden to environmentalists. (Recall that in his final failed attempt to run for mayor, the Sierra Club supported Roberts's opponent.)

With hindsight, one wonders why the environmentalists did not work to unseat Roberts instead: his district was the only one where Democrats significantly outnumbered Republicans, making him uniquely vulnerable. Replacing him wouldn't have been the prize of getting rid of Horn, but it would have left Horn partially isolated.

The Goals and Policies, Interest Group Style

In February, 2002, the interest group began revising the steering committee-drafted and board-endorsed goals and policies. The environmentalists were unenthusiastic about opening them up for changes. While they recognized problems with specific wordings, they generally found them acceptable. Matt Adams of the Building Industries Association, however, was the driving force behind the revision. He wanted to eliminate what he considered to be the steering committee's systematic bias against development. With the help of several others on the committee, he created a developer version of the goals and policies that outlined in red ink the changes they wanted. In the housing and land use sections (the ones most critical to the building industry), there was as much red ink as black.

Staff took a curious position. Pryor had long said that they could tinker or wordsmith but not make wholesale changes. As the committee slid down the slope towards completely rewriting the goals and policies, however, staff encouraged significant amendments, even though they were putting themselves in a crossfire by having to adjudicate between two substantially different versions from two different committees. The interest group revisions, however, reflected some of staffs concerns, which gave them a bias towards the new version.

Tom Harron, County counsel, who otherwise rarely spoke at the meetings, made many comments on the goals and policies and contributed significantly to the tone the committee established. He had two objectives: to keep the County from getting sued, which meant that the goals and policies should commit the County to as little as possible, and to avoid putting small developers in absurd situations. His views, then, were compatible with the development side. Environmentalists, on the other hand, were closer to the steering committee and worried that developers would play with shades of meaning to circumvent the intent behind the goals and policies. They were accordingly skeptical of Harron.

Planning Director Gary Pryor argued heavily for a position similar to Harron's. He wanted anything that was related to implementation, including definitions of terms, removed and placed in ordinances and standards to be written or revised later. What he wanted was abstract language with qualifiers. Absolute statements were potential headaches for the DPLU.

Between Harron, Pryor and the developers, the steering committee land use goals and policies were rewritten into a more developer-friendly version. For example, Matt Adams wanted to change the steering committee's policy from "[p]rovide standards to maintain ridge lines" to "[p]rovide *criteria* to maintain viewsheds and ridge lines *where appropriate.*" The words "criteria" and "where appropriate" would give the DPLU and developers room to maneuver. To the steering committee's "Maintain viewsheds and ridge lines," was added the word "significant," which gave developers the chance that a particular ridge line or view that they wished to disrupt was not substantial enough to protect.

As each goal and each policy led to a reenactment of the same battle, rewriting the goals and policies took a grueling five months and a dozen meetings. (During the winter Olympics, one member quipped, "curling is not the most boring sport.") By the conclusion in July 2002, the committee was frayed. The trust and consensus that Scarborough struggled heroically to maintain grew harder to sustain as the willingness to engage in give-and-take wilted and the process degenerated into a series of split votes. For some, this reluctance to compromise became permanent. Others would eventually catch their wind again. When they did, alliances would be much different.

Towards the end, the environmentalists and professionals became more thorough in using proxy votes to cover each other's absences. This created a voting bloc that just outnumbered the developers, leading to a long string of votes of 8–7, 8–6–2, etc. in favor of the environmentalists' language. This led to the use of breakout sessions to hammer out details before voting. These meetings, designed to fall below the committee's quorum, were usually held at the DPLU. No minutes were kept and the public wasn't invited. While they struck community groups as conspiratorial, I was told no decisions were made, just prep work to encourage people, in a safer setting, to consider other viewpoints. Given the disagreements that continued to plague that committee at this time, this seems credible.

While the split voting occurred after revisiting the goal statement and policies for the land use element of the general plan—the most important element—it weakened the consensus that gave the committee whatever legitimacy it had. Two events epitomized the deterioration.

At the June 11 meeting, Karen Scarborough brought a cake for the committee but only if, as expected, they finished the goals and policies. Instead, several perfectly split votes deadlocked the group and no one budged, meaning another meeting on the same subject. In a burst of passive-aggressiveness, the frustrated staff took the cake back to the DPLU and ate it themselves.

At the July 9 meeting, while tremendous wildfires in Arizona and Colorado were burning tens of thousands of acres, the committee went back and forth on the fire safety policies. One dealt with encouraging secondary access roads; the other, with letting fire safety influence the siting of housing. The siting issue was especially contentious. The environmentalists objected to having everyone subsidize expensive efforts to preserve the remote homes of the few. At one point, the developers accused Bowlby of trying to use fire restrictions to stop growth. He snapped back that no, he wasn't trying to stop growth, they were trying to grow smarter, which was met with a sarcastic "ooo."

A motion, however, finally passed 13–0–3.

The New Map

While the interest group was spending winter and early spring 2002 chewing itself up over GP 2020's goals and policies, the steering committee was in a de facto recess, as staff did not call a meeting for three months. In April, Supervisor Jacob held a meeting with the planning and sponsor group chairs in her district. For a stint in the late 1990s, she did such meetings regularly but had not done so for some time.[3] The chairs complained that they felt disengaged from GP 2020, shunted aside while the action took place at the interest group committee.

Staff called a meeting for April 20 to introduce the digital version of the new land use map. This map, almost two years in the making, was to replace Alternative III. The new map was more sophisticated, in both a political sense (the process included a wider range of interests including a number of more powerful ones) and a technical sense (e.g., new census data, which showed a lower current population than had been believed). The steering committee was to have the first look at it.

3. This doesn't mean that Jacob was out of touch with these planning groups. They had numerous reasons to be in contact. One chair told me that he was at least in the same room with her for a meeting once a month. While I was interviewing him in his home, her office called him.

At the beginning, Bryan Woods, again the chair, explained the lack of meetings: the interest group was slow and had to play catch up. They were merely wordsmithing the goals and policies, he assured them (as he had been assured by staff).

People were then invited to look at the 6' by 8' map marked "DRAFT" in huge letters. Some were clearly more unhappy than others. One steering committee member complained to the staffer standing beside him that the map didn't recognize what was on the ground, to which they replied, "It recognizes the fear of lawsuits." Pictures, of course, were snapped, as people did not want to wait for the DPLU to get around to making copies available to the public.

Ivan Holler introduced the new land use map. Its foundation, he explained, was still the population targets the board had endorsed years earlier for both the individual communities and for the overall unincorporated county. While conceptually based on the interest group's Concepts A to D and their grand compromise of redirecting growth to within the County Water Authority line, the map included feedback from the steering committee, the interest group and members of the public. (It was not unusual for staff to meet with individual landowners.) Holler stressed that it was a work in progress: when staff was to give the supervisors a progress report the next week, they weren't even going to show them the map.

The meeting was contentious. The representative of Potrero (a rural area to the east near the Mexican border) complained that the map ignored his group's input and that his community was as unhappy as hell. He blasted the interest group for having input into his community when they spent all of twenty minutes there (on their October tour). He wanted to know who told the consultant to shade certain areas green, to which Planning Director Gary Pryor snapped back that staff did: they have obligations to the county as a whole. (Potrero was east of the CWA line.) The community representative argued against the changes, leading to a heated discussion of the build-out based on the community's input versus based on the new map.

Others expressed a range of frustrations. They complained that when they talked to the staff person assigned to their area, they were told to bring up problems at the steering committee, and, at the steering committee, they were told to talk to staff. Jack Phillips had been told that the interest group had a secret meeting to view the map yet there was staff claiming that this was its first public appearance. Staff's responses only fueled his suspicions.[4]

The biggest issue was how to handle the maps for individual communities. Part of the problem with Alternative III, staff decided, was the maps, in isolation, tended to be egregiously misunderstood and be treated as a final version when they weren't. To avoid panicked responses, staff were to be present whenever someone looked at the map. They could answer questions and personally assure people that it was just a draft. But this meant keeping all the maps under DPLU control at all times. The steering committee members were incensed that even they, as elected officials, would not receive copies. They thought it difficult to interpret the maps at meetings and wanted to take them home for proper review. Pryor argued strongly against this. After the break, however, on the assurances from the chairs that they could avoid a blow up, he reversed himself. To assuage concerns that "draft" meant it was all but complete, Pryor changed the name to the "working copy" map.

The Map Goes to the Communities

In April, the DPLU sent out a flier notifying all 154,000 County property owners that GP 2020 workshops were about to be held in their communities. The flier said nothing about how decisions were made in the general plan update or how the plan could impact land values. Property rights activists complained that the fliers were

4. What happened was that the interest group agreed to postpone discussion of the new map until after they were done with the goals and policies. Staff offered to let them examine the map at the DPLU individually in the meantime, and some did so several days before the steering committee meeting. During the map review process, this was a standing offer to anyone in the public.

sent out too close to the earliest meetings and that because they did not alert people to what was at stake, they would be tossed as just more junk mail. Given how concerned staff was with containing controversy, it's hardly surprising that they forwent an opportunity to send people suspicious of government a flier from the County with the tone of "Be afraid. Be very afraid."

DPLU staff took the maps to each community twice. First was at a formal meeting. Then, at an open house held at a later date, members of the public could come in and view the maps. Staff ultimately held sixty-one meetings between May and August.

To make it easier to collate public input, staff encouraged people to submit comments on preprinted forms, an approach that also made it more difficult to get angry at individual staff members, as staff could take the position, "Yes, yes, your views are very important. Here, write them down so we make sure we have them."

While not a fount of enthusiasm, the introductory meetings lacked the focused anger of Alternative III. It is hard to say how much was the result of staff's approach and how much was merely the result of exhausted acquiescence, shock, relief or uncertainty about the proper target for anger. The poorly attended Spring Valley meeting, for example, was a generalized vote of no confidence in County planning. The audience complained about their abysmal treatment by the County. Since they were uninterested in what staff said or the niceties of the general plan update process, they effectively had no opinion on GP 2020.

Anger over the new map was slow to build, but build it did. (Alternative III took from June to September 2000 to reach a frenzied state.) Staff's limiting of access to the maps became central to the controversy. It upset not just the steering committee but members of the public as well. I witnessed an especially intense case while researching at a counter at the DPLU. A volunteer for a group of landowners came in, thinking that she could pick up a copy of the Ramona section of the new map. When told that the DPLU was not giving individuals copies of the map, she exploded. She had seen the map at the local workshop and couldn't believe that now she couldn't get a copy. The staff person tried to explain that there were reasons for the DPLU's policy on the map—to which the woman replied that there were reasons for the Holocaust. In her tirade, she likened the DPLU in its secretiveness to the Gestapo. She demanded to see Ivan Holler or Gary Pryor. Staff told her that they were in a meeting with the deputy CAO, so she called the man's office. The deputy CAO apparently said that Pryor and Holler had left. She vented and said she'd hate to see this turned into a Brown Act issue (that is, she threatened to sue). Finally, the staff person relented enough to walk with her to the reproduction office in the same building and let her pay to have it copied (not a cheap proposition).

While the comparisons to Nazism demonstrated a total loss of perspective, staff frequently did not help matters. Before and after meetings, members of the public would approach them and demand justifications for specific things. A common way out of this uncomfortable situation was to take a "please don't behead the messenger" attitude. In doing so, staff members tacitly reinforced the perception that the update was guided by arbitrary unseen forces.

The correspondence from the public about the new map dwarfed what the DPLU received about Alternative III. While the letters lacked the shocked outrage of the earlier controversy, they were generally negative. Developers again wrote detailed letters, even with aerial photos, explaining the appropriate densities on their clients' properties. Dozens of property owners sent or faxed a small form letter that read:

TO: DPLU Staff and Members of the County Board of Supervisors

I **STRONGLY** PROTEST HAVING MY PROPERTY DOWNZONED BY THE G.P. 2020 PROCESS! I ASK FOR NOTHING MORE THAN TO BE LEFT ALONE!

Then the form had spaces for name, contact information, property description, signature and additional comments, usually blank but occasionally containing observations like, "You don't pay taxes on my land—I do!! If you render it of less value you have to cut my taxes or eliminate taxes altogether."

Positive comments were sporadic. One letter might explain why there weren't more: "I was under the impression that if we were happy with the plan we didn't need to make comments. Apparently I was wrong. :-)" Organized efforts to support GP 2020 were localized, such as that by the Friends of Hellhole Canyon in Valley Center, who liked the lower densities around the canyon preserve.

The planning and sponsor groups saw the new map as solely the product of the interest group (which was no more true than Alternative III being solely the product of the steering committee). Since they felt the map was imposed upon them, they were unlikely to like it. Some, however, felt they could live with it. Spring Valley passed a motion rejecting all of the DPLU's proposed changes, decrying both the lack of rationale for them and the way they ignored problems like steep slopes. Ramona passed a motion saying that they weren't bound by County deadlines for input because the members of the planning group hadn't received personal copies of the new map.

In short, the new map was unpopular. Yet, within a year, staff would create the momentum to move forward, despite opposition, especially from property owners, and despite a lack of enthusiasm from the board of supervisors. It was a complex and tedious process, akin to making a sand castle with a pair of tweezers, all the while knowing that a big wave could wipe out the whole thing.

CHAPTER TWENTY
FROM LONG SEDUCTION
TO THE ENDLESS PLAN

We did okay but didn't get our full agenda. We did the best we could.
Not a home run, that's for sure. Maybe a double.
—*Developer and SOLV member (2013)*

As the years passed, more people continued to be sucked into GP 2020. The expanding number of subplots, shifting alliances and backroom deals made it harder to grasp the entirety of the plan. Decisions and deals of all kinds were made, but it was unclear which ones would ultimately be respected by the board of supervisors. At the center of the vortex was the increasingly sophisticated DPLU staff. They had become negotiators extraordinaire as they labored to craft a politically viable plan update.

The frequently stated goal was to reach an agreement on one land use map and one set of documents (goals and policies, standards, etc.) before the plan went to the planning commission and then the board of supervisors. The failure to do so would put the commissioners and supervisors in an unenviable position of adjudicating between conflicting groups that had decided that they could not compromise. Not only would this be politically costly for the commissioners and supervisors, they simply weren't in a position to do it: the technical data was too overwhelming for them to micromanage. (One developer on the interest group described the complexity of a plan update by saying it was like trying to plan for an area the size of the state of Connecticut when Connecticut didn't even try to plan for Connecticut.)

Staff's long-seduction approach to doing the impossible—reconciling the community planning and sponsor groups with development and environmental interests—was so incremental that its motion was easy to miss. And it was dangerous: while people made small steps towards compromises, they did not change their underlying beliefs. For instance, in a letter dated October 1, 2002—in other words, well along into the new process—the development side argued for virtually the same positions they always had. This meant that as the working copy map became more concrete, it became tougher to maintain everyone's commitment, as each refinement of the map diminished the hope of people who perceived themselves to be the plan's losers.

This included participants from all three camps. Individual landowners were running out of ways to avoid downzoning. At least a few of the environmentalists on the interest group were uneasy with the dilution of the one firm thing they got out of the plan update: a population cap of 660,000. As it went from 660,000 to 670,000 and then 678,00 and, as that number was seen to exclude redevelopment and as the number increasingly became seen as a conservative estimate, it became less clear what they were achieving through the process.[1] (Their truly hardline brethren in SOFAR had no commitment to the plan update process whatsoever.) Likewise, some planning and sponsor groups didn't like what they saw being done.

The perennially unhappy steering committee met about once a

---

1. The calculated maximum population based on the current plan, however, shrunk over time, from 855,000 persons down to the 770,000, thus reducing the apparent scale of downzoning.

month through the end of 2002 and then was essentially recessed until the end of April 2003. Its discussions were highly technical and concentrated on the implications of arcane changes in the wording of the new plan. Just as the interest group grew repetitive in its discussion of the goals and policies, the steering committee played out the same battles over and over: staff tried to innovate— or support innovations worked out by the interest group—and the steering committee dragged its heels, concerned that the changes meant a loss of control.

By agreeing to not discuss the new map until after completing the goals and policies, the interest group was delayed so long that the official public comment period on the latest map had ended before they had begun. Their discussion was so overdue that when they finally began, Scarborough opened with, "If I had a drum, I'd roll it."

Dan Silver of the Endangered Habitats League presented changes, based on hours of pouring over the community maps at the DPLU, that environmentalists wanted to see in the working copy map. The changes (corrections really, Silver claimed, of deviations from the group's agreed upon principles) were so minor that they presented no housing supply issues. Apparently caught off-guard, the developers plowed ahead with their own agenda, saying that their list of corrections would soon be forthcoming—while giving the distinct impression that they hadn't considered giving the same kind of detailed response to the map. The developers in fact never formally presented a list of corrections to the committee. Instead, they eventually gave them directly to staff.

With Silver's presentation, the map split into two. On one hand was the working copy map that had been shown to the communities and on which the public gave input. On the other was the "interest group interim" map, essentially a combination of the environmental and development wish lists. The latter, despite its name, was never endorsed by the interest group and didn't represent a consensus. The maps lived parallel lives for half a year.

To try to bridge the differences between the planning and sponsor groups on one side and the interest group committee on the other, staff organized meetings between a subcommittee of the interest group and select planning and sponsor groups. Both sides found this illuminating, but the planning and sponsor group members believed it was more of an eye-opener for the interest group members, who had a limited understanding of the difficulties involved of creating GP 2020 at the community level.

Changing Plans

GP 2020 subtly evolved as adoption inched closer. First, as already mentioned, the population target that the County was striving to achieve was drifting upward. Second, the maximum housing densities decreased again. With Alternative III, the existing highest housing density in the 1970s plan—43 dwelling units per acre (du/ac)—was eliminated, making the highest 29 du/ac. To prevent local jurisdictions from claiming land was for affordable housing and then permitting expensive single-family homes to build upon it, a 2002 state law required that any land designated for affordable housing in the housing element must be built at its maximum density. In response, the County lowered the highest density from 29 du/ac down to 25. While this was high by the standards of owners of single-family homes, it was low for apartments and condos.

Further, recall, as described in the previous case study, when SANDAG's population projections for 2020 had been lowered, San Diego City Council rejected the need to accommodate more housing units. For years, the County had claimed that its downzoning wouldn't hurt the regional housing supply because the City was willing to take the housing. After that was no longer true, DPLU staff simply claimed that what the County did was independent of what the City did. This meant that a higher proportion of the regional growth would be in the unincorporated county.

On the whole, these changes meant GP 2020 was then moving towards more housing at lower densities. Sprawl was making a creeping comeback.

The Planning Commission Hearings, Take Two

Three days of planning commission hearings were scheduled to give the go ahead to conduct the environmental impact report. Since EIRs needed to have a preferred alternative that would be the basis of the study, starting the analysis meant picking a plan with a few other versions analyzed so that decision-makers could see the difference. In the alternate reality of GP 2020, however, there wasn't a truly preferred alternative. Rather, it was emphasized that the planning commission was not approving anything in its final form. Rather, if the plan passed muster at the commission and the board of supervisors—be "accepted for further refinements" as staff liked to put it—the EIR analysis could begin in earnest, a process that would likely take at least nine months, given the size of the project and the near certainty of being sued by whoever considered themselves losing out in the plan update process (and, perhaps, SOFAR).

In preparation for the commission hearings, the interest group met twice in January 2003. (In December, the steering committee had signed off on as much as they were going to.) Tensions were high. At the tools subcommittee before one of the meetings, developers turned on each other over their inability to agree on how to fund TDR and PDR (purchase of development rights) programs. Instead of reaching a broad agreement as hoped, the committee developed a motion whose qualifiers meant in effect that no one was bound by any particular agreement if the overall result was unacceptable to them. The environmentalists wanted language saying that further increases in population in one place had to be equaled out with decreases elsewhere, but the developers rejected the idea that the map was balanced enough to make that kind of agreement. SOLV voted against supporting the land use map, saying that it did not contain enough density increases to make a TDR program work.

In many ways, the hearings before the planning commission were the repeat of the filibustered meetings that broke Alternative III: SOLV was out in force against the plan; the commissioners were visibly not in agreement themselves; the working copy map was, in a number of areas, not dramatically different from Alternative III; the hearings had to be extended because so many people—mainly unhappy landowners—wished to speak. The objections to the plan were recycled: landowners' property was near infrastructure and appropriate for development; the densities on their lands was inconsistent with their neighbors'; the downzoning was arbitrary and was a taking.

The meetings, though, were different in critical ways. Staff was much better prepared. Instead of just facilitating grassroots planning, they worked within an overarching conceptual framework that justified their actions. The chairs of the planning and sponsor groups generally stressed the great lengths to which staff had gone to assist in developing a viable plan for their communities. And where they continued to disagree, staff worked with them. Complaints of not being informed about GP 2020 were fewer and received less sympathy.

Although by no means a majority, many public speakers supported the plan, quite a change from Alternative III. They stressed the countless meetings and claimed that GP 2020 was the product of their communities. Others noted that wells were going dry, and there simply wasn't the water for additional growth. Most colorfully, an environmentalist from Valley Center argued that since his community was so divided that the commissioners were guaranteed to upset someone no matter what they did, they might as well do the right thing. He ended his two minutes at the podium with the plea, "Please downzone me!"

Despite the growing support, the underlying conflict between landowners and those opposed to much more growth remained. Dave Shibley of SOLV, who had done much to encourage discussion of TDRs, spoke directly after Patsy Fritz described how a transfer of development right program could solve many of their problems. He dismissed what she said as, "beautiful words," and admitted that he too had been seduced by TDRs. It had, however, become apparent that the County was not serious about creating a viable program. Shibley's reversal was significant: the interest group's compromises were predicated on preserving economic equity in land, and, without a TDR program, all the equity would have to bought, something clearly wasn't going to happen because there just wasn't the money.

The commissioners appointed by Supervisors Cox and Horn made their hostility to GP 2020 clear. They often asked landowners "clarifying questions" which in effect extended their time to speak. At one point, Cox's commissioner called the DPLU's justification for a proposed density in Borrego Springs "the dumbest thing he had ever heard." After Dave Shibley of SOLV spoke on the second day, one of Horn's commissioners turned on his microphone and added, "I totally agree with your position."

Although it may not have been premediated, several commissioners made a series of small decisions that added to the delay of GP 2020: when a landowner or their developer made a compelling case that their land had been erroneously downzoned, the commissioners began asking staff to reexamine their situation. By the end, they were referring all the property owners' cases back to staff. This was the beginning of what would be known as "the referrals."

At the final hearing in March, the commission supported the following motion:

> Recommend that the Board of Supervisors support the direction in which GP 2020, the maps and its concepts are headed, and direct Staff to continue resolving the concerns indicated in the list of referrals received during this series of Planning Commission Workshops.

Board of Supervisors

At its April 30 hearing, the board of supervisors deleted one of its policies (I–59) and reduced another (I–63) down to a page. The policies had required that the relevant planning or sponsor group be involved from the beginning whenever a developer brought forward a large-scale project. They also established a procedure by which general plan amendments were made, requiring that they meet at least six of ten criteria. All this was eliminated. Developers praised the streamlining; planning and sponsor groups decried their loss of input. In a June 5, 2003 editorial in the *San Diego Union-Tribune*, former steering committee member Gordon Shackelford argued that these changes were evidence of developer corruption and that the new general plan would be made meaningless by the ease with which changes could be made. "What can be done?" he asked. His reply: "When representative government breaks down, the people can become the powers that be, through the Ballot Initiative Process. The time has come."[2]

On May 21, 2003, the board opened testimony on the plan update before an overflow crowd. Cox was the chair for the year, making him speak much more than usual on GP 2020. Supervisor Horn made it clear where he stood by quoting Locke on how government had no other end than the preservation of property.

Staff gave its initial presentation. It was unusually snazzy and coherent. Instead of simply trying to make sense of an amalgamation of public input, staff made the case that the map was motivated by a vision of concentrating growth west of the CWA line. (The current plan had 40 percent of the future growth east of the line; the working copy had 20 percent.) Second, staff made the politics of GP 2020 overt: they said that "achieving a broad consensus" in support of the plan and "balancing competing interests" were two of their goals. Third, staff only mentioned a PDR (purchase of development rights) program as a possible equity mechanism, thus in effect coming out against a TDR program that for several years had been claimed to be *the* mechanism by which downzoning would be made politically palatable.

What made the staff presentation a landmark event, however, was the emphasis on the public costs of the plan. For years, Planning Director Gary Pryor had insisted on developing a plan and *then*

2. See also Marty Graham, "Supervisors Change Land Use Policies," *North County Times*, May 1, 2003.

doing a reality check against what was financially feasible. This meant delaying discussion of the public costs of growth. Since GP 2020 went for years without an agreed upon vision, landowners had focused debates on the costs of the plan to themselves, setting themselves up as victims and focusing attention away from the public costs of their own actions. Staff, however, was finally talking about the costs, and they were blunt: growth did not pay for itself; it generated $1.29 in expenses for every dollar of additional revenue. Concentrating the growth meant lower costs; dispersing it—sprawl—exacerbated the cost of infrastructure.

This strategy of the planners would profoundly impact the shape of the final plan. What the planners did was to steer the supervisors onto the horns of the dilemma inherent in their conservatism: the contradiction of their simultaneous support for development and low taxes. Putting the supervisors in an even more difficult position did not encourage them to make decisions any faster, but it would ultimately force their hand, tilting the plan toward respecting the desire to reign in the growth potential of the backcountry.

In short, the planners had discovered Smart Growth. It had been a long journey. The concept had been mentioned in passing for years and the planning director had said he did not want to see the backcountry covered over with homes. But "grassroots" was the watchword of GP 2020, and, unlike the City of San Diego, elected officials had not, occasional nods aside, expressed that much interest in Smart Growth. Smart Growth, however, was a ready-built ideology that gave the planners tools for justifying the compromises they had been trying to reach. When the grassroots are in disagreement, simply extolling democracy is not enough.

The rest of the initial presentations at the May 21 hearing were more along the lines of what was to be expected. Planning Commissioner Woods, who noted that he had the "dubious pleasure" of being both the chair of the commission and the steering committee, emphasized the spirit of cooperation and extensiveness of the committees and the commission hearings (471 speaker slips, 200+ speakers). The steering committee, he said, wanted community character respected. At the hearings, the commissioners had heard loud and clear about downzoning. Karen Scarborough, chair of the interest group committee, spent most of her time describing how the members of the committee needed "a complete package" to be able to support the plan and that their compromises on any given point did not hold out of context.

The chairs of the planning and sponsor groups offered a cacophony of views, ranging from glowing praise of staff and satisfaction with the progress so far to the claim that the plan had so many holes you could drive a Mack truck through it. They went from highly technical—the densities were wrong on a particular section of a community map—to the droll: before he became chair of his planning group, one man noted, he had a full head of hair and a lot more friends. Several complained that they were forced in particular directions by staff. Their planning group voted for changes, but the DPLU didn't incorporate them. The new Ramona chair said that people asked themselves, "What's the use?" and stopped coming to meetings. The Spring Valley representative said the steering committee was a misnomer "unless you thought we were being steered." The Lakeside chair, taking a cue from the board's discussion the preceding day on sexual offenders, ended his criticisms of the interest group with the call to "remove the predators from the playground."

Landowners blasted the plan. One received much clapping for his fire-and-brimstone sermon on how GP 2020 was destroying the land of opportunity with its "socialistic land policies" and SOLV spoke out against downzoning. SOLV's director, Jack Orr, had submitted over a thousand public speaker slips using preprinted address labels. Supervisor Cox thanked him for not having all those people speak (but made no mention of the thousands of postcards that the Sierra Club spent several years getting people to sign).

So many members of the public spoke that the hearing had to be continued for a second day in June and then a third day so the supervisors themselves could speak. The opinions varied: several contradicted their planning chair's Mack truck comment and said the plan was working; residents of Palomar Mountain bemoaned the impact of SOFAR's Forest Conservation Initiative on their area; some Lakeside business owners were concerned that the plan would drive them out of business.

Much of the time, however, was devoted to a handful of developers, all except one of whom had spent time on the interest group. The way the hearings were structured, anyone who wished to speak about a particular community could, even if they had already spoken about other communities, so these men with projects across the backcountry spoke again and again. (One said he submitted eight slips that day.) Each time, they described their clients' properties, down to their assessor's parcel numbers, in order to have the board put the parcels on the growing referral list. This contributed to the lifelessness of the hearings. Supervisors worked to hide their yawns.

The parade of developers and parcel numbers did show, however, that there were—contra the belief held by some residents—limits to the developers' influence at the DPLU: they had many clients who were to be substantially downzoned. It also showed why the developers worked so hard on GP 2020: their livelihoods depended on it.

One of these developers, Jim Whalen, spoke again on the second day when people were allowed to make final comments. He had five points, four of which were technical. The other, however, was political: "it is a bit unfortunate and it's as simple as this: it's that anyone on the interest group who publicly supports the initiative should be removed from the interest group." At the end of his comments, he returned to the matter:

> The initiative. It's a slap in the face to the environmental community who've played by all the rules within the system to have someone who is participating in the initiative process still be on the interest group.

The initiative was, of course, SOFAR's latest effort.

SOFAR had tried to influence the structure of the GP 2020 early on but otherwise did not involve itself in the plan update—nor was it asked to be. Members of SOFAR, in discussion with other environmentalists, drafted an updated version of the failed 1998 Prop B. They wanted it called "The Clean Water and Forest Initiative" but the registrar called it "The Rural Lands Initiative." The initiative would have created a zoning overlay that covered much of the backcountry with lots between 40 and 160 acres, which, with some exceptions, could not be changed until 2023 except by a countywide vote. If the experience of similar local measures was any indication, then the voting requirement would prevent any modification to the densities the initiative established.

On the Third Day

The third day of the hearing began with developers using the non-agenda item period to again protest the continued presence of the Sierra Club (Eric Bowlby) on the interest group, given the group's support for the SOFAR initiative. Like Whalen, they called it a "slap in the face." After the Speaker of the State Assembly, Herb Wesson, Jr., spoke to the board about the state budget crisis—to which the supervisors responded by opposing any tax increases, giving Wesson the management manual for the County and suggesting the state declare bankruptcy—the time had come for the supervisors to make a motion. Characteristically, Jacob made a motion, of which she gave copies to the other supervisors. Uncharacteristically, there was an awkward silence until Cox announced the motion dead for lack of a second. Horn then put forth a motion. It took him so much time to explain how it was different from Jacob's that she finally observed, "What I passed out is your motion. I think you just wanted to make it." After that drew some laughter, she added, "But that's okay."

The motion was a three-month delay by way of asking for many clarifications, including making really, really sure on the 210 referrals from landowners who felt wrongly downzoned. The referrals were likely to be labor intensive and not accomplish much, other than put staff in the position of trying to guess the politically correct amount to change so that they (a) didn't look like they were ignoring the referrals but (b) didn't give too much legitimacy to the complaints against GP 2020.

While admitting that everyone on the interest group had a conflict of interest, the supervisors also asked that staff look into the possibility of someone on the interest group working at cross-purposes with GP 2020 by helping with the SOFAR initiative (though they ultimately declined to make anyone a First Amendment martyr). They also asked staff to continue to look into PDRs *and* TDRs.

The supervisors were cautiously positive about the process, though Horn was flat-out opposed to any downzoning west of the CWA line. Roberts said they had "a good basic plan" and Cox compared GP 2020 Chief Ivan Holler to Rocky for withstanding a pounding from everyone.

From the Long Seduction to the Long Haul

If at this point you, dear reader, feel exhausted, confused about the blur of meetings and torn between the temptation to stop reading and the need to go back and reread some earlier parts to jog your memory about what the whole thing was supposed to be about— then you've grasped GP 2020 and the experience of living through it. The plan was starting to resemble a chronic illness at the point where not only are you sick and tired but you are sick and tired of being sick and tired. It was well past the point where it was annoying when it dawned on a newcomer to the plan update to make the joke that it would take until 2020 to get GP 2020 done.

The length of the plan update was talking its toll. GP 2020 was becoming expensive for the County. The passage of time also meant turn over among everybody but the supervisors. SOLV was on its third representative on the interest group and others had their replacements as well. Older staff retired or moved on to other jobs; recent college graduates filled new positions. Every two years there was an election for half of the community planning groups, and that challenged the institutional memory: it was a moment to groan when a new steering committee member expressed concern that the word "should" in planning documents was too rigid and didn't leave any wiggle room, when everyone else in the room had known for years that "should"—as opposed to "shall"—was entirely wiggle room.

In short, GP 2020 had become a vast and incoherent endurance test—one that faced many distractions. First was the carnival of a special election in which California voters recalled Governor Gray Davis and replaced him with Arnold Schwarzenegger. Three weeks later, a wildfire started near Ramona. It would become the largest in state history up to that point. The next day, another fire started in Valley Center to the north and a third started near the Mexican border. Before being contained, the fires burnt over two thousand homes and almost six hundred square miles. Many of the homes destroyed were in the unincorporated County, so the DPLU had to issue an enormous number of permits for rebuilding, which meant pulling staff off GP 2020.

And in the End…

Little is to be gained by describing in detail the *next seven years* of the general plan update to its adoption: the arguments presented to the board at the final round of public comment before the same five supervisors in 2010 could have been said before the planning commission in 2000 when Alternative III first erupted into controversy.

So what happened? First, the SOFAR initiative was crushingly defeated in May 2004, with 63 percent of the voters opposed. This would be the last major attempt to ballot box the planning process. Internally, much was happening at the County. Pryor and Holler left, putting a temporary halt to the plan update process. A County planner named Devon Muto ultimately took over. Under his leadership the plan zigzagged again, to the point that it's impossible to

306

look back at the population build-out target or the goals and policies that were fought so heavily to figure out who ultimately won.
The build-out was converting from a population target (the famous
660,000 figure) to a number of dwelling units, which isn't exactly
convertible. Likewise, instead of trying to compromise between
the steering committee and interest group versions of the goals
and policies, a new consultant was brought in to do one combined
set of goals and policies. That is, while the work at the community
level continued, the giant and increasingly sterile debates that this
book has documented were ultimately sidestepped.

Muto steered the plan to an adoption. Community planning
groups came to dislike conservation subdivisions as much as clustering, which was their main remaining concern when the steering
committee voted to support it.[3] Environmentalists got a modest
victory in the sense that less open space will be bulldozed than
would have been under the old plan. Like so many environmentalist
victories, however, it was a defeat of a hypothetical and what they
value (the natural world) is slated to take a slow hit over the next
generation. The DPLU continued its Smart Growth approach, which
basically forced the supervisors to adopt a moderate plan because
the costs to the County for a landowner-friendly plan were too high.
Landowners, developers and farmers sounded demoralized at the
final public hearings.

In 2005, I had written that "in effect, the supervisors had decided
to drag out the general plan update as long as possible (while
complaining about how long it took)." They couldn't pass a plan
without alienating anyone, and developer allies could continue to
(try to) build under the old plan. Did the supervisors passing the
general plan in 2011—long after "2020" had been deleted from its
name—contradict my 2005 assessment? That depends on whom
you ask.

3. The argument could be made that a conservation subdivision is a subcategory of
clustering, made more comprehensive and repackaged. On the national interest, see
Rayman Mohamed, "The Economics of Conservation Subdivisions: Price Premiums,
Improvement Costs, and Absorption Rates," *Urban Affairs Review* 41, no. 3 (2006): 376–399.

The plan, as community planning groups and environmental-ists now think of it, proved in the minds of many to be a decent plan. It should have been: it's a likely contender for the most delib-erate general plan in American history. Every possible issue, every possible compromise, was exhaustively discussed and considered. Satisfaction varies by individual planning groups, of course. Many who were critical of the planning process ultimately had a grudg-ing respect for it—perhaps because they were suddenly faced with what in their minds was something worse.

In 2003, the referral process, in which individual landowners could protest the zoning on their land and have the DPLU's deci-sion referred back for further review, was started more or less by accident but then continued and continued. It was much like Xeno's arrow covering half the distance in each time interval. Planners developed a recommendation. Landowners protested. The board told the planners to compromise. Then the planners went back and analyzed the recommendations again and compromised again. This was repeated ad nauseum, leading to epic planning commission and board of supervisor hearings in which individual parcel after individual parcel was discussed. One might have expected that this endless rehashing would have been put to rest with the adoption of the plan. *It has not been.*[4]

Landowners and developers who saw themselves as losers in the plan—not all did as a number were upzoned—got Supervisors Horn, Roberts and Cox to do something unusual. Over the opposition of Jacob and the now hyphenated Slater-Price, they agreed to have the County foot the bill for a general plan amendment that would include many of the referrals that could not be incorporated into the general plan because they would have been so substantial. Developers tend to downplay the significance of these "property specific requests" (PSRs). A founding member of SOLV, when reinterviewed in 2013,

4. In 2014, when given this "Xeno's arrow" interpretation of the referral process, a long-time County planner challenged its accuracy because it implied that property owners only got part of what they wanted when many times they got everything.

said they see the plan as basically the final word and as something of a loss. They feel that they were able to do a decent job of protecting the landowners they were able to mobilize but that their broader political aims fell short. They argue that the after-the-adoption general plan amendment, in seen from the broader perspective of total growth throughout the County, as relatively insignificant in its impact but quite important to those landowners.

Environmentalists and homeowners, however, have been scandalized by the amendment, doubly so for the County's willingness to pay for it. The County, in their view, no sooner adopted a general plan than reopened it at the behest of special interests. They criticize the method by which the amendment was initiated as under the table and believe it fundamentally calls into question the notion that the County in fact has a general plan. One leader of the community planning groups argues that the amendment "means that there is no general plan. . . They never really adopted a general plan."

The amendment might never get completed, however. The entirely Republican board of supervisors not surprisingly has had strained relations with public employee unions. In 2010, labor helped get on the ballot an initiative to impose term limits on the supervisors. It won. Slater-Price, however, retired in 2012 and threw her support behind the Democrat running for office, Dave Roberts. Given the changing demographics of the county, Ron Roberts's and Greg Cox's districts could very well elect a Democrat in the future (though Roberts ran opposed in the 2014 primary). If the GOP loses its grip on either of those seats, then there will likely be three supervisors who would move to stop funding the general plan amendment, putting the landowners in the position of having to pay for work done on it by Planning and Development Services (PDS), as the DPLU was renamed when combined with Public Works and Parks and Rec (to create "a new approach to doing business and a new culture" as the website puts it). From the point of view of the County, however, this general plan amendment may be responsible for saving it from a long awaited horror: by giving the people who felt they lost out in the final plan a forum for pursuing their claims, it reduced the incentive to file suit against the plan's environmental impact report. Only Rancho Guejito, admittedly the largest property in the county, filed suit. (Stonegate, which sounded the alarm on Alternative III and provided the seed money for SOLV, was unable to gain approval for its Merriam Mountain development, with Ron Roberts casting the deciding vote against its general plan amendment in 2010, citing principles that sounded a lot like Smart Growth.[5])

There were several other important threads to the general plan update. The County did create a Purchase of Development Rights pilot program for farmers. (The Farm Bureau felt compelled to oppose the final general plan because of concerns of the loss of land values.) There were doubts about whether any farmers would be willing to sign up, but the interest was greater than anticipated. It seems like a ballot initiative for a modest County-wide parcel tax to fully fund the program is something that everyone involved in the general plan update could support, which could potentially draw significant urban support as well. Whether any serious attempt will be made to that end remains to be seen.

The politics of the general plan also increasingly splashed outside the confines of the official plan update process. As they increasingly felt that they would lose out in the planning process, farmers, developers and landowners consolidated into fewer groups, largely focused on North County, and stepped up attacks on the plan and planning. Their criticisms, perhaps inflamed by the rise of the Tea Party movement, grew harsher and took new angles. Supervisor Horn did everything he could to assist, from fighting parcel by parcel against downzoning to working hard to get a controversial road inserted into the plan. He helped create the Red Tape Reduction Task Force, which included as one of its recommendations either the elimination of or severe term limits for the community planning groups.[6] This recommendation was not directly acted upon, but a

5. Allison St John, "Roberts Votes To Scuttle Merriam Mountain Project," (March 24, 2010): http://www.kpbs.org/news/2010/mar/24/roberts-votes-scuttle-merriam-moun-tains-project/.

6. During the final stages of the adoption of the plan, development interests lobbied

new requirement for ethics training was put into place, which could discourage participation on the planning groups. Environmentalists and homeowners were critical of these developments, which they felt were disrespectful of democratic processes.

In short, the adoption of the general plan was but the shortest breather in the politics of growth. Like mortal enemies continuing to fight after the grave, the different factions that fought over the general plan for well over a decade still are at odds. In a sense, GP 2020 can never end until all buildable land is exhausted and it becomes time to "build up and not out." Then it will be time for another plan update, perhaps one to be called the County of Villages.

hard and successfully to eliminate language from the plan that required projects to be consistent with community plans. As one leader of the community planning groups put it, however, the community plans were in fact part of the general plan, which every development had to be consistent with anyway, so the impact would be minimal.

CONCLUSION

For the City, the plan was passed but rendered toothless, primarily as a face-saving measure. For the County, no vote was had, primarily as an ass-saving measure.

—A UCSD student's response
to a San Diego politics class
final exam question
on the general plans (2006)

General plans don't guide growth. Politicians do.
—A County staffer (2013)

In a book on the absurdity of trying to divide the dynamic planet into static units of property, Theodore Steinberg takes advantage of the concept of *involution*. He borrowed it from an anthropologist named Alexander Goldenweiser who defined it as "what happened when a cultural form (art, ritual, and music were his examples) developed in such a way that it became increasingly complex, yet at the same time rigid, monotonous, and unable to change in any fundamental sense." Steinberg saw in this concept a perfect description of American notions of property rights in land:

Like Maori art, property too is a cultural form. It rests, as we have seen, on the ideas of ownership and possession, very old ideas, but ones that have grown all the more tenacious in our own century as they have been pressed hard to colonize the planet's more distant reaches. In the process, the law of property has grown all the more technically complicated and ornate. More than three thousand amendments were made to New York City's original zoning ordinance by the time it was replaced by a new law in 1961. So much has been written about water law that the entry for the topic in one legal encyclopedia stretches to over one thousand pages long. Property law is a vast exercise in what Goldenweiser called "technical hairsplitting." It is a virtuoso performance but also in many ways a rigid and dreary one that does not benefit everyone equally and further, may well hamper our future ability to adapt to changing environmental conditions.[1]

San Diego planning epitomizes this. But how did planning for where buildings would go become exercises so vast and so ornate that they turned into temporizing exercises—as if additional time was the missing ingredient that would make them all work out? Understanding this requires stepping back.

1. Theodore Steinberg, *Slide Mountain, Or the Folly of Owning Nature* (Berkeley: University of California Press, 1995): 173–174. Something that deserves more attention is the way in which planning extends the time line for projects to such an extent that it limits the ability of government spending to stimulate the economy as the time it takes for the planning and lawsuits of a major project is now often longer than a business cycle (or at least half of one, which is what matters). As a result, the stimulus spending in response to the Great Recession did not leave legacy projects in the manner of the roads, dams, bridges and the like of the New Deal. The execution of the American Recovery and Reinvestment Act instead became a funding stream for planning (of which I was involved with, of all things, assisting with changing the City of San Diego zoning code) and a grab at "shovel ready" projects.

What Happened?

At the beginning of the twenty-first century, both the most populous city and the geographically largest jurisdiction in the San Diego region each attempted to reinvent themselves by rewriting their plans for future development. Neither jurisdiction began with far-reaching intentions. The initial rationales for revising the general plans were simple. The City was modest and vague: bring the plan up to date. The County was precise and immediate: stop lawsuits from environmentalists opposed to further development.

In both cases, mission creep from within the planning departments swelled the ambition of the plans. The City planners responded favorably to SANDAG's population projections that called for a million more people in the region by the year 2020. Since following the current general plan would lead to a shortfall of housing for the new people, the planners and their allies took it for granted that they must prepare for additional housing. At the County, planners concluded that a legally defensible document based on public input meant a massive overhaul and embarked on a thorough revamping of the general plan, including a near total reexamination of undeveloped parcels of the land under their control. City planners embraced Smart Growth from the beginning; County planners facilitated a hodgepodge of community-driven plans and only belatedly began talking about Smart Growth.

The combined effect was to be a bold change: in comparison to what the current plans suggested, much of the anticipated growth was to be shifted away from greenfields and redirected into existing communities. Open space and rural communities were to be preserved, infrastructure costs were to be reduced, and existing neighborhoods were to develop the finest qualities of European cities. This would have profoundly changed how all San Diegans went through their daily routines.

Both plans ran into trouble. The process for public input at the City kept the reins in the hands of the advocates for a denser San Diego, preserving the purity of their ideals at the cost of having no tools to co-opt critics, who fought the plan to an ambiguous stand-still at city council. At the County, planners interpreted orders to be community-driven to mean that they should allow the community planning and sponsor groups to lead the process. As these groups were disproportionately stacked with people who believed in the sovereignty of local communities and were skeptical of the ben-efits of additional growth, the product of their efforts antagonized developers and landowners who saw their economic investments jeopardized. To incorporate the landowners, the board of super-visors threw out the offending maps and gave developers almost half the seats on a new advisory committee. Thus began a lengthy process of negotiating and delaying, as the planners became de facto diplomats who thanklessly mediated between homeowners, environmentalists, developers and landowners.

These plan updates were simply inadequate for the massive chal-lenges facing San Diego. The most glaring way is that they were not completed in a timely fashion. Both started, after two years of prepa-ration, in 1998. The County's GP 2020 went on for so long that they stripped "2020" from its name before it was (mostly) approved in 2011. Someone born when the general plan was started would have been a year from high school when it was formally adopted. The City of Villages, which was supposed to just be an initial vision for a more thorough plan update, took two years longer than anticipated and all the other elements were not updated until 2008. And these are plans for guiding growth to the year 2020.[2]

What delayed the plans was the efforts to gain acceptance from the mobilized members of the public. The time put into gaining their approval only led to tepid support. The Strategic Framework Element gained the City's planning department few friends. Instead of developing trust as hoped, the planners alienated people and inspired opposition. At the end of summer 2006, the plan's new

---

2. It should also be noted that the first flex-trolley line, discussed in the City case study, was being put into place as this book was going to press in 2014.

housing element went over poorly at the Community Planners Committee and was accused of being a developer giveaway and punishment for not supporting the City of Villages. When the full general plan update was adopted in 2008, it received relatively little public attention as the housing market was imploding, and, like the bumper sticker saying that it's better to be over the hill than under it, even dumb growth was starting to look not so bad. (The environmentalists who sued over the EIR for the Strategic Framework Element felt that they had a strong legal case to do so again in 2008 but not the resources to carry proceedings to their conclusion.)

The County effort to garner public support was a mixed bag. The first attempt at creating the plan, which led to the aborted Alternative III, antagonized just about everyone, though sometimes for contradictory reasons. The second attempt at creating the plan continued to displease some, and its intensive shuttle diplomacy, in which planners and supervisors had many backroom discussions with a wide range of interests, provided grist for conspiracy theory mills. It led to much more acquiescence to the plan. This, however, is a far cry from enthusiasm. Several years into this phase (perhaps 2003 or 2004), people started to become resigned to whatever they thought the final outcome would be. Even then, it took another seven years to complete the plan.

Can Smart Growth Make Planning Sustainable?

Beneath the vexing but ultimately surface-level dilemmas of how to gain consent of mobilized interests were acts of bad faith that made sustainable development unlikely. First, advocates of Smart Growth persistently conflated the *potential* for scale economies in infrastructure with the *existence* of that infrastructure. Smart Growth envisions redirecting growth into communities that already have infrastructure. In theory, it's cheaper and less wasteful than having to install entirely new infrastructure in what a few months earlier was corn or coastal sage. Unfortunately, San Diego was and continues to be hardly unique in neglecting the infrastructure in existing communities. Urban communities might have, for instance, sewer pipes that could take additional capacity, but they're just as often short on parks, libraries, seats in schools and the like, and additional construction exacerbates these problems.

The second reason Smart Growth planning was unlikely to lead to sustainable development was that in the context of limited and uncertain revenues to commit to infrastructure, planning can be little more than an intellectual exercise. One of the main purposes of a general plan is to create a stable framework for planning capital improvements. Even more than voters in most other states, Californians have displayed a pervasive unwillingness to pay for the public services they demand, meaning that the state's enormous wealth has not translated into well-funded government programs.[3] Historically, San Diego has been particularly tax averse. At the risk of modest hyperbole, the general plans were guidelines for spending money that there was little enthusiasm to collect.[4] The participants in the plan updates did not face this squarely. The County's GP 2020 focused heavily on private costs. It wasn't until 2003—five years into the plan—that public costs began to be considered in a serious way. To the credit of the County, this did ultimately influence the direction of the plan, though it was only one of many influences. At the City, the Strategic Framework Element never calculated the costs of growth, only the cost of catching up with past growth.

Third, jurisdictions were well aware that they had serious problems but refused to act. For many reasons, San Diego is a profoundly

3. This was not always the case. For a history of this shift in government spending and taxation in California, see Peter Schrag, *Paradise Lost: California's Experience, America's Future* (New York: The New Press, 1998).

4. For a sustained critique of San Diegans' unwillingness to pay taxes for proper infrastructure, see Steven P. Erie, Vladimir Kogan and Scott Mackenzie, *Paradise Plundered: Fiscal Crisis and the Governance Failures in San Diego* (Palo Alto: Stanford University Press, 2011).

vulnerable place to have a major population center. Most notably, water was and continues to be an issue that San Diego shares with the rest of southern California and the Southwest. Because of technological and political obstacles, no future source of water is guaranteed, meaning that the region's population will be increasing without certain water supplies.[5]

More of an immediate problem is housing. Even with the plunge in housing prices caused by the collapse of the Bush era subprime mortgage bubble, high housing costs are a chronic issue for many San Diegans, but neither City nor the County elected officials have been willing to face this in a meaningful sense. In 2002, the City passed a weak inclusionary housing ordinance and began regularly passing a symbolic "housing state of emergency" measure. While the inclusionary housing ordinance will benefit the people who get the chance to live in the affordable housing units it creates, few are under the illusion that the ordinance will substantially improve housing affordability for a very long time.[6] The County government likewise did not and continues to not make the cost of housing a significant issue. SANDAG repeatedly forecasts population growth exceeding housing construction: their 2030 forecast predicts a 37 percent increase in population and a 30 percent increase in the housing stock; their current 2050 forecast predicts a 41.7 percent increase in population and 35.5 percent in housing stock. While such forecasts should be understood as predictions about an uncertain future, they give no grounds for optimism that housing affordability will improve over the long-term.

In 2000, I became the teaching assistant for the Urban Studies and Planning program at the University of California, San Diego. As the economy went into a recession but housing prices continued their upward climb, I noticed a disturbing trend among my students, one that was national: the number of hours they worked

5. The Carlsbad desalination plant, which took fifteen years of planning and permitting, was under construction as this book headed to print.
6. Lori Weisberg, "Affordable-housing Backers Chide City," *San Diego Union-Tribune*, August 5, 2004.

kept rising.[7] After several years, this became a serious problem: while working part-time has its benefits, more and more students were working full-time, which put them under a surreal amount of stress and diluted their education. For the ones who wanted to stay in San Diego after graduation, I discovered a surefire way to make them laugh: ask them when they thought they might someday own their own home. It was an absurd question: they couldn't envision reasonable scenarios in which they might be able to buy. The end of the housing boom might have temporarily prevented the situation from growing worse—at the expense of wiping out many first-time homebuyers—but the underlying volatile dynamics remain.

This was a breaking of the intergenerational contract. Instead of different generations being linked together by the care they could give and the care that they need, younger people increasingly were shaping their lives around paying the super-profits of older generations of landowners, homeowners and landlords.[8] In this context, the elaborate process of writing the general plans of San Diego was little more than fiddling while the region burned.

The problems of the San Diego plans, however, were by no means unique. Take, for instance, the following quote:

> Municipal spatial planning, and especially the local land-use plan, is performing poorly. The process of plan preparation takes too long, more often than not the local land-use plan is too detailed and already

7. On trends in the undergraduate experience, see Rebekah Nathan, *My Freshmen Year: What a Professor Learned by Becoming a Student* (New York: Penguin Books, 2005).
8. And, of course, the challenges facing younger persons makes it more difficult to hold up their end of the intergenerational bargain. Someone with chronically high rents or mortgage payments is not in a good position to help their own parents and will be less likely to have the slack resources that makes them feel they could support government programs that primarily benefit older citizens, a point made repeatedly in Herman M. Schwartz and Leonard Seabrooke, eds., *The Politics of Housing Booms and Busts* (New York: Palgrave Macmillan, 2009).

out of date when adopted, the article 19 [variance or exception] procedure has become common practice.[9]

Article 19 is a section of Dutch legislative code.

David Johnson's study of the 1929 New York City likewise reached conclusions similar to the ones that could be drawn about San Diego. Despite it being a much more explicitly patrician plan, the New York plan embodied the aspirations and dreams of the upper middle class and its execution would most benefit them. Johnson notes that given that the planners aspired for upward social mobility:

> The Regional Plan was trapped in a dilemma: it could acquire influence only by gaining the support of those who possessed influence, but it could only gain this support by appealing to the values of those with power or wealth. Thus the Regional Plan, initially motivated by a rhetoric linking aesthetic and redistributive goals, ended by being dominated by a concern for engineering efficiency and for the perpetuation of an administrative organization.

The hope was to harness the energies of the business community to support the plan, which would also help poorer residents. Instead, "[w]hat happened to a considerable degree was just the reverse. Efficiency and growth-related elements of the Plan were enhanced in their acceptability by being linked to a rhetoric of concern for amenity and redistributive objectives."[10]

In San Diego, the plans were participatory, yet participation was limited mainly to one segment of the population: middle-aged and older Anglo homeowners. The tensions that the plans tried to resolve were between factions within that group (community

9. L. van Damme, M. Galle, M. Pen-Soetermoer and K. Verdaas, "Improving the Performance of Local Land-use Plans," *Environment and Planning B* 24 (1997): 836.
10. David A. Johnson, *Planning the Great Metropolis: The 1929 Regional Plan of New York and Its Environs* (London: E & FN Spon, 1996): 278, 279.

activists, environmentalists, planners, elected officials, landowners). The only real recognition of the needs of renters, minorities and future generations was the City's attempt to find room for more housing, an abstract need that could be sacrificed at the end of the day. Indeed, the elite groups often tacitly defined their sense of community *against* these groups. The plans then became exercises in efficiently handling future growth without changing the social order. The County plan was a matter of handling traffic and preserving rural character; the City of Villages was about getting the benefits of growth without touching single-family neighborhoods.

The plans represent major strands of urban planning. The City was top-down rational comprehensive planning that could not handle public participation. The County started off with grassroots planning and then replaced it with what's called *communicative planning* in which the planners conducted negotiations among the major organized interests. Neither approach worked particularly well, though through sheer exhaustiveness the County's plan had a kind of thoroughness to it.

This raises the question, is there a better way into the future of cities than comprehensive plans for Smart Growth? The answer is yes, we can see the outlines of something better, but it requires recognizing the poverty of both planning and Smart Growth. Land use planning as a vehicle for human betterment, especially Smart Growth, is just too literal.

The Limits of Smart Growth

The approach used in San Diego and throughout the country has been too dependent on the traditional urban planning approach of writing local plans to be implemented through zoning. It ignores the wastefulness of current building practices and designs; it sidesteps any national debate on how, where, and whether we should even be growing; it neglects how people vary in how they interact with their environments; and it ignores anything beyond the normal purview of planners, like the mortgage industry or the quality of public schools in large cities. Thus ignored are hard issues like the absurdity of continued growth in the bone-dry Southwest, the low cost of gasoline and the profligate consumption of resources that high-rises entail. Instead, too high of expectations are pinned on several broad changes in regional land use, ignoring that the cities that Smart Growth planners harken back to had the form they did did because of a confluence of conditions—political, technological, cultural—that no longer obtain. The centripetal forces that pulled great masses of humanity together by and large do not exist in the United States anymore.

A remarkable thing about the period when the City and County of San Diego were writing their plans and their fellow planners across the country were pushing for similar Smart Growth plans was that at the very same time, in Europe, there was beginning to be an unease about what was and still is called the *compact city*, which is all but indistinguishable from Smart Growth.[11] The European criticisms of this ideal, however, barely filtered over to this side of the Atlantic.

Curiously, most of the individual criticisms noted in Europe (and Canada and Australia) have been mentioned in passing in the United States, but little significance has been attached to them. Perhaps this is because governments in Europe embraced the compact city, makings its shortcomings more pressing and obvious. In the United States, the debate about sprawl and Smart Growth has been largely ideological, with planners on one side and libertarians and property rights activists on the other. Sympathetic criticism of Smart Growth has been rare.[12]

11. On the compact city, see Mike Jenks, Elizabeth Burton, and Katie Williams, ed. *The Compact City: A Sustainable Urban Form?* (London: E & FN Spon, 1996). On a rare US discussion of the European work, see Michael Neuman, "The Compact City Fallacy," *Journal of Planning Education and Research* 25 (2005): 11–26.

12. See Thomas Bier, "Urban Sprawl and Decline: Prospects for Change," *Public Works Management and Policy* 6, no. 2 (2001): 83–87; Timothy J. Dowling, "Reflections on Urban Sprawl, Smart Growth, and the Fifth Amendment," *University of Pennsylvania*

In comparison, the discussion of the compact city has lacked rancor and partisanship. Instead of ideological posturing endemic in discussions of Smart Growth, the European researchers have presented a gamut of focused criticisms that offer a very sobering portrait of our ability to build sustainable cities by regulating land use. For instance, one scholar undercuts the sense of uniqueness of the compact city by putting it in its historical context, namely that it is just the latest installment in a hundred-year-old European intellectual cycle that alternates between favoring urban concentration and favoring dispersion, with each new wave being seen as the cure-all for the problems the last trend caused. There are specific criticisms as well: one study notes that compact city discourse is "strangely deficient" in its explanation of how trucks fit in. Another sees limits to how much growth can be accommodated by infill and to what kinds of redevelopment residents are willing to take near them. Researchers also argue that compact cities are not necessarily more equitable (a point San Diego developers have suggested for years). Attempts to measure the benefits of the compact city have proven ambiguous. The compact city has not clearly and consistently shown reduced energy consumption or reduced driving. And even if these reductions are large enough to measure, the results aren't always an unvarnished good: one study concludes that compact forms create less air pollution but the higher concentrations of

---

Law Review 148 (2000): 873–887; Anthony Downs, "Smart Growth: Why We Discuss It More Than We Do It," *Journal of the American Planning Association* 71, no. 4 (2005): 367–380; see also the previously cited Michael Neuman, "The Compact City Fallacy," *Journal of Planning Education and Research* 25 (2005): 11–26.

The opening pages of Bruegman are even-handed and make some intriguing arguments about suburbanization that challenge Smart Growth. The book, which received a fair amount of attention in the popular press, slowly morphs into a familiar libertarian critique with predictable arguments. Robert Bruegman, *Sprawl: A Compact History* (Chicago: The University of Chicago Press, 2005). If the height of Smart Growth produced a classic critique, it would probably be Randall O'Toole, *The Vanishing Automobile and Urban Myths: How Smart Growth Will Harm American Cities* (Brandon, OR: The Thoreau Institute, 2001).

people mean that more people breathe what there is.[13]

All these and other disparate criticisms are tied together by a semi-explicit theme: the compact city is simplistic. The problem is that increased urban density does not necessarily lead to sustainable behaviors. Instead, what looks like a compact city can merely be layers of sprawl piled on top of each other. People's lifestyles are still fundamentally car-oriented. A number of researchers have pointed this out in different ways. Stead and Titheridge believe it is necessary to stop thinking of people's travel behavior being directly connected to land use and transportation and instead emphasize how socioeconomic conditions play a role. Katie Williams's assessment of the same point has perhaps the most brutal italics in planning

13. On criticisms of one uniform model of urban development, see Simon Guy and Simon Marvin, "Models and Pathways: The Diversity of Urban Futures," in *Achieving Sustainable Urban Form*, ed. Katie Williams, Elizabeth Burton, and Mike Jencks, 9–18 (London and New York: E & FN Spon, 2000); on the historical cycle of planners advocating concentration and deconcentration, see Michael Breheny, "Centrists, Decentrists, and Compromisers: Views on the Future of Urban Form," in *The Compact City: A Sustainable Urban Form?*, ed. Mike Jencks, Elizabeth Burton, and Katie Williams, 13–35 (London: E & FN Spon, 1996); on disappointing energy consumption, see Mirjan E. Bouwman, "Changing Mobility Patterns in a Compact City: Environmental Impacts," in *Compact Cities and Sustainable Urban Development*, ed. Gert de Roo and Donald Miller, 229–240 (Hampshire, England and Burlington, VT: Ashgate Publishing, 2000); on disappointing driving results, see Peter Headicar, "The Exploding City Region: Should It, Can It, Be Reversed?" in *Achieving Sustainable Urban Form*, 160–173; on paradoxical air pollution, see Vincent Fouchier, "The Case of the Paris Region, and Its Urban Density and Mobility: What Do We Know? What Can We Do?" in *Compact Cities and Sustainable Urban Development*: 146; on the lack of trucks in compact city thinking, see Geoffrey Dobilas, Richard M. Soberman and Alan Waterhouse, "Heavy Vehicles in the Compact City: A Combined Advanced Information/Land Use System," in the same volume (pp. 275–286); on doubts about the equity of the compact city can be found in Elizabeth Burton, "The Potential of the Compact City for Promoting Social Equity," in *Achieving Sustainable Urban Form*, 19–29; on infill, see Gert de Roo, "Environmental Planning and the Compact City: A Dutch Perspective," in *Compact Cities and Sustainable Urban Development*, 31–42; Gert de Roo, "Compact Cities, Environmental Conflicts and Policy Strategies: Complexity as a Criterion for Decision Making," in *Achieving Sustainable Urban Form*, 229–241.

literature: "there is considerable uncertainty about the extent to which spatial planning or the manipulation of urban form can contribute to sustainable mobility *at all* in the face of broader socio-economic and cultural trends.[14]

Another implicit point of the compact city literature, related to the above, is that people and communities have a history. It might be one thing to be able to calculate the energy consumption an abstract urban form may have, but creating that form on top of an existing town is vastly more complicated. People may live within walking distance of a grocery store, but it might not be the one they frequent; they may live at high densities and be able to walk to many nearby homes, but their friends might be living in equally dense communities miles away.

Researchers on the compact city also organized an edited volume around an obvious but damning observation: Asian cities are well-described by the compact city ideal—dense neighborhoods, widely used mass transit—yet few would call them sustainable.[15] One of my own breaks from living in San Diego, almost a year in Hong Kong between 2004 and 2005, supports this skepticism. Hong Kong's extraordinary density made possible an extensive and rapid mass transit system. Furthermore, what outsiders often did not appreciate about Hong Kong was that it was also mostly green space: the land available for construction was just slivers between the steep hills and the ocean, and the government was measured in releasing more for new construction. It was, in short, Smart Growth so intense as to border on caricature. In many ways, it was an amazing

14. Dominic Stead, Jo Williams and Helena Titheridge, "Land Use, Transport and People: Identifying the Connections," in *Achieving Sustainable Urban Form*, ed. Katie Williams, Elizabeth Burton, and Mike Jencks, 174–186 (London and New York: E & FN Spon, 2000); Katie Williams, Editor's introd. to *Spatial Planning, Urban Form and Sustainable Transport* (Hampshire, England: Ashgate Publishing, 2005): 2.

15. Andre Sorensen, Peter J. Marcotullio, and Jill Grant, "Towards Sustainable Cities," in *Towards Sustainable Cities: East Asian, North American and European Perspectives on Managing Urban Regions*, ed. Andre Sorensen, Peter J. Marcotullio, and Jill Grant, 3–23 (Hampshire, England and Burlington, VT: Ashgate Publishing, 2004).

city and I retain considerable affection for it.

But it was an environmental disaster. Although the stunning compactness meant it was possible to go months between riding in a car (without any sense of sacrifice), the residents were largely indifferent to obvious environmental problems and their own intense consumption. Examples abound. We lived on an estate of approximately ten-thousand residents; it had three recycling bins and those seemed to be mainly used by foreigners. Recycling by Hong Kong residents was mainly limited to clothes: it balanced the desire to not throw away money spent on old fashions with the desire to free closet space for new styles. Our flat overlooked a channel partially covered with the black, nauseating slime of raw sewage, and my suggestion that people ought to complain was just further proof that foreigners were strange—stranger, apparently, than fishing in the contaminated water. (And woe to any endangered species believed to have medicinal properties.) Renting movies was all but unheard of; people bought bootleg discs on the cheap and then tossed them out if the movie was no good. Since virtually everyone lived in a high-rise, housing wasn't a particularly effective way of displaying high social status. Instead, hi-tech gadgets and latest fashions (or at least knock-offs) were paramount in many social circles. This meant tremendous consumption.

Observing these situations made me ponder the limitations of Smart Growth as an environmental movement. But what really gave me pause was the power of cars. True, if you didn't own a car, it was liberating not to have to worry about fender benders, insurance, rush-hour traffic and limited parking. But even in this dense urban environment, cars were quite convenient, especially when shopping for more than one bag's worth of goods, and were frequently still faster than mass transit.

My other time away from San Diego warns of another possible illusion. I lived for ten months in a small college town in upstate New York that had a charming, walkable downtown. Indeed, as a resident of this several-block downtown, I did not need a car. Although local planners would undoubtedly disagree with me, the experience hardly supports the viability of Smart Growth. Many of the apartments above stores were empty because it was not worth the cost to bring them up to code, which meant that the main drag, despite its Victorian loveliness, was in effect a strip mall in disguise. And the renters living in the occupied apartments were bombarded by so much noise that only those with hearing problems and the heaviest sleepers likely had much enthusiasm for staying in their unit for more than one lease. It was difficult to rent out the shops below, and this was before massive big box stores being built on the outskirts of town were finished. As a vision of the future, Smart Growth was such a mild reform program. It barely touched upon the region's biggest problems, including enough poverty to make the area feel like a flat version of Appalachia.

Visionaries for American cities are starting to appreciate the limitations of what they've been advocating for over the last several generations. Andre Duany, the leading proponent of New Urbanism, which is in many ways the architectural equivalent of Smart Growth, has recently written:

> Detroit is now the city where the risk-oblivious millennials can get things done. Elsewhere, over the last three decades, there has arisen a regulatory regime so comprehensive that it is impossible even to make a cookie for sale without a certified kitchen, an accessible bathroom, and constant inspections. Almost everywhere else, the slack that once allowed revitalization to evolve organically has been exterminated by bureaucracies. If this is not obvious, it is because most of us elders have grown up within the rising tide of regulation. We are inured—and we even know how to operate within it—but the young folk do not.[16]

16. Andre Duany, "The Pink Zone: Why Detroit is the New Brooklyn." (February 14, 2014): http://features.blogs.fortune.cnn.com/2014/01/30/the-pink-zone-why-detroit-is-

Duany calls this "lean urbanism" and wants to situate it within a giant cycle of rejection of stifling rules ("risk oblivious"), ambition within rules ("risk aware") and conformity ("risk aversion"). But even this is modest.

As European researchers have noted, the shape of cities are deeply impacted by broader social conditions, social conditions that planners are, like so many other people, loathe to discuss. Immigration is responsible for much of the country's population growth, yet we can't seem to have grown-up, bipartisan conversations about what the ideal level of immigration and population growth should be. Also key is the size and number of households. This has an enormous impact on the demand for new housing as smaller households need more housing units than larger ones, yet what causes changes in household formation and whether certain household sizes or living arrangements should be encouraged has been off the Smart Growth radar. In particular, we should especially be discussing the causes and impacts of the rise of people living alone, as they magnify the amount of housing needed to serve the same population. Perhaps Arthur C. Nelson's recent *Reshaping Metropolitan America* will jumpstart this conversation: it does not discuss the family dynamics but does draw attention to the way that decreasing household size has been an important driver of household growth.[17]

In an insightful article, Michael Neuman complains that the compact city literature does not "raise the level of the game." In other words, it lacks the ambition and originality to actually solve the problems that it is intended to address.[18] This failure of imagination is not only based on a narrow way of looking at urban

the-new-brooklyn.

Duany, incidentally, is not exaggerating about the cookies, a point liberals ought to find sobering.

17. Arthur C. Nelson, *Reshaping Metropolitan America: Development Trends and Opportunities to 2030* (Washington, DC: Island Press, 2013): 49.

18. Michael Neuman, "The Compact City Fallacy," *Journal of Planning Education and Research* 25 (2005): 22.

problems but the equally narrow range of techniques considered as possible tools to solve them.

Much of this lack of inspiration has to do with the belief that densities determine cities, which implies if we could only control density, we can control many of the negative impacts of growth. In my life, I lived in everything from a forty-story high-rise to a detached house on a large lot. Everything about my experiences is consistent with Herbert Gans's conclusion from almost fifty years ago that density is meaningless.[19]

And to be blunt, Americans quiver at the mention of the word "density" but relatively few of them have experienced it. What Americans have experienced is anxiety over threatening environments and unpredictable change. So when Americans criticize density, they are like people who romanticize life in a small-town without ever having lived in one: they are not talking about land use but about the psyche. Density is an inkblot onto which people project fears; it dictates little. Low densities guarantee neither free flowing streets nor traffic jams. High densities can be pedestrian friendly or downright dangerous. Suburbs can be endless ticky tacky homes offering sterile lives or little castles offering sanctuary to growing families. High densities can be alienating and impersonal, or their anonymity can be liberating and allow for new kinds of social contacts. These are all possibilities.

General plans, as they are currently done, encourage one-dimensional solutions to sustainability problems along the lines of Smart Growth: just as regulatory complexity begets more involuted regulatory complexity, conceptual oversimplification begets conceptual oversimplification, creating political conflict with those who have to live with the consequences. While some jurisdictions

19. Herbert Gans, "Urbanism and Suburbanism as Ways of Life," in *Readings in Urban Sociology*, ed. R. E. Pahl, 95–118 (New York: Pergamon Press, 1966). On how the distinct trajectory of the United States (compared to Europe, which had major cities for centuries) led Americans to conflates cities with the ills of industrialization, see Leo Marx, *The Pilot and the Passenger: Essays on Literature, Technology and Culture in the United States* (New York: Oxford University Press, 1988).

include no land use map in their plans to avoid controversy—or to pretend that it does not exist—as general plans are often done, particularly for largely jurisdictions, the core of a general plan is its land use map.[20] All the other elements are, in effect, there to make that map work. But such a map, by suggesting a use for all the land within a jurisdiction, creates a breeding ground for libertarianism by antagonizing propertied interests out of proportion to its demonstrated ability to make a community sustainable—or the map provokes environmentalists and homeowners with its visions of additional growth.

Not only are general plans more divisive than effective, they are inherently absurd in that they portray urban dynamics as static endpoints. Obviously, there are communities that are quite static. Zealous homeowner association enforcement in some of San Diego's wealthier communities leaves them feeling like they've been flooded with twelve feet of formaldehyde. However reassuring that is to a homeowner, especially as an investor, it is not a realistic approach for large jurisdictions.

When Smart Growth first became popular, arguments for it centered on the environmental and fiscal unsustainability of sprawl, and critics of Smart Growth replied that people simply did not want it. As the debate wore on, advocates have tried to reverse this, saying that a convergence of demographic and economic trends—increasing energy costs, Baby Boomers wanting to downsize, Millennials unenthusiastic about cars and homeownership (and less able to afford either anyway), etc.—will create tremendous pressure for Smart Growth. While this might be a good thing, it may also be an optimistic read of the data, and more to the point, it doesn't give the fears that Smart Growth generates among those with political power their due.[21] As the San Diego experience shows, the bureaucratic

20. Eric Damian Kelly and Barbara Becker, *Community Planning: An Introduction to the Comprehensive Plan* (Washington, DC: Island Press, 2000): 180.
21. A Pew survey that came out as this book was going to press offers some insights into the politics of the San Diego general plans. Seventy-five percent of those identified as "consistently conservative" preferred to live where the "houses are larger and further

inertia behind outward growth patterns is reinforced by competing interests—nervous about change—having extreme difficulties
reaching a consensus.[22]

Smart Growth and planning are not truly strong enough to deal
with the problems of American cities. This is true in a myriad of
ways. They do little, for instance, to confront segregation and the
limited enforcement of fair housing laws. Their profound weakness, however, is most obvious in the face of the sheer magnitude
of economic forces. In the years since the birth of Smart Growth,
American cities have been tremendously impacted by deindustrialization and financial speculation on a global scale, especially
the dot-com bubble and the subprime mortgage scandal. Indeed,
during the subprime mortgage collapse, a matter very much under
the purview of planning—housing—effectively tanked the world
economy. Planners were well aware that an unsustainable bubble
was rapidly expanding, yet they could do little to prevent it because
the actual problems (the selling and monetization of corrupted
mortgages) were not considered land use per se and not within their
jurisdiction or power.[23] Global speculation is simply too strong of a

---

apart, but schools, stores and restaurants are several miles away." Seventy-seven percent
of those identified as "consistently liberal" said they prefer to live where the "houses are
smaller and closer to each other, but schools, stores and restaurants are within walking
distance." Perhaps this merely indicates that people prefer to live where they currently
live. It also suggests that Smart Growth has become more distinctly associated with
liberals. Pew Research Center for the People & the Press, "Political Polarization in the
American Public," (June 12, 2014): http://www.people-press.org/2014/06/12/political-
polarization-in-the-american-public/

22. Despite recognizing the dangers of bureaucratic inertia, Nelson, for instance, is
quite optimistic about demographic changes leading to Smart Growth. Arthur C.
Nelson, *Reshaping Metropolitan America: Development Trends and Opportunities to
2030* (Washington, DC: Island Press, 2013): 111.

23. For a history of Fannie Mae during this time period, see Timothy Howard, *The
Mortgage Wars: Inside Fannie Mae, Big-money Politics, and the Collapse of the American
Dream* (New York: McGraw Hill Education, 2014). What is fascinating about this book,
written from the point of view of a risk management specialist, is how little attention it

force to be contained by the power that Americans are willing to vest in their planners.[24] It's as if urban development is a canoe in which the planner's ability to paddle in a straight line is severely compromised by sharing the craft with a very inebriated Rich Uncle Pennybags whose constantly shuffling perpetually threatens to capsize them both.

So where does this leave Smart Growth? At a minimum, the criticisms of the compact city suggest that advocates of Smart Growth, especially environmentalists, will likely find themselves disappointed in the results, particularly in light of the amount of work necessary to convince people to accept higher densities. The compact cities literature suggests that the further a desired result is from what a policy directly changes, the less the impact will be: Smart Growth, which is mainly a redirection of growth, might preserve open space, but it is over-optimistic to hope that this will dramatically change travel patterns or increase social justice. The connection between the change in policy and the intended effect is too remote, too prone to other influences.[25] As housing markets heat up again, we can expect cities to turn again to Smart Growth as the obvious tool to deal with the unwanted effects of development. This is an understandable impulse, but we should not expect too much from Smart Growth or be content with it.

---

pays to anything unique about housing as a commodity. It's a story of interest and credit. For a broader look at the Great Recession in the context of the intellectual history of economics, see John Cassidy, *How Markets Fail: The Logic of Economic Calamities* (New York: Picador, 2010).

24. For an excellent book on the rise on the massive amounts of capital swishing around in the globe since Eastern Europe, China and India entered the developed world markets over the last several decades, see Daniel Alpert, *The Age of Oversupply: Overcoming the Greatest Challenge to the Global Economy* (New York: Portfolio/ Penguin, 2013). On the impact of this money pouring into US mortgage markets in particular, see p. 16.

25. Katie Williams, "Does Intensifying Cities Make Them More Sustainable?" in *Achieving Sustainable Urban Form*, ed. Katie Williams, Elizabeth Burton, and Mike Jencks, 30–45 (London and New York: E & FN Spon, 2000).

Life after Smart Growth

If Smart Growth is of limited utility, then where is it better to focus energy? We need to recognize that Americans, perhaps more so now than ever, are deeply suspicious of government but likewise don't want themselves or people they care about to be crushed by the indifference of market forces.

Specifically, there are four areas in which work can be done to improve American cities and their hinterlands:

1. Decrease planning regulations.
2. Tax car travel and real estate speculation.
3. Accept that some regions are better for continued growth than others.
4. Aggressively combat inequality.

Deregulation

The first matter we must address is the devolution of property law. The complexity of land use regulation calls into question the legitimacy of government and is too convoluted for anyone's good. Simplification of too complex rules will be extraordinarily hard. Once a rule gets on the books, it represents specific, organized concerns. The prospect of eliminating the rule raises the hair on the back of their necks, and there's a way in which banning something and then retracting a ban creates a sense of tacit approval when it could have been more effective to have frowned upon it from the beginning without passing a rule.

The truth is that we don't know how to stand down from overregulation. Laws are intertwined in complicated ways and streamlining them would require reformers to know the law intimately both as code and as enforced. Streamlining would have to be done carefully, and it would have to be widely discussed and researched before it was done. (Historically, there have been bursts of deregulation, especially under Reagan and Thatcher.

These could be useful largely, but not entirely, in understanding what to avoid.) A balanced, nuanced approach to deregulation would be slow and laborious—and advocates of Smart Growth and New Urbanism have, in fact, been working on it.

They call their idea *performance zoning*. At face value, it is one of the strongest cards in their hand. Instead of having each project follow highly baroque regulations imposing a mind-numbing number of conditions, developers are obligated to make sure their construction meets a city's goals. For example, instead of having regulations specifying the width, slope and the like of a street, a city could specify how much traffic a road should be able to handle at what speed, how much run-off the gutters must handle, etc. At first blush, this is enormously appealing. At second blush, it's still not bad. It ignores, however, that one of the reasons why regulations tend to become more specific and measurable over time is that they lower the number and intensity of disputes and make it clear to people when they are complying with the law or not. Indeed, performance zoning often relies on a point system, so it contains within it its own possible method of ossification. This reconceptualization of zoning, however, is something that needs to be done—with the expectation that eventually the laws will lose their crystalline clarity and need to be restated yet again.[26]

But even recognizing that performance zoning will someday become a beast that needs to be slain does not go far enough. Regulatory complexity, regulatory exhaustion, is a problem across the board, though how bad it is varies by state. California seems to be one of the worst. A particularly troublesome case of exhaustive Golden State regulation is the California Environmental Quality Act, the law that undergirds the environmental impact reports that played such a role in the San Diego case studies. A friend of mine works on EIRs at a firm that was bought by a larger company

26. The classic essay on how laws fluctuate between being "crystal" (clear, rigid) and "mud" (nuanced, impenetrable) can be found in Carol M. Rose, *Property and Persuasion: Essays on the History, Theory, and Rhetoric of Ownership* (Boulder: Westview Press, 1994).

several years ago. When an out-of-state planner came to inspect their new acquisition and saw what California planners had to do for environmental analysis, they said, "You guys overkill overkill." There have been rumblings of CEQA reform again in Sacramento the last several years, but unfortunately the issue gets framed as a pro-business/anti-environmentalist effort. It's hard to see how an effort that in effect touts itself as a way to steamroll environmentalists will go anywhere. Environmentalists clearly need to be at the table, putting their imprint on CEQA reform from the get-go. Anything else should and probably will fail. The tradeoff to be made seems fairly obvious: less baroque regulation and more actual environmental protection.

Performance zoning is one beachhead into standing down from overregulation and CEQA reform is another. Something else that should be done is to stop making laws so complicated in the first place. This is a challenge because we don't have any systematic way of distinguishing between legitimate concerns and paranoia during the legislative process. As a result, each piece of legislation runs a gauntlet of committees, hearings and votes in which somebody being able to imagine a problem is treated as the same thing as the problem actually existing—and the main strategy of responding to criticisms of a bill is to add language to try to address the concerns. California and its jurisdictions exemplify this: one state-level bill that I worked on in 2012 in a modest capacity was based on a one-page Ohio law. The law that passed was fifteen pages long—and worse for it (including an asinine restriction spelling out, in a dollar amount that does not adjust for inflation, the maximum amount of goods to be sold, meaning that another law will have to eventually be passed correcting it when it becomes so restrictive that the people affected howl).

This is an area where academics could play a key role. While the claim that "more research is needed" usually deserves skepticism in the policy arena, research designed to help understand how regulation comes into existence and how it can be simplified with minimal negative impact are matters that warrant considerable study.[27] Such research could include the conditions under which deregulation has historically served the interests of the republic (as opposed to unleashing special interests), the accuracy of different kinds of the claims made during policy debates and the actual impacts of laws. Little in my experience of observing and participating in campaigns to change public policy gives me much reason to believe that policy-making is a rational process, but such research, if done well and if the results were widely disseminated, could help contain emotions in politics and decrease the rampant political polarization of recent years by making it easier to tell which kinds of claims can be rejected out of hand and which are legitimate criticisms that, even if inconvenient, people committed to the greater good have to take seriously.[28]

Eating Your Broccoli or: Raising Taxes

Deregulation may be worthy in its own right. It could make the legislative process more timely and the experience of living with legislation less of a hassle, which can have positive economic impacts. Indeed, abandoning planning in its exhaustive and exhausting detail could free up energies to focus on social issues whose symptoms become expressed in land use. In itself, however, deregulation does nothing to help ordinary residents nor does it address the concerns that led to regulation in the first place.

This is where more thoughtful tax policy comes in. Taxes, because they leave people alone after an exchange of money, can be a way to achieve social policy objectives without binding them with heavily detailed regulations. Indeed, some people, especially economists, already advocate one form of this: congestion pricing that makes it

27. For a provocative argument about why academic research often only makes policy conundrums worse, see Emory Roe, *Narrative Policy Analysis: Theory and Practice* (Durham and London: Duke University Press, 1994).

28. For instance, there's evidence that there's an inverse relationship between someone's confidence about a prediction and the likelihood that a prediction will come true: the arrogant are more likely to be wrong. Dan Gardiner, *Future Babble: Why Expert Predictions Are Next to Worthless, and You Can Do Better.* (New York: Dutton Adult, 2011).

more expensive to drive during peak traffic.

One could forgive the reader for thinking, "If there's something that makes Smart Growth look downright popular, it's the taxman." As George Orwell put it, "No one is patriotic about taxes."[29] This must be faced squarely, as must people's specific grievances against taxation. How to make the case for taxation in general is well beyond the scope of this book, but a few points can be made. First, fairness is absolutely essential. While high taxes have played their role in many a revolution, the United States is probably the only country in the world founded in reaction to unfair taxation. Second, work has to be done to improve the standing of taxation with the American public, especially the political right. Conservatives used to stress balanced budgets and accepted tax increases as a tool for achieving them. Since the 1970s, they have simply become hostile to taxation—period. They've gone from "No taxation *without representation*" to "No taxation." It's won them many elections, but fiscal anorexia is not a credible long-term governance strategy. Its difficult to have reasonable discussions about taxation, but advocates for American cities have no choice but to make the attempt.

The argument here is that taxes, when paired with a measure of deregulation, represent a useful approach for improving American cities. The idea is to scale back on intrusive or clumsy regulations, instead putting broadbrush incentives and disincentives into the structure of taxes—with the expectation that people will innovate in response. This would encourage pro-social behavior without government becoming too elaborate. (The danger, of course, is that over time, the temptation to excessively fine-tune the taxes will increase.)

If the goal of Smart Growth is to reduce reliance on cars and on oil, the Archimedean point is the cost of a gallon of gasoline. Advocates of Smart Growth don't talk about it, but the fundamental problem in their logic can be stated baldly: *there will be no Smart Growth as long as gasoline is cheap.* Cars are so much more convenient than mass transit that people will drive as long as they can

29. George Orwell, *A Patriot after All, 1940–1941* (London: Secker and Warburg, 1998): 225.

afford to—doubly so if they have kids. Indeed, the argument could be made that price spikes in gasoline, like during 2007–08, do more to promote Smart Growth than planners have been able to do.

What is appealing about raising the cost of car travel through taxes is that while not much fun to pay, they are relatively unintrusive and get at community goals without making landowners feel individually targeted.[30] We have seen from the 2000–01 energy deregulation scandal in California and from gasoline spikes that people respond to price increases creatively. If discouraging gas consumption is the goal, then gas and vehicle ownership should be made expensive and then let people respond as they best see fit. People would likely do things like try to live closer to work or change jobs to shorten commute times and use more mass transit and taxis while developers would build more close-in housing. If gasoline is expensive for a sustained period of time, it would eventually be reflected in the built form in ways that work for people. People would innovate and take the cost of gasoline into account when making decisions. In other words, people would respond with something similar to Smart Growth without the massive complexity of attempting an all-knowing general plan. The real challenges would be to make gasoline and vehicle ownership expensive in a way that was fair—and not punish poorer residents or small businesses—and to be savvy about where the benefits of keeping complex land use in place outweigh the disadvantages, such as in historic districts. That hybrids and electric vehicles are calling into question traditional vehicle tax policies creates an opportunity to bring this to the forefront.

But without a national consensus to reduce reliance on automobiles—there is certainly no such thing today—planners are left making the tweaks to the urban landscape that can be done in the absence of widespread political support, things like reducing parking requirements in older communities to encourage the densities necessary for

30. An economist will recognize that this is as a political argument for a variant of Pigouvian taxes. (Pigouvian taxes—often spelled without the "u"—are taxes on the negative effects of an activity to try to force the person who benefits from it to also pay the negative costs instead of being able to get away with forcing the public to shoulder the burden.)

viable mass transit. These tweaks, however, are likely to come across as petty misguided idealism because by themselves they're unlikely to have much impact but will annoy someone.

In addition to vehicular traffic, another area where Americans need to seriously consider higher taxation is in real estate markets. Housing in urban America will be always be suffering from one crisis or another as long as it's driven by speculation. Markets are an efficient means of linking production and distribution for certain goods, but it's hard to make the case that urban housing is one of them. Finite supplies of land, very long production times and high resale values make housing markets act in ways far from ideal models of supply and demand. Higher taxes on real estate is one way to suppress real estate speculation and more generally address the problems of inter-generational inequality.

This can be achieved in several ways. One approach is supported by many city planners and pursued much more aggressively in Europe: inclusionary housing in which a specified percent of each develop-ment has to be set aside for affordable housing. This is in effect a tax that captures, for the public, some of the increased value of land that results from property becoming more desirable as a result of social improvements like roads and schools.[31] This has the added possible benefit of increased social inclusion but is narrowly focused on new development. A broader approach would be to raise real estate taxes across the board but *slowly*. The California experience of the 1970s demonstrates why abrupt real estate tax increases are a bad idea and will encounter widespread opposition. But slow measured increases would decrease the appeal of speculation and allow a higher percent-age of the money devoted to real estate to be spent on things like schools, sidewalks, public safety, parks and bike trails.

The advantage of higher taxes—cars or real estate—is that it does not directly force substantial immediate change in how Americans

31. See Nico Calavita and Alan Mallach, eds., *Inclusionary Housing in International Perspective: Affordable Housing, Social Inclusion, and Land Value Recapture* (Cambridge, MA: Lincoln Institute of Land Policy, 2010).

go about their daily lives. The cost-basis housing of other countries, especially in Scandinavia, combines the best features of renting and owning. Americans should consider them more seriously even though they don't offer the apparent certainties of outright ownership. But Americans are likely to balk. In my experience, homeowners find cost-basis housing unappealing (and would have no need or motivation to participate unless they felt crushed by their mortgages), but renters who have abandoned hope of ever owning their own homes are much, much more open to the idea.[32] Realistically, however, it would take extraordinary efforts—and generations—to make cost-basis housing a middle-class option in this country.[33] Taxes offer a thinner intervention.

Where to Grow

Abraham Shragge's history of San Diego growth argues that the success of city's civic boosters in promoting growth was very much in the face of environmental constraints or logic.[34] It makes sense, to be sure, to have some uses related to the bay and to winter tourism in San Diego. But it does not make sense to put a major American metropolis in such a dry place.

This harsh reality should be put more directly: the most affordable housing in San Diego, California is in Detroit and Buffalo. That is,

32. European countries have been in full retreat from the notion of "housing as a social right" and instead are shifting toward the American paradigm of housing as a form of welfare through wealth creation, a scenario that has exacerbated intergenerational inequalities and increased homeowner resistance to a more fully developed welfare state. See the debates of Herman M. Schwartz and Leonard Seabrooke, eds., *The Politics of Housing Booms and Busts* (New York: Palgrave Macmillan, 2009).

33. An interesting possible use of cost-basis housing is to lock in the economic competitiveness of low-cost areas of the country. In places like Detroit, where land is being abandoned, cost-basis housing projects could purchase land on the cheap (though likely requiring subsidies) and then if the economy could be improved, housing costs would not escalate as much, reducing the need for outsized wages to compensate for high living costs.

34. Abraham Shragge, *Boosters and Bluejackets: The Civic Culture of Militarism in San Diego, California, 1900–1945*, PhD diss., (University of California, San Diego, 1998).

if we as a nation are going to grow, it should be in the Rustbelt, not in environmentally fragile, high housing cost regions like coastal California. Throughout the Midwest and the Northeast, there are cities and villages hurting from deindustrialization. They could benefit from growth. It is also on the list of things that would not be easy, but a Marshall Plan for the Rustbelt, perhaps made politically feasible by being paired with programs to combat southern poverty (the worst in the nation), could strengthen the country as a whole.

Combating Inequality

Finally, there needs to be a larger movement for the people who are routinely excluded from participation in land use. Despite how powerless and frustrated participants in the general plans felt, they represented the *haves* of American society. For many, their social position is more tenuous than in the past, but their sense of frustration or victimization was made possible in part by their social distance from the people who really struggled in the San Diego economy.

Those who care about American cities must squarely face the growing inequality between the top and bottom of the economic ladder. Much of what gets criticized about American cities—sprawl, privatized space, concentrated poverty, etc.—is the result of those with resources trying to claw free from those who are economically sinking. There is great debate about how to best eliminate poverty, and this book cannot resolve such matters. An aggressive approach to poverty would be a tough sell today, but it's naïve at best to think any vision of a better future for metropolitan America has a chance of becoming reality while pretending that our social contract is intact. It might be best to build coalitions around discrete issues: the uneven distribution of educational opportunities, the weak enforcement of fair housing laws, the prison-industrial complex, the tilt of policy in favor of homeownership and against renters, etc. Or it might be better to build a climate in which it is possible to go at them all at once when reform is in the air. It would take another book to figure that out, but it's a far more important use of progressive energies than subtle reforms to planning regulations.

Indeed, what all of the positives suggestions here—from raising taxes to deregulation to tackling poverty—what they all have in common is that they are politically difficult. The ones that are most likely to succeed are the ones that resonate with our broader ideals, like fairness and equality before the law. Tackling challenging issues would require more candid discussions of American attitudes than our gaffe-driven politics currently allows. Inequality between schools has much to do with racial anxieties, and our attitudes towards the environment are paradoxical: the most destructive consumption practices are also highly valued. Much of what is undesirable about suburban development is what Thorstein Veblen, in observing the robber barons of his day, dubbed *conspicuous waste*: displaying wealth by the profligate use of resources. The SUV, the large lawn, the McMansion—they all are high status social displays. Indeed, that may be their main point: SUVs seem rarely used to their capacity; large lawns, especially in front yards and around suburban businesses, are usually only there to be looked at; and the massive square footage of McMansions is being used by historically small families.[35] But this social flaunting is widely accepted; indeed, we're complicit in it. We fantasize about being rich, we admire people who are, we keep off their grass.

But let us take for granted for the moment the largeness of the American republic. Despite deeply rooted tensions, despite ambiguities and conflicts in our political attitudes, we have over the last two hundred years done much to make a reality the overheated rhetoric of equality used in the fight for independence and subsequent founding of the republic. It's often been against the will of entrenched interests, and, when it comes to the shape of our cities, interests are most certainly entrenched. Indeed, with increased frequency and

35. A friend of mine who has worked on large production homebuilding has said that their company calculated a price for the home and then based the square footage on it. Then they duplicated the basic rooms until they reached the target. Little thought was given to how people would actually use the space.

frustration, discussions of how to improve our country, regardless of the actual matter at hand, all seem to eventually turn to the issue of election reform, especially of campaign financing, as a precondition for meaningful change. This does increasingly seem to be the case, though campaign finance reform in itself is not enough if many urban and rural residents cannot participate because they have to hustle so hard to make ends meet that they don't have the time to look beyond their immediate survival.

The changes proposed here are all so difficult that they are unlikely to occur in the short term. This is no cause for discouragement. Most dramatic shifts in the American history had long periods of gestation before a crisis made them possible. And, if the writing of general plans teaches nothing else, they teach patience.

INDEX

www.ingramcontent.com/pod-product-compliance
Lightning Source LLC
Chambersburg PA
CBHW031458270326
41930CB00006B/145